Licence Denied

Licence Denied

RUMBLINGS FROM THE
DOCTOR WHO UNDERGROUND

edited by

Paul Cornell

This edition published in 1997 by
Virgin Books
an imprint of Virgin Publishing Ltd
332 Ladbroke Grove
London W10 5AH

ISBN 0 7535 0104 X

Cover illustrations by Paul Griffin, Nigel Thomas, Lee Binding, Adrian
Salmon and Amanda Kear

Typeset by Galleon Typesetting, Ipswich
Printed and bound in Great Britain by Cox & Wyman Ltd, Reading

Contents

Acknowledgements   vii
Introduction   1

 1 Sad/Not Sad   7
 2 Love Bits   61
 3 Fanlife   67
 4 Rude Bits   83
 5 Tom and Graham   90
 6 Oddly Fond But Also Mocking Bits   117
 7 Analysis   127
 8 Interactive Bits   153
 9 Raves   165
10 Days Out   179
11 Leftover Bits   193

Epilogue   199

For someone who can't be named.
'A gentle answer turns away wrath.'

Acknowledgements

Fandom made this, but some people put in a special effort. Thanks must go to: Peter Anghelides, David J. Darlington, Jackie Marshall, Jon Preddle, Keith West, Martin Wiggins (especially), for provision of articles. John Binns, Vanessa Bishop, Carrie O'Grady, Jac Rayner, Jim Sangster, for typing help. Miria Aman, Sandra Hastie, Peter Linford, Matt Jones, for scanning. Tom Beck, James Bow, James Margitich, Kathy Sullivan, Shannon Sullivan, for help abroad. Jeremy Bentham, Anthony Brown, Cate Caruth, Martin Day, David Gibbs, David Howe, Dominic May, Steven O'Brien, Nick Pegg, Paul Simpson, Paul Winter for help finding people. Rebecca Levene, John McLaughlin, Keith Topping for other stuff.

Two of the writers that I wanted to contribute to this book, Gary Russell and Nick Pegg, declined, very politely, feeling that their past should remain behind them. Thanks must go to them anyway for their contribution to fandom.

The shape of this book took many twists and turns during editing, and the process had to balance many things, so apologies to the many people who were passed over for reasons other than quality. Some of you were even told you were in and then disappointed (Mark!). Sorry again. If I get to do another volume, you'll have another go. Unless that volume is about the fandom of the Americas, which, as I discovered when sampling it, deserves a book of its own since it's so different. I made the decision not to make the tremendous stretch that it would have taken to include it. Apologies.

The fine art of pastiche. Script by Alan Barnes, art by Adrian Salmon and lettering by Annabel Jowett from the *Cottage Under Siege Yearbook* (which had Deirdre from *Coronation Street* on the cover).

Introduction

The word 'fanzine' was once featured on *Call My Bluff*. Joanna Lumley defined it as an Italian word for 'basket'. The opposing team believed her, finding the idea of magazines produced by fans on an amateur basis extremely improbable. It's wonderfully apt that this first public definition of this book's subject matter was by the actor who played Patsy in *Absolutely Fabulous*, that character being a polysexual, drink-and-drug-addled gay icon. It's also fab that, through telling a lie, Joanna got it absolutely right. Fanzines are baskets. They carry a bundle of social, political and fanpolitical meanings; they're a basic tool for those wishing to move from one place to another; they're a symbol of our culture. The culture of fandom, that is. A splendid place to come from, a splendid place to stay. Like the peasant Mafia who weave those fictitious fanzines in Joanna's imagination, if you gave us an island, we'd know how to rule it, from the police down to the thieves. That's why I say culture, rather than subculture. The Isle of Fandom is a sunny, sheltering place, but it's continually at war with itself. It produces many great artists, many of whom go unrecognised, because the world outside looks down on it.

Let's abandon that metaphor and talk about the real world. There was once a photoshoot for the *Observer* magazine, featuring a number of selected representatives of fandom. The paper brought them from all over the country. 'Have you got any space guns?' the photographer asked them. The final photo shows many of the great and some of the good of our culture as it was then, arrayed in scarves and space helmets and monster costumes in David Howe's back garden. The piece that went with it was about freaks and eccentrics. It wasn't us laughing at ourselves. It was *The Black and White Minstrel*

1

Show. A few of those present had the good sense to storm out.

That's the first subversive lesson that many fans learn. That when we cuddled up to that Zygon for the press photographer, we were having a laugh with our mates, but when the photo appeared in the newspaper, we had suddenly become sad obsessives. It makes many fans aware at a very early stage that what's done to us is also done to other people: that the greater culture's parameters are enforced through ridicule and peer pressure.

The reason the greater culture does this to us is sheer psychological projection. They want to portray fans as mad consumers, people who accept everything the television gives us, without question. That's them, I'm afraid. Fandom is the culture that takes what television gives us, chops it up, laughs at it, pulls it apart, makes its own art with it, and eats it.

Fanzines, not being allowed or licensed by the powers that be, are the main area where this violent deconstruction takes place, where the boundaries of our culture are neurotically and secretly advanced. I'm going to say 'our' and 'we' and 'us' a lot in the following pages. That's because I'm unashamedly part of, and still passionately in love with, fandom. Any academic distance I took in this book would be an affectation, and a lie, in that this isn't in any sense a definitive history or guide, just a feverish grabbing of brilliant bits, a very partial and individual sample. People from other sections of fandom, or other eras, might find that their experience is different from mine. I hope that their accounts will become available too. Cultures are big things, and they need many chronicles.

Above all, this book is about the difference between the official perception of what fandom should be like, and what it's actually like. It's about not having bought a licence, and thus having complete licence to say everything. Here we can chuck all the rubbish and present the scary, monstrous and gorgeous face of fandom.

It's about the way that fans really experience the series.

The show, I mean.

Doctor Who.

I should have used those words earlier. But it didn't seem important.

This book samples various articles from *Doctor Who* fanzines, mainly of British origin. The articles are largely presented as they originally appeared, rubbish grammar and all, but in certain cases the authors were allowed to make small changes, and sometimes I got fed up and made similar interventions for the sake of clarity, understanding and *not getting sued*.

Let's start with a story review from the old days, from 1976 to be exact, when the voice of the president of the *Doctor Who* Appreciation Society was the voice of all fandom, and when there was still a living television programme getting in the way of our culture. It shows that a lot has changed, but that some things, hilariously, have remained exactly the same. Readers from outside fandom should take note of the clear division the author makes between the fan way of viewing television and the way everybody else does it.

That was then . . .

Television Review of 'The Deadly Assassin'
Jan Vincent Rudzki, Society President
(*TARDIS*, Vol #2, #1)

Few *Who* stories go very much against what has been done before, but recently this has changed. First, there was 'Genesis of the Daleks', then 'Revenge', 'Morbius', and now 'Deadly Assassin', or rather 'Deadly Continuity'. But first let us look at the programme as someone who hardly ever watches. The costumes and sets were quite effective, but a little too *Flash Gordon*. It had a good cast and was well acted. The story was fair but did not hold together too well.

Now let's look at the story as *Doctor Who* viewers. The following is not only my view, but that of many people (including people who aren't avid fans). First, congratulations to Dudley Simpson for using Organ Music for the Time Lords, but thumbs down for not using his excellent Master theme. Then there's the more than usually daft title. Have you ever heard of an assassin that *isn't* deadly?

On to the 'story'. Before we even started we heard the same boring cliché: 'the Time Lords faced their *most* dangerous crisis'. I suppose Omega was a minor nuisance! The next blunder was the guards. Why *were* there any? The Time Lords were supposed to be *very* powerful, so much so that anyone strong enough to invade would swat the guards with ease, and Time Lord technology should be able to deal with minor intrusions. Then came the TARDIS. Before, it was a Mk 1 and the Master's and Monk's were different marks. So why type 40? OK there could be different marks of type 40 TT Capsule, but why

3

only one missing? As for such an advanced race being unable to find someone in a 52 (sometimes 53) storey building. Ridiculous! I've always thought Time Lords' names were secret and unpronounceable, so why do we suddenly know their names? 'C.I.A.' was certainly not appreciated, or Time Lords with bad hips. There is a time and a place for humour, and this wasn't it. Particularly Runcible whose demise I was certainly not sad about. This story really showed up the infatuation for Earth people in *Doctor Who*. It could have been set on Earth and no one would have known the difference. Doesn't R. Holmes realise that Time Lords are *aliens* and do not need to conform to human motivations whatsoever? This fact was well brought out in 'War Games', but ignored here.

Elgin said that premonition does not exist. Yet the Doctor had them in 'Time Monster', 'Frontier in Space', 'Evil of the Daleks' and 'War Machines'. I was surprised by the Doctor saying that Time Lord machinery was 'prehistoric'. Mr Holmes seems to have forgotten that the whole Time Lord way of life is to 'observe and gather knowledge'. So apart from the fact that they are supposed to be one of the most advanced civilisations (brought out so well in 'War Games' and 'Genesis') they could have easily copied more advanced races. For instance in 'Three Doctors' the Time Lords were amazed that there was a force more powerful than themselves. They *were* pretty powerful pre-'Deadly Assassin'.

In 'Deadly Assassin' the Time Lords seem to have forgotten the Doctor yet we've always been led to believe it's *very* rare for a Time Lord to leave Gallifrey. So he should be remembered, particularly as in 'Three Doctors' he saved Gallifrey (and the universe *of course*!) from destruction, and Borusa said they needed heroes. The trial of the Doctor was another R. Holmes farce. The 'War Games' trial was so excellent, but of course this had to be in Earth norms, and was pathetic. Then later the Doctor and co. go to look at the public register system to see what really happened at the ceremony. Now we were, I believe, dealing with *Time* Lords, so why couldn't they go and look at a time scanner and see the truth? Also, why need the brain machine to predict the future? Another fact forgotten is that Time Lords *are immortal*. In 'War Games' the Doctor said they could 'live forever barring accidents'. This had never been changed until 'Morbius' where we learnt that the Time Lords used the Elixir if they had trouble regenerating. So why didn't the Master use the Elixir? We also saw in 'Morbius' eleven incarnations of the Doctor ('though in 'Three

4

Doctors' Hartnell was *rightly* the first) so now we're left with one more Doctor, according to 'Deadly Assassin'.

Then there *wasn't* Part 3 which must be the biggest waste of time *ever* in 'Doctor Who'. A ten-minute trip into the matrix would have sufficed, but 25!

One minute Elgin was saying there's no way to tap the machine, the next he was taking the Doctor down to the 'old part of the city' which looked just like all the other parts. When Goth was discovered we heard the daft reason for him helping the Master, for an exchange of knowledge. Again ignorance of the Time Lord way of life is shown by R. Holmes. Goth should have been quite able to go to the extensive library and sit at a Time Scanner for a few decades or so, and find out everything for himself. He could even have followed the Master's travels on the scanners! Borusa recognised the Doctor, but since the Doctor and the Master were at school together wouldn't Borusa remember the Master? Also what's this rubbish about the Doctor being expelled? We know he has a Time Lord degree in 'Cosmic Science' (and that was revealed in a R. Holmes story!).

I was stunned to discover that the Doctor doesn't know his own people's history! The Time Lords would have their own history completely documented. After all, they can look back at time, so what's all this nonsense about myths? And surely somebody would have wondered what that lump and two holes in the Panopticon floor were.

Of course, Part 4 saw the return of the same old story. It couldn't just be Gallifrey in danger, it had to be a hundred other planets in danger.

You'd have thought that not much else could be wrong with the story, but there *was* more to come. Time Lord power sources are well known to be novae etc., as Omega produced, not some silly black box with tubes. I would also like to know how the Doctor managed to climb up a 100′ shaft with smooth sides, and with plastic rocks falling on him. Also, even if the Master was protected by the sash when everything was to be swallowed up, what point would there be to floating around in space – not much! Things get *even more* ridiculous when the Master falls down the deep hole (his yell lasted a long time) and he's back very soon, regenerating (due to absorbing energy). If all he needed was energy why didn't he use his TARDIS, like anybody else, to regenerate?

For some of these blunders you could argue that the story was set far into the future at a time when the Time Lord race is degenerating. But it can't be as the Doctor was recognised. No. *The new rule* for *Doctor Who* seems to be the reason, which is 'anything pre-Holmes needn't exist', which can't be good for a script editor.

What must have happened was that at the end of 'Hand of Fear' the Doctor was knocked out when the TARDIS took off, and had a crazy mixed-up nightmare about Gallifrey. As a *Doctor Who* story, 'Deadly Assassin' is just not worth considering. I've spoken to many people, many of whom were not members, and they all said how this story shattered their illusions of the Time Lords, and lowered them to ordinary people.

Once, Time Lords were all-powerful, awe-inspiring beings, capable of imprisoning planets forever in force fields, defenders of truth and good (when called in). *Now*, they are petty, squabbling, feeble-minded, doddering old fools.

WHAT HAS HAPPENED TO THE MAGIC OF *DOCTOR WHO*?

1: Sad/Not Sad

And this is now! Whew! The above wasn't a minority opinion, either. 'The Deadly Assassin' came last in that year's *Doctor Who* Appreciation Society Season Poll. These days it's widely regarded as the ultimate classic, one of a handful of contenders for the best *Doctor Who* story ever made.

By those fans who believe in such things as 'classics'.

The above review is a rather blunt introduction to the way fans watch television. We're certainly aware of qualities such as strength of performance, direction, design and so forth, to such a degree that many fans have gone on to successful careers in the media. But, uniquely, those qualities don't cover everything we look for in a television show. One of the things we like is continuity, as the above demonstrates. We enjoy (far too much) the idea that *Doctor Who* is one big story. Another thing we look for is the presence of elements that support our own fanpolitical points of view. In Jan's case, this meant a horror at the way the Time Lords were changed from godlike beings into a race of squabbling bureaucrats. While I don't wish to speculate on Jan's particular needs or larger politics, of which I know nothing, these fanpolitical viewpoints are often connected to a fan's everyday political and social viewpoints.

Which is why two fans meeting for the first time can tell if they're going to be mates pretty instantly by comparing favourite stories. If the other fan says 'Planet of the Daleks' and 'The Time Monster' then one might make one's excuses. If they say 'Androids of Tara' and 'Kinda' then one has instant common ground. Because there are so many, very different, *Doctor Who* stories, many different shades of opinion can be expressed through one's favourite story.

That's why fans are continually at war with each other. We're actually fighting the same dinner-party battles as everybody else does – about politics, art and society – only rather more fiercely and suddenly.

Of course, Jan's piece also demonstrates one of the worst tendencies of fandom: a pathological nostalgia. Nothing can be any good until it's a decade old, and change is always a bad idea. The main body of this book is taken up with a radical response to that tendency, by a new wave of fans who appreciated change. I call them the New Fandom.

Some Fan History Heard Third-Hand From Dubious Sources

Fandom is supposed to have started with the William Hartnell Fan Club or something, but it's only with the *Doctor Who* Fan Club (around the time of Jon Pertwee's stint as the Doctor) and its transformation into the *Doctor Who* Appreciation Society (DWAS, usually pronounced 'Dwass', around the time of Tom Baker) that we arrive at recognisable fandom of the sort we know today.

Let's divide fanzine production into some handy eras, while we're dealing with the mythology that passes for fan history. Initially, in the seventies, we have 'zines like *Oracle* and $E=MC3$, all rather gosh-wow and pleased just to exist, competing with the dinosaurs and all that. Then, from the early eighties, comes a glorious era of A5 fanzine production. Everybody was in the Dwas in those days, everybody got their newsletter, *Celestial Toyroom*, and winning that periodical's annual Fanzine Poll was the Holy Grail of fanzine editors. In this era, we have the original *Skaro*, *Ark In Space*, *Frontier Worlds*, *Cygnus Alpha*, *Shada*, *Aggedor*, *Space Rat* and many others. These fanzines got a huge boost from the vast collision of fandom that happened at the Longleat Celebration for the twentieth anniversary of the television series. Our Woodstock. Where over 20,000 members of the public crowded into an exhibition meant for 200. Everybody in fandom seems to have been there, even if they didn't know each other then, and the anarchistic, hothouse conditions of the event in question led to the creation of organisations, gangs and new fanzines. This is at the Dawn of Video, when trading pirate copies of stories on VHS tape was the standard excuse for fandom's existence. In the A5 fanzines of the time, old episodes were reviewed, letters pages (a very slow version of Internet bulletin boards) flourished, and fan fiction blossomed. (I'm going to ignore the vast field of fan stories, because it deserves a book of its own.) Their budgets were tiny, they aspired to photographic – and, usually on the last issue, colour – covers. There was little in the way of literary criticism. Fandom itself, bar the odd angry letter about people charging for videos, wasn't seen as a worthy subject for discussion. Appreciating the series was the entire point of the fanzine business then.

People left Longleat energised and gossiping. The anniversary, and the first new Doctor in years, had brought lots of new people into fandom. John Nathan-Turner was a producer who talked to fans, and listened to them. Something new was going to happen.

A few indicators of what this boom was going to look like were already visible. Nick Cooper's *Star Begotten* had always featured articles about fan politics. *The Black and White Guardian* had always made jokes about fans.

But it took *DWB* to change everything. *Doctor Who Bulletin*, as it was then, was, for its first few issues, a rather cheap-looking fanzine, extraordinarily positive about John Nathan-Turner, as the vast majority of fandom was back then. The only rude incident concerning the new producer had been a strange booing at a convention, fanzine-editor-led, but more a product of the usual contrariness and bile of fandom than anything organised. If the producer was *listening* to us, why then, he couldn't quite be the Olympian figure we required in that post. That self-hatred is what often stops meaningful communication between production staff and fans.

Then something happened, a moment of Promethean creation, a big bang if you will. JNT and *DWB* fell out. And the seeds of the New Fandom were sown.

DWB in itself wasn't very appealing, with its tabloid language and new-found aggression. Fans had always hated whatever the current version of the show was (as the review above shows), but saying it so forcefully and repeatedly was extraordinary. Throughout the late eighties, it attacked JNT with one negative headline after another. And it grew successful on that basis, creating an audience of very cynical fans.

Thus, the best thing about *DWB* was that it split fandom into tiny pieces. You were either for it or against it. Rows broke out all over. It was as if the formerly passive fandom had been empowered by JNT's desire to meet with and understand it. Unfortunately, the power fans found they had was largely the power to criticise and shock.

The Dwas, coincidentally, went through upheavals and bitter factionalism at the same time, and never recovered its former position as the unanimous voice of fandom. An alternative body, the Whonatics, arose, prospered for a few years, and then vanished.

So, from being one unified body of passive saddos, fandom became a mass of truly disparate warring cliques. The tensions of the 1980s had split the fault lines in the culture wide open. And the wars that resulted started to create what might be called war poetry.

The first reaction to *DWB* was *The Frame*, a rather dry collection of facts about *Doctor Who*. Both these publications were A4, glossy, with a professional look to them. Neither, for their differing reasons, felt quite like a fanzine any more.

It was the reaction against these two opposing principles – iconoclastic anger and the desire for a calming authority – that allowed fandom to finally find its own voice.

That voice was the New Fandom.

It began with a fanzine called *Purple Haze*.

Its editor, Stephen O'Brien, had formerly been responsible for *Peladon*, a sort of classy second division A5 'zine. With *Haze* he wanted to do something different. You could write about anything in this fanzine. Music, other TV, politics, fan politics, cinema, your life. Critical theory and humour weren't dubious excursions: they were *necessary*. *Doctor Who* was something you *did*, as opposed to something you watched or were.

You didn't have to be pro- or anti-*DWB* or -JNT. You didn't have to be that sad. There was more to this culture than fighting. *Haze* played a game of football across the trenches, started to enjoy the new empowerment for its own sake. Had fun.

The standard reason fandom existed became that it was because we liked each other. From this starting point exploded dozens of different 'zines, including *Brave New World*, *Alien Corn*, *Top*, *Private Lives* (material collated by Tony Gallichan, but 'remixed' by a different editorial team every issue), *Club Tropicana*, *Circus*, and more, some of which continue to this day.

In the early nineties, when there suddenly wasn't a show to appreciate any more, the New Fandom found that fans themselves were interesting. So the 'scene that celebrates itself' had its own gossip column (in Amanda Murray's fabulous *Sunday Frontios*, which also featured cartoons and satire about fandom). When Stephen O'Brien produced a booklet of photos taken at a convention, they were entirely of the fans, without a 'celebrity' in sight. Fandom as art lab or literary circle had arrived. And yes, while it was great at the time, it was a relief that everybody graduated after a couple of years.

One of the most important results of this fandom was a fanzine called *Cottage Under Siege*. Openly queer (so much so that a disclaimer in one issue announced that participation was not to be taken as a sign of sexual orientation), continually taking the piss, proud and sarky, *Cottage* led to a number of other Queerzines, such as *Anti-Matter Chicken* and *Sarah Jane*, and was part of the movement that included the gay fan group, the Sisterhood of Karn. (As if it needed a group! Fandom is almost entirely queer – but more of that later.) The latest standard reason for why fandom exists is because we want to shag each other. We finally got there!

Influenced by the post-*Haze* New Fandom were the new version of *Skaro* (A4, colourful, glossy) and *Matrix* (A4, solid, dependable). Between them, these two 'zines form a sort of synthesis of fan criticism in the present day, each reacting to the other's last issue in exciting ways, and presenting a kind of developing forum of fanlife. It would be bad if only one 'zine represented a so-called 'consensus', but with two of such near-newsstand quality, we can have debates, slag off, remain at war with ourselves. And that's how it should be.

The Following Pieces

To illustrate some of the basics of fanzine writing, I've chosen a fanzine article about each of the eight Doctors. They're not in order of Doctor, or even chronological. Here's a quick guide to where they come from.

One of the major differences between the old and New Fandom concerned how these movements each regarded Graham Williams's time as producer of the series. Then: shoddily made, childish, embarrassing rubbish. Now: postmodern adult comedy masterpiece. This new fashion was about cutting oneself off from people who couldn't laugh with, or at, the show, and Gareth Roberts outlines almost a manifesto for it in the piece I've picked.

Nick Pegg, through his fanzine *Perigosto Stick*, invented the Anti-Pertwee-Era movement as a weapon along similar lines. A weapon, that is, to divide one sort of fan (the series as Classic Serious Drama, collectors of facts and compilers of lists) from the other (the series as our first love, load of old tosh that it is, takers of the piss). This new view held the Jon Pertwee years to be rubbish, and laid scorn at the feet of everybody involved. Pegg's movement turned fandom around within two years. Then, the Pertwee era was the height of Classic *Doctor Who*. These days, even the most dedicated Pertweephile admits that certain elements of the show then were a bit rubbish. Positive reviews are *defences*, railing at the new majority of Pertwee-era-haters. So much so that Pegg and co. have started to get rather embarrassed at all the bandwagon-jumping, and may soon decide to adopt the opposite opinion again. In this chapter we have Amanda Murray, editor of *Frontios*, reminiscing about the anti-Pertwee movement in a piece written for this collection.

Why Nottingham should be the home of Fan Crit no one knows. But it was there that Tat Wood, Nick Pegg, Dave Hughes and many others refined the concept of using literary theory to examine *Doctor Who*. Alec Charles, Thomas Noonan and Martin Wiggins had done this in the A5 era, but the practice reached its zenith with *Spectrox*, Tat Wood's irregular book-length dissertation in the form of a fanzine. Initially, it can be a shock, seeing such theoretical big guns wheeled out to attack such a tiny target as *Doctor Who*, but the conclusions, and the journey taken, peppered with self-deprecating humour, asides and love, is always worth it, and the authors are invariably aware of the irony involved in what they're doing. Recently, a number of academics have started to examine series like *Who* in books like *The Unfolding Text* and (the closest anybody has got to describing what fandoms are really like) *Textual Poachers*. But it takes critics from inside, who know the ropes, to do it really well. I've selected a piece of Tat's that's not from *Spectrox* itself (which, while incredibly rewarding, is not exactly a starter slope for new fanzine readers – sample one via the address at the end of the book) but from elsewhere, concerning the strange version of science in David Whitaker's universe.

I just loved the innocence of Justin Richards's Troughton-era set visit, and how, when he meets them, all three of the show's leads react exactly like the cartoon versions of themselves that fans think they know via gossip and so enjoy bitching about.

Matrix these days specialises in long, in-depth, deeply interesting articles. John Binns's recent piece on 'Trial' shows another fan speciality: the willingness to rewrite the texts we're given. And the talent to do so most effectively.

And, beside *Matrix* as always, comes the new *Skaro*. Matt Jones came out in *DWM* recently, and from the letters they received afterwards you'd have thought he was the only gay man working on that magazine, or even in fandom. Whenever I say in print that all *Who* is gay, I always get angry letters from some Local Group or other saying 'well, none of us are!' (I can imagine the meetings where they ask around. It must be a bit like *The Crucible*.) Let's be more precise, then. The *vast majority* of *interesting Who* is gay. Including many of the authors in this book. But let Matt speak for them here.

Jackie Marshall, together with Val Douglas, edited the multimedia fanzine *Space Rat*, which became the *Doctor Who* fanzine *Queen Bat*. Their largely female, multimedia culture (the fans of *Blake's 7* and *Robin of Sherwood*) were the Eloi to the (largely male) *Who* fandom's Morlocks. They brought wit, happiness, fan fiction and continuous, layered, in-joking with them. (In the past, the point of entry to *Doctor Who* for women was often via the connection between our fandom and the fandoms of those other shows. Post-Davison, many more women entered fandom for its own sake. This book reflects the fact that, although women are still in a minority in this fandom, they produce some of the best work.) The piece I've picked has Jackie herself musing on Davison.

We finish with a poem, a sweet and ironic link to the next section. William Keith is the (now exposed) pseudonym of the poem's author. 'Menky' is an adjective, another example of the wonderful language that's developed around the culture. It's a very particular and fond sort of 'sad'. Perhaps the poem speaks a little of betrayal. The idea that professional broadcasters, Americans at that, would try to take the Doctor off us again! And then make him heterosexual!

Tom The Second
Gareth Roberts
(*DWB* #122)

'There's humour, which for cheerful Friends we got, And for the thinking Party there's a Plot.'
William Congreve, from the Prologue to *Love for Love*

'Contact has been made.'
Bob Baker and Dave Martin, 'The Invisible Enemy'

1. The Mission
'It stands to reason. Why? Why can't it lie down to reason?'

Criticism of *Doctor Who* within fandom retains the vocabulary of its origins in the early eighties. The series is seen as a succession of discrete blocks, depending on who the producer was or who was playing the Doctor at the time. The edges of what is known as 'the Graham Williams era' are particularly frayed.

For the purposes of this piece, I'm stretching the definition backwards to 'The Deadly Assassin' and forwards to 'Warriors' Gate'. On the fictional level, the twenty-seven stories within that bracket all take place in the same wondrous SF universe. And for me, they represent the highpoint of the series. The later Tom Baker stories tend to provoke extreme reactions. The traditionalist stance (shoddy production, slapstick, send-up, childish, season eighteen a 'return to adult drama', blah, etc.) has been redressed slightly over the past few years by an opposing argument. This sees the Williams era as an artefact of postmodern forces combining to produce works of semiotic thickness through usage of meta-textual signifiers. Hmm. I think the answer lies somewhere else entirely, and that what both arguments are missing is that the *Doctor Who* stories of the late seventies are hugely, magnificently and squarely entertaining.

2. Origins of the Universe
'What's for tea?' 'Tea?' 'Yes, tea!'

The universe of the Williams era is entirely middle class. Even the Gallifreyan Outsiders and the Swampies obviously come from the Home Counties. There's an abundance of royalty and aristocracy, particularly princesses and ladies. The only commoner we ever see is Drax, and he is a (Time) Lord dressing down. Naturally everyone speaks English except the French and their news is in English. Twentieth-century England has eccentric spinsters, mumbling rustics, villains with perfect manners and bemused commuters who promise their wives they'll be home in twenty minutes. It's a universe where an almost bloodless revolution can take place in thirty-five minutes, where time can be checked, slipped or tied in a knot, where machines can be friends. Yet it seems more real than any period of *Doctor Who* before or since.

Good characterisation is one of the hallmarks of the Williams era. The motivation behind the manoeuvres of characters such as Scaroth, the Graff Vynda-K, and Pangol are discussed and debated as key points in the narrative. And in our daily lives we meet people like Kimus or Thawn or Rorvik. The attention paid to detail is most pleasing, giving the fictional worlds portrayed roundness and credibility that allows the drama space to function the more convincingly. Examples: Vivien Fay's previous aliases; Pangol's study of the Foamasi; the 'courtesy' once shown to Lamia by Grendel. Characters as diverse as the Pirate Captain, Professor Rumford and Binro have backgrounds, beliefs, lives of their own. What drives most of the stories is a desire for love or money or power. The characters lead the plots; the science fiction, as Lalla Ward has said, just happens to be there, a distinction unfortunately lost on subsequent scriptwriters.

Imagination and science are interchangeable here. The camp horror of the Hinchcliffe seasons was replaced by often outrageous ideas. The warpsmash that releases the Mandrels, the nature of the Vardans as beings who can travel along thought waves, a pirate planet sucking others dry. One of the clichés wheeled out regularly to explain the longevity of *Doctor Who* is its concentration on the conflict between good and evil. This conflict is at its best when the oppositions are a bit more complex than Dark versus Light. One of the many reasons why the Master is such an unsatisfying character is that he makes the Doctor look too strait-laced. The Guardians are the backbone of the Williams universe, but they never come close enough to make us realise how silly they are. What's more, the first appearance of the White is underplayed so deliciously. He displays an attitude of indifference utterly contrary to his words of warning, neatly summing up in one scene exactly what makes this era so satisfying. To the Guardians, the Doctor and his enemies are insects and their battles have no moral dimension. Their war is between balance and chaos. White (or is it Black, or both or neither?) selects the Doctor only because he is successful. Against all the odds. On the Doctor's immediate level, the battle is between him (along with his friends), representing jokes and improvisation, against the villain or villains, who represent lack of humour and grandiose schemes that are too complex for their own good. This is the backdrop provided by the scripts. The regular characters interact with this. And what goes on in the rehearsal room and on the studio floor adds another dimension.

3. Vulgar Facetiousness

'Listen, when your life has been threatened as often as mine, you'll find this is much more fun!'

The Doctor, by his own admission, will soon be getting middle-aged. He's seen it all, done it all. In 'Pyramids of Mars' we glimpsed the enormity of his responsibilities as a time–space traveller. The lifestyle he chose is its own trap. The change in the character from season fourteen onwards is that he starts to react to his dilemma in a different way. Ultimately, as he tells Captain Rigg, he wants to have fun. Whereas Sarah Jane had been a good friend and sparkling company, the Doctor, at least consciously, preferred to be alone. Leela brings out his lonely, contemplative side even more, mainly because they can't really communicate on the same level. His behaviour in the time of their acquaintance grows ever more bizarre, but crucially, they know each other and how the other behaves almost too well. Leela's instincts tell her that the Doctor is shamming to the Vardans, just as he expects them to. In 'The Invasion of Time' it is K9 to whom the Doctor turns as a confidant, simply because he has no mind in the accepted sense.

In many ways, this story serves as a template for the character of the Doctor. The narrative revolves around him, his past, his opinions of others, others' opinions of him, and his great strengths and weaknesses as a person. In the eyes of his peers, he is a half-forgotten nobody; Theta Sigma, the slow starter from the class of '92 who scraped a doctorate from Prydon Academy with 51% on his third attempt. But five hundred and twenty-three years of practical, on the job experience of life as it is lived rather than observed on a thought channel has given him something far superior than a dusty certificate of graduation. He has learnt to feel, and with that feeling came humour and imagination. It has also made him smug, opinionated and moody.

The character of Kelner gives us a chance to see the kind of cloying parochialism that spurred the Doctor to reject life on Gallifrey in the first place. And the Doctor's revelation to Borusa of his true motives in staging the Vardan invasion reveal something else about him. Although the script suggests this was something that had to be done, there's more than a trace of gloating in the Doctor's treatment of the Time Lords. He is showing them, he thinks, that his way of life has equipped him to deal with anything, even to save their skins. Then comes the final irony, as the Sontarans appear in the Panopticon. As

16

ever, the Doctor has overlooked one vital detail. His capacity to make mistakes, as Romana would later suggest, not only makes his victories more unlikely but also more uplifting. He is flawed but endearing, which is very useful for a long running hero in any medium. The final shot of the story sees the Doctor looking rather morose at Leela's departure, but there will always be something to keep him going, such as building a new K9 to keep him company.

The motif of conflict between experience and book learning is continued into the following three seasons with the character of Romana. Her first incarnation is constantly exasperated by the Doctor's apparently warped priorities during their search for the Key to Time. In fact, as the audience knows and as Romana comes to learn, the Doctor never does anything, however odd it may appear, without a reason. His motive is usually confusion. In 'The Power of Kroll' his prattlings on the influences of early Samoan architecture conceal two simultaneous attempts to escape from the Swampies' seventh holy ritual. 'He's got piggy little eyes and a piggy little mind behind them', he says of Ranquin. 'It's very difficult to hypnotise somebody with piggy little eyes.'

The rapport he enjoys with the regenerated Romana is rightly legendary, and owes a lot to off-screen events. They are totally at ease with one another. Both characters are intelligent and witty. Whereas the first Romana's non-technical reading stretched only as far as the lifecycle of the Gallifreyan flutterwing, the second has obviously taken a crash course in literature. Forgive me as I gush like the Lalla fan I am. Advocates of a female Doctor would do well to remember that Romana virtually is the Doctor. They are two aspects of the same personality, and during their time together she uses a sonic screwdriver, wears his clothes and even starts to react like him. Her conversations with Rorvik – 'That's a very interesting philosophical question!' – are particularly worthy of her mentor. Shortly afterwards, she makes the decision the Doctor made hundreds of years before, and sets off to rove time and space with a robot dog on missions of mercy. Doctor two, Time Lords nil.

Her departure leaves the Doctor deflated, and without her and K9 he becomes a tired old man, sombre once again. He tolerates Adric rather better than his successor, but isn't afraid to let the boy know how he feels about his unorthodox entry to the TARDIS. Aware of his imminent demise, the Doctor is simply marking time until his end, preparing for the moment.

Whatever the case, a high level of attention was given during this period, by production team and actor, to the character of the Doctor, his beliefs, his friendships and his motivation.

4. Its Wonderful A-functionality

'All this fuss over outside appearances . . . it's what's inside that counts, isn't that right, K9?'

Part of the critical vocabulary of *Doctor Who* fandom that I mentioned earlier is the inevitable, 'Well, as for the sets and costumes . . .' As the Doctor says, these external details aren't all-important but it is nice to get them right. In defence of seasons fifteen to seventeen, I think that the sets wobble just as much if not more both before and after, and that the reason *Doctor Who* fans picked up on these particular wobbly corridors and zip-up monsters is more to do with not liking the scripts and the actors. Season twenty is a feast of tackiness, for example. It doesn't bother me that the Shrievenzale isn't very convincing or that the model of the Empress/Hecate crash doesn't come up to George Lucas standards. It's nicer when effects and things do work, but the directors of this period rightly favour the performances and the construction of a narrative. That's far more important.

5. Time Tots

'I must try to bring him up properly this time.'

Anethans aside, children are another grouping almost absent from the Williams era, something that made the arrival of Adric and the Outlers doubly unexpected and embarrassing. Despite its increasing sophistication, the series was nominally still for children. K9 is the most obvious point of appeal for youngsters, but his appeal is not lost on adults. I just can't see how this period of the series, which contains the most intelligently argued and concise plotting, could ever have been written off as kids' stuff. Importantly, the series was functioning very efficiently as a family show, with the Doctor's disrespect for authority and bubbling optimism of appeal to all groups.

I was ten when season sixteen aired. It's still my favourite. From somewhere, I can't remember where, I got the address of the DWAS and joined. I was a bit confused when I received my first few issues of the newsletter. These people didn't realise that *Doctor Who* was supposed to be funny. They didn't like Romana or K9 or even the

Doctor. They believed that *Doctor Who* should be more like something called 'the Barry Letts era', whatever that was. I didn't know who Barry Letts was. The series was a childish farce, which was a shame because when Jon Pertwee had been in it, it had been a gritty realistic drama and the Master had been really scary. And the black and white stories may have been a bit dusty but they were much better than the latest episode of the Tom Baker show. And the worst story of the season was 'The Androids of Tara' because Count Grendel was a silly villain and the whole thing was a bit of a joke, really, not like classic stories like 'The Space Museum' or 'The Daemons', which were proper serious *Doctor Who*. And Graham Williams, whoever he was, was dragging the whole thing down.

I didn't renew my DWAS subscription.

Eventually, some years later, these people got what they wanted. They got a story that was about adults struggling to stay alive, with guns and policemen and gritty backstreets, and plenty of references to old monsters and past stories because bringing back anything from the series' past got their vote. They got an actor who took the part of the Doctor seriously. They got a script that would help them compile lists and theories about the history of the planet Telos. They got 'Attack of the Cybermen'.

6. The Critics

'What these people (the fans) are conceding is that they don't understand actors or programme makers.'

Tom Baker, *Starburst* #17

'Listen, when I retire from politics, I'm going to set up a business, it'll be called Rent a Spine.'

Margaret Thatcher

'Go on, Doctor. Run like all the rest. Lily-livered, faint-hearted do-nothing cowards. I'm finally getting something done. Ha ha ha ha ha, ha ha ha ha ha.'

Rorvik

Why didn't the fans I mentioned earlier like Graham Williams' time on *Doctor Who*? Here's my theory. The academic definition of fandom is 'an excess of pleasure'. What I think this means is that fans are people who respond unusually to a text. We enjoy it too much. There are several different ways of enjoying things too much. Some ways are more respectable than others in the wider community. At least in its first twenty-one years, *Doctor Who* was a family adventure series. It was designed to provide twenty-five minutes of fun every week. Some *Doctor Who* fans tend to like lists and guides. Lists of extras' names and guides to how many episodes Deborah Watling appeared in including flashbacks and specials. Some *Doctor Who* fans think the series is a serious science fiction drama. For them a story or group of stories without jokes, and preferably with soldiers in, will always be better than any, no matter how well executed, with jokes in. For them the series should be more grown up. But adult, like progress, is a word that can mean just about anything depending on who's using it.

The main butt of the humour of the Williams era is at the expense of people who grew up without a sense of humour or sense of proportion. The Graff, Hade, Adrasta, the Daleks, etc. People with the backblast attitude to life. Unfortunately other periods of *Doctor Who* glorify this approach to things, the Brigadier and his butch chums being a prime example. If your favourite story is 'The Mind of Evil' you probably aren't going to like 'The Creature from the Pit' very much. The early eighties saw Williams slagged routinely. In preparation for this piece, a friend lent me a few fanzines of the period. One included a dartboard of Graham, his punishment for the production of 'embarrassing crap' like 'Underworld' and 'The Power of Kroll'. It was right next to a favourable review of 'Time-Flight'. The Longleat convention programme contained a piece by Ian Levine on the history of the series which slagged Williams before going on to praise 'the new golden age' overseen by his successor. In *The Unfolding Text* Eric Saward expressed a belief that the Williams era 'insulted its audience'. What upsets me slightly is how much this attitude still prevails.

7. The Producers

'Well, I can't get everything right.'

'The Leisure Hive' is very different to 'The Horns of Nimon'. But 'Meglos' is very different to 'The Leisure Hive'. I think that the series' big change begins with 'The Keeper of Traken' and the start of the Davison soap. JNT brought control to the studio floor, which suggests oddly that he may have been more suited to Douglas Adams as script editor, who could have done with that.

JNT's real successes of later years ('Caves', 'Happiness Patrol', etc.) have a Williamsesque feel to them. But the earlier part of season eighteen has a lot more in common with what went before than what came after. The received wisdom on this subject sees Williams wheeled out of the edit suite of 'Shada' in a white coat (presumably screaming 'Fools! Nothing can prevent the catharsis of spurious intertextuality!') as JNT and Bidmead slip in rather like Graham Chapman's *Monty Python* Major: 'Now, this is getting far too silly. Stop all this silliness!'

Why do I think Graham Williams was the best producer of *Doctor Who*? Because he and his three script editors thought about the series and emphasised the essential theme that makes it so special, messages present in almost every other period before and since but not capitalised on; that growing up shouldn't mean cutting off your emotions, that friendships are important, that the most dangerous thing in the universe isn't a shower of dianane acid or a redirected neutron star or even a chronic hysteresis, but people who have lost the capacity to laugh at themselves.

8. Tomorrow
'The future lies this way.'

At the time of writing, I note that 'Planet of the Daleks' has been selected for rescreening on BBC1. This choice fits in perfectly with the thirtysomething nostalgia cult currently growing so tiresome at the BBC. Nobody's going to be watching anyway because Raquel is back at the Rovers and there's a possibility of a Ken/Deirdre reunion. But if the BBC want to gather viewers for *Doctor Who* repeats rather than alienate the uninitiated with a bewildering jump through wildly differing casts and approaches, here's a suggestion. Start with 'The Ark in Space' and run Tom in order. It's worked before.

Pertwee
Amanda Murray

Let's start by facing facts – *Doctor Who* fans are never happier than when they are in disagreement with each other. Consensus, either in print or in person, would be unthinkable in fandom. What would we say to each other? No one would publish fanzines, and even fewer people would want to read them.

Perhaps it's because *Doctor Who*, as a body of output, covers such a cornucopia of eclectic styles and themes. Fandom has numerous actors, writers and production teams to compare with each other, so it's not really surprising that the majority of fans can't actually agree on anything. I can recall a few of my own arguments with other fans (drunkenly trying to convince anyone who would listen that 'The Robots of Death' is the superior Boucher story is only one of many examples that spring to mind). Indeed, on that rare occasion when we find another fan who actually shares our own opinion, we tend to form little coalitions against the opposition, digging our heels in twice as hard.

So it's not really surprising then that fandom has passed through cyclical phases of opinion, what could be loosely termed trends. Vilifying the Graham Williams era, and then placing it on a pedestal, protesting that 'The Gunfighters' was the worst story ever produced in the history of the series, then declaring it a forgotten 'classic' are only two examples. Therefore it should have been no surprise that fandom actually condemned a whole era to be despised in print and person, with a great deal of blame for the perceived failures laid squarely at the door of a single man – Jon Pertwee.

The accusations have been wide-ranging, swinging from the sublime to the ridiculous – everything from chauvinism, sexism, bad acting, and imperialism to meanness, Toryism, arrogance and even making little children cry. Reviews, discursive articles, poems, and even whole fanzines have been seemingly devoted to criticism of the actor who is not even allowed a first name in conversation – he is simply 'Pertwee'.

Typical local group exchange:

Fan One: I went to that *Doctor Who* convention last weekend.
Fan Two: I couldn't afford it. See any good panels?
Fan One: Well, I saw Colin and Sylv in the bar. Tom made one of his first appearances for years! I missed Pete's panel, but I saw Mike and Anneke – they told some great stories about Pat and Billy! Oh, yeah, and Pertwee was there as well . . .

Yet it's not just fandom who deny him a first name – popular comedians, Harry Hill for example, refer to him as just 'Pertwee'; the radio tribute upon his death rarely referred to him as Jon; and next time you're in your local HMV, take a look in the *Doctor Who* video section – you'll find a copy of 'Terror of the Autons' or 'The Sea Devils' lurking in the section marked simply 'Pertwee'.

Still, having surveyed my extensive library of fanzines (well, the ones from the big box in the back of the wardrobe), on the surface it would be hard to tell there was ever any antipathy towards the third Doctor era. There were more articles or letters of comment attacking an unnamed faction of fans who 'slate' the Pertwee years, than there was actual criticism, and there were a vast number of positive reviews and discursive articles.

It would seem that any published criticism of the era appeared in a small number of fanzines, and that subsequent opinion, and indeed outrage, fed from that body of work, snowballing into a sort of 'cult'. The 'big three' pieces of important Pertwee criticism that have generated the most feedback or debate are Chris Newbold's review of 'The Daemons' in *Perigosto Stick*, Paul Cornell's review of 'Terror of the Autons' and Tat Wood's 'Hai! Anxiety' piece, both from *DWB*. Indeed, *DWB* is largely responsible for legitimising what it describes as the 'significant minority' of anti-Pertwee fandom. By suggesting to a largely unaware body of *DWB* readers that there was actually something akin to a movement in existence within fandom, it actually helped propagate what feeling there was. People who had never felt the need to form any strong opinion on the era suddenly seemed to polarise into 'for' or 'against', and we were suddenly awash with letters and articles that were more concerned with reviewing the reviews, or even the reviewers themselves.

Pertwee – The 'Cult'?

It has to be admitted that, to a great extent, Jon Pertwee set himself up as a target for fandom. Compared to many of the other actors to have appeared in *Doctor Who*, Jon was perhaps the most exuberant and extrovert when it came to making convention appearances. Indeed, there was hardly a major convention (or conference, as he liked to call them) that he did not attend, and when he did appear it was in character, complete with costume. 'I am the Doctor!' he would cry whilst taking the stage, clad in flowing cape and frilly shirt.

For many fans, the actor and the character were one and the same, and it was easy to associate the worst of the third Doctor's character traits with the actor himself. The fact that when guesting at an event he was always in character off stage and on helped to reinforce this. Jon always seemed to see those weekends as working engagements, treating them with all the seriousness of a new play or film he was appearing in. He even had a script: a well-rehearsed list of anecdotes and amusing stories that he would vary only slightly, and trundle out for every convention panel he attended. From eyepatches, to lions and Draconian half-masks – the stories would emerge each time.

A typical piece of Lee Binding lateral thinking from his *Anti-Matter Chicken* #1.

Made Again
As a result of such frequent appearances and oft-repeated reminiscences, his familiarity bred a sort of contempt in many fans. He became unfashionable, if you like (why bother with Pertwee when we can ooh and aah over new people like Caroline John, or Anneke Wills?), and by making himself part of our public domain he gave us the opportunity to re-invent him in an image of our own choosing. As Paul Cornell observed in an article in *Cottage Under Siege*, we actually 'detourned' Jon Pertwee, reversing the messages, images and context of his era of *Doctor Who*, creating a sort of evil twin of the third Doctor – he was ours, we made him. We even loved him, albeit in a grudging manner.

According to Paul, this detournment occurred at much the same time as the actor made his presence felt at conventions, enabling the fiction to merge seamlessly with the reality. This was aided by bad jokes, rumour and scratch videos lampooning *Doctor Who*, which attached themselves to our perceptions of his personality. Unlike others (Nicholas Courtney springs to mind) Jon had no comprehension of our perception of him, or his character. I think fandom enjoyed its creation too much to share it, to spoil the secret. Maybe it was also because, deep down, we realised that 'our' Pertwee, and Jon Pertwee, actor, were separate people. I was present at one of the last conventions Jon ever attended, in fact he was the main attraction. I was standing behind a fanzine table manned by friends who were plying the convention-goers with their latest publication, one that just happened to contain a series of jokes about 'Pertwee'.

(Hopefully libel-free) Example:
Q. Why did the chicken cross the road?
A. To get away from Pertwee.

Anyway, we observed Jon wandering about the Dealers' Room, chatting to fans. He got nearer and nearer then stopped at the table next to ours (to flick through an album of photographs of Gillian Anderson with great interest). Immediately I watched copies of previously mentioned fanzine vanish from the table with great speed. Just in case he didn't see the funny side.

As well as the phenomenon of detournment, I think the nostalgic label of 'the UNIT family' had a lot to do with our derision of the character, and by association the actor. We were spoon-fed with this image of the Brigadier as the jolly, but reserved uncle, Jo, Mike and Benton as the brothers and sister you would have liked to have had, and the third Doctor as the head of the household. He was the patriarchal figure, even matriarchal (how many times has he been referred to as the mother-hen, clucking around his brood?). The third Doctor was certainly a father figure, and let's face it, how many people get on with their father? Especially one who's always quick to jump to conclusions, slightly grumpy, often sarcastic, a show-off and wears funny, embarrassing clothes.

But now, perhaps we've all grown up a bit. Lost some of our rebelliousness and worked out our anger. Perhaps as we can now see ourselves emulating our parents (getting jobs and mortgages and families) we no longer want to criticise the father figure. Or maybe that's a train of thought best left for psychiatrists with a Freudian bent.

Yet with the passing of the actor, the great crashing tidal wave of anti-Pertwee-ism has seemingly slowed to a few ripples here and there, replaced with a warm after-glow of nostalgia, and the belief that yes, most of the Pertwee years weren't VERY good, but we know that, and love them anyway. The same way people can still love a threadbare teddy-bear with a missing eye and one arm. It's still intriguing, however, that such feeling was able to form itself into a noticeable enough subculture in the first place, enough to create the momentum for Cornell's suggested act of detournment to actually occur.

Why Did You Want To Climb Everest? Because it's There!

Hypotheses as to why such feelings faded are easier to suggest than why they started. Maybe the small(ish) group of protagonists have had their say, myself included. We've just run out of steam. Perhaps there are fewer fanzines, and those that come out do so infrequently. Or maybe we're all just too busy thinking about the New and Missing Adventures from Virgin, the BBC novels or the implications of the telemovie. Or maybe many of those who had most to say have gone on to bigger and better things, and the rest have jobs now, and just don't have the time. Or maybe we don't want to speak ill of the dead.

But where did it all begin? It would be fairly safe to say that fandom's reinterpretation of the Pertwee era, and indeed of any aspect of the series' history, can find in its origins a similar motivation to that of a man who climbed mountains just because they were there. We criticise things because we *can*, because someone else years before us made sweeping assertions that we feel are there just for us to challenge them. Anyone who has ever written for a fanzine wants to be noticed, to be contentious. We love to play devil's advocate, and in many cases end up believing our own publicity, as do vast numbers of other people, who read what we write, and then write letters or articles in reply.

Surely there can be no smoke without fire? Was the Pertwee era *that* worthy of our criticism? It's hard to believe that an entire era, an entire five years' worth of output could be of the poor quality and questionable morality some people in fandom have made out, and I've been as guilty of jumping on the bandwagon as anyone. It's so much easier when reviewing something to point out why it's bad, rather than justify why it's good. Moreover, it's all too easy to conveniently disregard the context of the seventies when watching Pertwee-era stories now. Perhaps it's worth stopping and remembering that *Doctor Who*, especially in the pre-video age, was intended to be watched once

– twice if there was a repeat – and then to be dispersed into the ether for good. It was made largely by people to whom working on the series was just a job, not a vocation.

It was not until the advent of regular BBC releases of stories, and repeats on satellite and cable channels, that much of *Doctor Who*'s output from the pre-VCR age became available. Many fans were too young to remember the early seventies, or held half-remembered nostalgic images in mind. Others were not even born. So we read the novelisations, and gorged ourselves on the opinions of those few people who had actually seen the programme at the time, or later on had copies of stories on video, and were in a position to have published their opinions for the rest of us to read. As a result, certain stories attained an almost legendary stature, many Pertwee stories among them. When the rest of us finally saw third Doctor stories for the first time, out of context, perhaps watched at one sitting, many must have been disappointed.

I was, for one. For me, much of the Pertwee era just never lived up to my expectations. I grew up with Terrance Dicks novels as my staple diet of reading material. Indeed, my fondest memories of childhood are of snuggling up in an armchair on cold afternoons with a hot ribena and a pile of new Terrance novelisations that I had saved up my pocket money to buy or had borrowed from the library. One of the librarians was a huge *Who* fan, and she ordered in all the new books. So I think it's true to say we tend to remember the Pertwee era as being good, simply because the novelisations were so great, the authors increasing characterisation and depth, or even making sweeping changes. Indeed, many, myself included, believe some of the books to be better than the actual serials.

Take 'The Claws of Axos', for example. In the novel the Axons seemed so threatening, Bill Filer seemed such a glamorous and dashing US government agent, the Master was frightening and UNIT was a powerful military force. When I saw the real thing, I felt like crying. The Axons looked like left-over spaghetti, the Doctor was pompous beyond all belief, the Master was dull and Filer was a middle-aged man with a thickening waist and receding hair-line.

But I'm not the only fan who found the transmitted stories lacking. 'The Daemons' was perhaps the Pertwee era's greatest sacred cow, one of those stories to which the imprecise label of 'classic' was casually applied. As a result it became a soft target, ready to be ripped into by the likes of Chris Newbold, who, in *Perigosto Stick*, would have us believe it was approaching the worst story ever made. However, the truth of the matter concerning 'The Daemons' (and many of the stories from seasons 7 to 11) is that it's not the greatest story ever made, but nor is it the worst – as pointed out by a pre-Shelf Life David Owen in *Frontios*.

Coming Out Of The Closet

Like many events now past, from revolution to royal wedding, our interpretation of them is now tainted by our own social and cultural influence. It's easy to look back at *Doctor Who* of the early seventies and condemn it as sexist, or racist or isolationist. In his article on sex in *Doctor Who* for *Purple Haze*, Nick Pegg described the third Doctor as the height of oppressive male dominance. I find this rather hard to swallow when looked at in context. Fair enough, he was bossy, opinionated – arrogant even – and capable of breaking out into spontaneous cheese and wine parties, but compared to his television peers he was not any more sexist. Jason King, Steed or the *Doomwatch* team were all as capable of sexism, and other non-telefantasy programmes of the time held similar sensibilities.

As this article started off by pointing out, fandom has taken more than one or two major U-turns in its time. For example, after years of protesting otherwise, we're now happy to accept that *Doctor Who* is a children's programme that we all just happened to like. (Personally I think this is a move to disassociate the programme from the pigeon-hole of 'TV Science Fiction' where it is lumped together with *Babylon 5*, *The X-Files* and the various incarnations of *Star Trek*, and place it firmly where it belongs, in the realm of the kitsch, camp and cult along with *The Avengers*, *The Clangers*, *Sapphire and Steel* and *Chorlton and the Wheelies*.)

So perhaps fandom has changed. It's now all right to actually *like* the Pertwee era of *Doctor Who* as well as write about it. We've accepted that we'll probably never see new *Doctor Who* on television, and we've reconciled ourselves to the medium of the novel and the fan-produced video as the only way we'll gain any new output to argue about. These are offered to us in a more adult format than we have been used to, one we can exert greater control over, and fandom has adapted as it has learned to accept this, grown up, and as a result our perceptions of the series' past, the third Doctor included, have been influenced by a new maturity.

New fandom. New Pertwee.

Whizz for Atoms
Tat Wood
(*Skaro* (New) #11)

OK, so you've got to make a new adventure serial, a go-anywhere, do-anything family show, hip to the zeitgeist of Mersey-beat, the Kennedy administration's New Frontier and style, the Space Age, Pop Art, the Ford Anglia, everything. You're discouraged from anything that looks too much like bug-eyed monster stories but can go into space, across history and through any known genre of story-telling.

There is a bijou snagette. You've got the budget that would pay for three weather forecasts or coffee with Christine Keeler.

Don't let this daunt you! The BBC has an automatic stamp of authority, so anything you show those people 'looking in' will be believed. Richard Dimbleby says spaghetti grows on trees, therefore it does. They'd believe that Russ Conway was charismatic if you told them often enough. Everyone knows that the world has become more exciting, more colourful, more nearly perfect since the War. A dozen years ago, there was the Festival of Britain, when people who didn't remember the thirties were shown what the country had been like before (sort of) and how it was going to be with Atomic Power, a Welfare State and Jaeger underwear. The same 'everyone' knows that science-fiction is something Americans do, like playing the bongos and saying *'Swell!'* Well, Americans in commercial television. *Pathfinders to Venus* and stuff like that. *Quatermass* doesn't count, as Nigel Kneale swears blind to this day that it wasn't science-fiction, which is something Americans do, etc., etc. The thing about *Quatermass* or *A for Andromeda* for that matter is that they were for grown-ups, so they *can't* be science-fiction. For the BBC to do 'an adventure in Time and Space' is like doing rock'n'roll with British accents.

To begin with, this was an asset, because if they were watching at all (and there was only one other channel, and it would take ages to retune the telly), they would accept anything you showed them as being exciting, realistic and The Future (or, indeed, The Past, set in concrete and incontrovertible). The sounds, the sets, the sig. tune, all unrecognisable as anything the BBC might have lying around so it must all be 'right'. You didn't so much watch *Doctor Who* as swim in it, imbibe it, visit it on a weekly basis. The only other programme to use its televisionness and mix of sound and atmosphere to make itself less a programme than a place was *Top of the Pops* (well, on BBC at least, but this is half the point; being in the context of the rest of BBC scheduling and style it is far more abrupt, strange and exclusive-seeming, making the viewers feel like a tiny clique that just happened to include the whole country. *Ready Steady Go* had the home advantage since pop style was supposedly the exact opposite of everything BBC) Removed from this context, both *Top of the Pops* and *Doctor Who* were in trouble.

You get anyone under fourteen (to be honest, anyone under twenty-eight) to sit patiently and watch black and white stories. The story-telling seems so . . . languid. Plot, in Hartnell and Troughton stories, is an optional extra, as relevant as the plot of a Busby Berkeley musical.

If you watch a lot of sixties children's television, as I do, you will notice a type of scene which might be called 'Isn't-The-Future-Keen-Huh-Dad?', or *Thunderbirds* scripting. Aficionados reckon the best example to be the episode 'The Mighty Atom' (there's a whole lost world in that title), in which a fully automated, oceanic – desalination – Sahara – irrigation station (nuclear powered, of course) is staffed by just two, that's *two*, people, both highly trained experts. One of these turns to the other and says *'It's fantastic, isn't it, to think that this entire oceanic desalination Sahara irrigation station is fully auto-mated and only needs the two of us to operate it!'* and proceeds to explain the station's operation and design to someone who already knew. Amongst writers of proper science-fiction, this is called the 'info-dump' and is generally done more skilfully. The info-dump is always a problem. Just at a basic practical level it is important that everyone addresses everyone else by name until at least the first death – in fact detective stories have as much trouble as alien planets, and there's a very good example of (deliberate) bad info-dumping right at the start of *The Real Inspector Hound* where Mrs. Drudge answers the phone: *'Hello? The drawing room of Lady Muldoon's country residence one morning in early spring?'* Sticking to *Who* for the moment, it's easy to list examples of clunkingly unrealistic, awkward, stupid dialogue which would never occur if there weren't viewers; my favourite is the First Elder of the Sensorites: *'Do these humans have their hearts on the left, the right, or in the centre as we do?'* (or words to that effect: I haven't seen it for seven years so it might be politic to check). And who can forget 'Timelash' (not me, try as I might) and the *'What? All five hundred of us?'* incident?

Returning to the original point, however, the sixties have another problem. As if creating an alien world with plywood, Motosacoche tape

30

loops and slow, patient explanations (two schoolteachers and a girl from the future result in a rota system for patronising each other and nodding politely when Billy launches into a spiel) wasn't arduous enough, they have to have people inhabiting these wonderworlds who speak as if they belong there. Most of them speak as if they belong in weekly Rep. as it is, but with the regular cast taking on the bulk of the verbal back-fill they can converse amicably in future-speak. The thing to remember is that most of what sounds like info-dumping is in fact a kind of verbal sound effect. There is, for instance, no logical reason why the Taltarian airlock on Aridius should be called a Taltarian airlock, unless some visiting Armenian airlock designer with a good patent lawyer insisted, but it sounds all spacey and futuristic and not a bit like 'Tarrant'.

The writers have landed themselves with a problem: how to build up a picture of a world which differs from ours because of as yet undiscovered scientific principles without themselves having a clue about the science that *has* been discovered. Not excluding Kit Pedler, who knew a great deal about optics but chose to ignore popular and important laws of physics when the story needed it (see Innes Lloyd's comments on why he picked Pedler, in Marvel's 'Winter Special' of '83). Most writers are content to brazen it out with lines like *'Fold back the continuum loop'*, which fill the space where an explanation would have been. Some, like Douglas Adams and Steve Gallagher (not usually bracketed together), use the degree to which characters spout this stuff without knowing how and, more importantly, why things work as a character point. Adams and his posse filled the Williams stories with throwaway gadgets which suggest marvellous technology being taken for granted (a 'conceptual geometer' is presumably something which maps imaginary spaces, such as the TARDIS interior). Conversely, some writers fall flat on their faces trying to fashion solid science. Brian Hayles is an unfortunate victim of Viking, having made the Ice Warriors in the image of Mariner IV's Mars, but his Ice-Age due to super-efficient industry couldn't work in the computer controlled future he suggests, simply because somewhere there would have been a computer monitoring CO_2 emissions.

David Whitaker, though, has gone a stage further than most in replacing science. I once heard about a fringe play where stage-hands holding toy spaceships crossed the stage wearing placards which said 'Special Effects'. Many *Who* hacks do this, making the characters behave as if what they're saying has reasons and an orderly causal

This issue of *Paisley Pattern* was a pastiche of an annual, complete with obviously sourced art, rubbish quizzes and simplistic stories. Cover by Alistair McGown.

logic like that of known science. Whitaker-science, taking its trappings from Renaissance mages and fairy-tales, suggests an entirely separate order.

Like any branch of physics, Whitaker-science has three laws:

1 Mercury can do anything. It can make police boxes bigger than they have any right to be, enables the Daleks to conquer static electricity (see below) and even makes a handy casserole for when those unexpected visitors arrive. It's metal, it's a liquid at room temperatures and it reflects things like a mirror, so obviously it's magic.
2 Static electricity can do everything else. It can repel the image right out of a mirror and back in time, can power Daleks, stick people to Bessie and makes clocks melt. Or something.
3 If a job's worth doing, it's worth constructing a big white box with flashing lights specially for that one purpose. One for haircuts by radar, one to mix flavours like colours and make white Mars bars that taste of bacon and egg (a merchandising opportunity Verity Lambert missed), a fault-locator (how can you tell if it's broken down?), an oil-and-water jet shower-and-massage (presumably including Biactol) and – apparently – a clothing regenerator. One almost weeps with remorse for the confidence, the thrill, the sheer swagger of this exciting Derek Cooper-narrated future, where the British space programme reached Mars and Dido unaided by the Yanks.

It may just be that he couldn't be bothered to think up any more 'patter' than was in Nation's original 'Dead Planet' script, so the basis of the Daleks' power in, erm, 'Power of the Daleks' is that 'they've mastered Static'. A safe conclusion might be that C.S. Lewis, keen as he was on neo-Platonist writers and Victorian fantasists who borrowed their trappings, took from them and that Whitaker read Lewis (who was one of the few respectable writers at the time to have written about science-fiction and was author of the gruelling, Ovaltine-flavoured but dimensionally-transcendental 'Narnia' tweeness). The point is that, fascinating though the properties of these three items were, they were all familiar to children who would be watching. What Whitaker did with these 'props' was to deploy them as if they were part of a scientific perspective, as different from that of the 1960s as Relativity and Quantum Theory were from the work of Faraday. Imagine sitting in an Edwardian drawing room explaining the Atom bomb: *'You see, there's this special metal, which doesn't naturally occur, and in small doses it's the most poisonous stuff ever, but thirty pounds of it in one lump completely destroys a city. So you get two bits which amass thirty pounds, separate them by a few feet, then set off a small charge to hit them together. Boom! Bye bye London.'* If they believe that, move on and try telling them how penicillin was discovered.

Where it all falls down is in 'The Wheel In Space'. From the moment they launch into the umpteenth re-run of the 'Food Machine' scene (excising this from 'Power of the Daleks' kept Dennis Spooner in work) and the lousy 'square meal' gag, you know the script is in trouble. The problem is that the viewers are watching in a different way. What had been *'Blimey! The Future!'* was now *'Blimey! That's what it'll be like when I grow up!'* Around 1968, people suddenly realised that 'The Year Two Thousand', remote and wondrous as it sounded, was something they could expect to see. Zoë Herriot was a tease/ warning of what the children of the kids watching could be like – no, not could be, would be. The rhetorical features of setting a story in 'the Future' were clarity and overstatement. Setting it in a 'near Future' is like putting a story about oil barons in a fictional Arab state rather than a real one, it has to ring true yet justify being there rather than in any known country. The crew of the Wheel have overcome the Cold War (not as far-fetched in 1968 as ten years later) but have defences against neural attack (Silenski capsules, myriad drugs, Zoë's conditioning) as if it were necessary even without threat of invasion by two stiff Cybermen. There's talk of parapsychology and Venusian flowers, and Zoë's unflummoxed by the Doctor mentally projecting 'Evil of the Daleks'. If they've got all this, and socko-boffo lasers, how else is that level of science used? How could a loony like Bennett not have been screened (a problem also endemic in *Star Trek* where rigorous training and no end of telepaths have removed racial prejudice and cellulite, but failed to weed out dozens of psycho Admirals hell bent on starting wars). The near future is as glamorous as the twenty-eighth century (and better dressed) but with no indication of how we got there from today and nothing to suggest that science is anything but a story-telling device. People behave as if the paradigms and procedures have not changed since the 1940s and yet they would have to have done. Jarvis Bennett in particular, although largely there to articulate the nasty side of the 'brain-versus-heart' argument which substitutes for drama here, follows a hard line positivist dogma incompatible with most of the science apparently going on. Down to specifics: when Jamie's being asked about his journey in 'Silver Carrier' (what a stupid name for a spaceship), and later when he spacewalks with Zoë, the big worry is enough food and water. What about oxygen, electricity and whatever they use to process waste? This, like Zoë's colossally crass question about piloting the ship ninety million miles with fuel for only twenty million, assumes that space is just the sea but a different colour (once the ship's moving you don't really need fuel again unless you change direction, or run into a big gravity well – and that can actually help if you use it for a slingshot manoeuvre).

OK, I know this probably sounds like nit-picking, doesn't it? The question is, with the series basing its appeal on aesthetics rather than on rigidity (I mean, time travel is hardly kosher physics), did it matter that the writers didn't know Newton's three laws if it sounded as if the characters were conversant in something post-Einsteinian? Yes and no. If the story was far enough away, enough could be swept under the carpet to allow it to get away with plain story-telling. If the story relied on the 'charge' of being around the corner, derived its moral clout from polemicising about current issues and trends, then it was a different matter. Whitaker was nothing if not morally didactic, and if a moral point was made better by aliens who could make radiation behave like electricity (or at least something everyone called 'radiation' 'cos it sounded scientific), so be it.

(Risky paragraph of speculation: you, dear reader, may dump this if necessary, as this is not Whitaker-science, more Whitaker-philosophy.) The Renaissance mages mentioned above were often Hermeticists, i.e. following the meld of NeoPlatonism and Christianity implied by the Hermetic corpus, a text supposedly older than Moses, written – perhaps – by Hermes Trismegistes. Hermes was the Greek name but he was deemed to be the Roman Mercury. Whitaker's contribution to the first *Doctor Who* annual included a piece on 'Who Is The Doctor?' suggesting that he was searching the universe for something. This emphasis on quests, with the idea common in Whitaker's scripts that his motives weren't clear to the companions, was – dare I say it – proto-Cartmel. It's interesting, though, that Hermes has several attributes peculiar to the Doctor (again, noticeable in Whitaker's scripts). Some accounts have him as father of Eros, who, like Dad, gets himself to wherever there's something beautiful or good, or where knowledge is kept. They both disrupt societies which are too orderly. Hermes is in charge of speech, silence, writing and secrets, guides souls to the underworld and is in charge of 'the distinction, newly-discovered between one thing and another' and supervises both commerce and theft. By noon on the day he was born, he had invented the lyre and pulled a fast one on Apollo. In giving the new Doctor the ability to change shape (like Eros, often mistaken for a beggar), a hat and a recorder, it is possible, just possible, that Whitaker was suggesting that the Doctor was a servant of Hermes, or maybe even a messenger for some other divinities (as, of course, he later became). That mythology may be in play was hinted by having the Daleks start a workshop on . . . Vulcan. I said it was risky.

I recently had my eyes tested by a machine into which I peered whilst the shape of my eyeballs was registered on a printout. I could almost smell the mercury.

Going Underground
Justin Richards
(*Frontier Worlds* #17)

Sometime in 1967, somewhere in London, there was an exhibition. Right away, I'd better just emphasise that the events that I'm going to relate here are likely to be merely a mishmash of ancient memories; they will be neither accurate nor complete in all probability. The remnants of a small boy's memories, dimly and vaguely related some sixteen years later by a somewhat larger small boy. I offer my excuses, but no apologies.

Back then to this exhibition. I don't know what it was an exhibition of, but as I say it was in London, and it contained something to do with *Doctor Who*. Again, I have no memory of what. All I do remember is that it was plugged on *Blue Peter*, and I was at once determined to see it. Having convinced my younger brother (then four) that he too wanted to see whatever it was, I then had the rather more formidable task of convincing my mother that she too wanted to see it. She didn't. However, after some pressure (in the form of pleas, sobs and threats to leave home) she was eventually convinced that it might be best to make a short trip to the appropriate area of London.

So, one morning in 1967, off we went to the City. Having got there, we soon found the queue to get in wherever and whatever it was. It was a queue several miles long, and we had no hope of getting in. It was at this point that my parents suddenly remembered how much my brother and I had always wanted to see some obscure exhibition at the British Museum, something like post-Ming shadow-boxers' thumbprints, and off we were dragged, in a sea of tears and amid great protest, to see it. If this were a play by Samuel Beckett, no doubt it would end here and be praised as a great comment on the nature of culture in a socially-based, parental context. Luckily for anybody reading it, it isn't. The reason why that was not the end of the unhappy incident was that my mother took the trouble to write to *Blue Peter* (which must have needed courage even then) to ask if the exhibition would be on again or elsewhere. I seem to remember it was only on one or two days originally. The reply arrived, with the usual BBC rapidity of service, about six weeks later. The exhibition would not apparently be repeated. But, and this was the exciting bit, they were all very sorry we'd had a wasted trip to London (all the way from Bedford, so it wasn't actually that far) and if we liked, my brother and I, with a couple of parents, could go along to the BBC and watch a *Doctor Who* episode being rehearsed.

Eventually, the big day arrived, and at three o'clock on Saturday January 27th 1968, my brother, mother and myself, with my uncle in tow, presented ourselves in the foyer of (I suppose) television centre. After a while a man came and found us. He was late and he was tall. He had short blond hair and I can't remember who he was at all. (Probably with my memory he was short and fat and bald, but I think not.) He apologised for the delay, and led us into a lift. This brought us up to a studio that was almost certainly at Shepherd's Bush. Once in the studio, the chap explained it all in terms that a shy six-year-old and a precocious and noisy four-year-old could understand, despite the fact that he then had to explain in slightly less technical language the same things for their adult chaperones. This was a rehearsal, he said. It looked like a mess, and a half-built one at that. What then was going on? Well, we were told, this was a rehearsal for an episode midway through the story to be shown after the one that was presently being screened. This information raises several interesting questions. First, I always remembered him telling us that the story was rehearsed in batches of two episodes at a time: going on information now freely available, it seems that the episodes were then recorded one at a time, not two. So is my memory wrong, or were they rehearsed in twos and then recorded singly, or was 'The Web of Fear', for this was the story, an exception to the rule? The second point this raises is how tight the schedule was then, for the episode being rehearsed to be recorded, I think, that evening, or possibly the next day (for this was a studio, not a rehearsal room) was part four, part three having just been rehearsed I think. From the date I have given for this visit, you will realise that the episode transmitted on that evening was 'The Enemy of the World' part six. Therefore, they were rehearsing an episode that had to be shown on television in only four weeks' time (assuming I've got the episode number right).

The next thing that the man told us was that the story was set partly in the London Underground, and was about the Yeti. This of course sent us wild with excitement and anticipation, and we were shown a scene with a Yeti being rehearsed. This involved a man (Travers) being taken into a room by a Yeti and holding up a small pyramid or something, then telling the people in the room that he was the Intelligence. Something along those lines anyway. Two things struck me about this scene. The first was that there seemed to be a wall missing from the room, which inside looked very real, but from the outside seemed to be held together with bits of sellotape and glue. But the much more worrying point was that the Yeti was undressed! It had no fur on at all. In fact, and I hope I'm not giving too much away here, it was just an ordinary man, albeit a rather large one. I pointed out to our guide that it might be more frightening and realistic if they gave the man a costume or something to make him look just a bit more like a Yeti. To my amazement I was told that in fact someone had already thought of this, and the actor was not wearing it at the moment merely because this was a rehearsal, and he didn't want either to spoil the costume, or, more importantly, get too hot under the lights just yet. So where then was the actual Yeti – the costume that would give the actor something to act about or fill out? We were shown. It was a thing not unlike a large fur coat, only it was braced with wood, and set into the 'head' were two lamps. This we were told was the new-look, even more nasty Yeti, set some years after their first appearance.

Next, we were shown the other large set in the studio. It was a tube train tunnel. It was, I suppose, about thirty feet in length, and it struck me that the trains couldn't be all that big. It included a bend in it at one end, possibly to obscure the fact that it ended soon after. I don't remember there being a platform included, though. Perhaps there was another set for that section of tunnel, as there must have been for the stairs down to the station, although we did not see it. The interesting thing about this tunnel, though, was that it was open along one side for almost half its length. That is to say that part of it – the end without the bend – was built only of one wall and a ceiling. This was apparently to allow the camera free movement to film into the tunnel and show characters and (gasp) Yeti, from the side. When they were seen from in front or behind, they were to be in the completed section. Quite clever, really, I decided once I had understood all this.

That, along with the inevitable toilet facilities, was about all we saw in the studio. Before we left, though, we were introduced to a few more people; Frazer Hines, Deborah Watling and Patrick Troughton. I can remember little of the conversation we had with any of them, just a few odd things, and what a psychiatrist would make of my mental make-up from that, heaven only knows. I do remember Jamie telling me his kilt was a McCrimmon tartan. 'Really?' I asked, aghast. 'Well,' Frazer replied, 'sort of, anyway . . .' Deborah Watling gave me a kiss, and Patrick Troughton showed me his braces. This is the interesting bit for the trick cyclists, because I can remember those braces better than anything else that whole day. They were red: bright red. What made them exceptional, though, was that they had little gold animals embroidered on them. In fact, I think some of the colour centre-spread *TV Comic* strips from this time show them quite well, should you want to follow this up. What was most interesting was that Patrick told me that they were embroidered for him by his mother. Whether she also gave them to him, or even whether this is true, I'm afraid my fifteen years of intensive research have failed to unearth.

And that was about it, really. We went off somewhere else then and met two more people who were very kind and polite and wanted to know what we liked best in *Doctor Who*, and how much we'd enjoyed our visit. In fact, they (possibly Peter Bryant and Derrick Sherwin?) tried to persuade us to stay and have tea with them and chat some more. They even revealed that there was a television room where we could watch *Doctor Who*. 'What's going to happen?' I asked one of them, referring of course to Salamander's dastardly plans. 'Ah,' said one of the men, raising his eyebrows. 'Who knows, and probably no one else does . . .' My mother decided at this point that we had had enough excitement and monsters and tunnels and tea for one day, and we'd better go home. So we made our farewells, and were promised autographs from Frazer, Debbie and Patrick (which I still have, along with BBC photos of Daleks, Macra, the Slyther, Monoids and Menoptera which were also sent a few days later) and lots more exciting adventures for the Doctor and co. So off we went into the horrors of London to find my uncle's car, and get us home to find out what sort of a mess my father was making of the dinner!

I'm told that we also saw Lulu while we were waiting in the foyer, but that hardly seemed important at the time, any more than it does now. Give me a Yeti any day.

"Hot Pink Shorts"

Part of Amanda Kear's indexing of Peri's ridiculous wardrobe from *Queen Bat* #3.

Trial and Error
John Binns
(*Matrix* #51)

A little imp on my shoulder perked up and began shouting as I read these words in *Skaro* issue 9/10: ' "The Trial of a Time Lord" has been quietly erased from fandom's collective consciousness.' I mean, if only.

Oh yes I thought. Though it wasn't the point Paul Dumont was making, the idea of those 14 weeks in '87 taking a flying leap from my (and every fan's) memory into a chasm of oblivion, never to return, then took a dangerously seductive hold on my psyche. What if, the devil whispered in my ear, what if we could erase it, obliterate it, disseminate its particles (so to speak) with a mighty blast from some psychological

Magnotron? You see, you're already quivering. You'd like it too, wouldn't you? Only the mad witterings of conventional so-called wisdom persistently tell you that it isn't possible. Free your mind, I tell you! – no need to listen to them. It didn't happen. It never happened.

See how easy it is? And how good it feels? You know it makes sense! The whole thing was an hallucination, brought on by Michael Grade. He threatened to cancel it, our beloved series, and naturally we began to panic. So the twenty-third season was to be a final test, the day of reckoning, desperate measures or even (for those of you sad enough to spot the connection) a race against death. What were we bound to imagine? What would inevitably give us endless nightmares? That's right: the worst possible season that could ever be produced, the hypothetical end product of as many miscalculations and errors of judgement that any production team could feasibly make. 'The Trial of a Time Lord'. We dreamt it. Of course.

It's not as if this sort of thing hasn't happened before. Way back when the very first episode was broadcast in November '63, the entire viewing audience believed they had seen a twenty-five minute film of a cage full of baboons at London Zoo, spitting and grinning and breaking wind, such was the anticipation whipped up around the start of a new sci-fi series. So great was the illusory effect that a repeat showing had to be arranged on November 30th to cancel it out and restore sanity. Similarly 'The Evil of the Daleks' was originally perceived as a man vomiting trifle into an upturned army helmet for seven weeks, and only the repeat showing a year later could convince the public of the truth.

The so-called 'Trial' is another such instance, although the BBC haven't thought it necessary to repeat the true twenty-third season. Very few of the people who watched it at the time now give it a moment's thought; only the fans, labouring under a misapprehension to rival Flat Earth and a moon made of green cheese, continue to suffer in silence. Peter Darvill-Evans discovered the truth and deleted the Valeyard from the possible list of New Adventures villains; Terrance Dicks, when writing *Blood Harvest*, thought nothing of casting aside the myth and wrote for a Gallifrey set straight after 'The Five Doctors'. Mr Dumont's comment brings us slowly back to reality: the dream is over, and as Bobby Ewing emerges from the shower it's time to shake the fug from our heads and work out what really happened that year.

We can be pretty sure that Grade's cancellation took place: after all, we've got the tabloid reports to prove it. But that happened during season twenty-two and the next thing we can remember clearly is the casting of McCoy for season twenty-four. There is, therefore, a season missing there, a gap in our collective memories. Whether any back numbers of *DWM*, *CT* et al can shed any light on the matter is for others to decide since when I got up during the night to sift through my collections, reading by the flickering light of my burning candle, that mysterious phenomenon of spontaneous combustion occurred and the only remaining records in my house were, tragically, burned to a crisp and lost forever. Perhaps, tonight, you'd like to try the same.

That season we remember (Oh, don't worry, I remember it too: the fan community has developed and refined its own nightmares, through a process of something like self-induced hypnotism), 'The Trial of a Time Lord', had it really occupied that gap, would have explained how Peri came to part company with the Doctor, and given us some details of who this Mel character was, where she came from and how and why she joined the Doctor. Behind the scenes as well, it ought to reveal a few things: chiefly, the departure of Colin Baker, and the non-departure of John Nathan-Turner, as well as the continuation of the series itself. Presumably, the production was impressive enough to secure the series' future and give its producer a strong mandate to carry on, marred only by a performance from Baker (we must suppose) so poor as to make him resign out of sheer shame.

Further proof, then, that the 'Trial of a Time Lord' that we've been thinking of can't have been it. The changeover from Mel to Peri seemed to happen, but it's a bit of a blur: Peri's departure wasn't explained (we thought it was, and then it wasn't. Dreams can have this contradictory quality, sometimes) and Mel just kind of turned up rather than joined. Then she came back, from the future, out of time and into the TARDIS, after she'd met the Doctor, but before he had met her . . . which can't be right, can it? As for the rest, that doesn't work either: since if anyone was going to be sacked after the season we remember, it'd have to be the producer and not the lead actor (disregarding the possibility that the BBC was actively pursuing a policy of suicidal insanity at the time). The same goes for the decision to continue the series, as (if we remember correctly) the 'Trial' got ratings of three to six million, rather than seven to ten as it had previously been accustomed to (and for which it had been accused of 'flagging'). And besides, if they really had introduced a character like the Valeyard, and then had him take over the Matrix at the end, they would have resolved the storyline by now, wouldn't they? Well, of course.

Pinning down the exact moment at which reality gave way to fantasy is a tricky problem, but I'm afraid we must face the fact that for a lie to work, it must be shrouded in truth. So most of what we saw, right up to the moment of broadcast was true. Bonnie Langford really was cast; so were Joan Sims and Brian Blessed, though Honor Blackman might just have been our imaginations. Robert Holmes and Philip Martin did have their scripts produced: which, of course, sounded fairly promising. The episode count was indeed reduced to fourteen; the format was four, four, six, although the exact detail of the last segment wasn't revealed before we blacked out. And of course, we can't ignore the fact that the season was to have a running theme, to involve the Doctor being placed on trial for his life by a character played by Michael Jayston called the Valeyard, which really does mean 'doctor of law'.

That was where our paranoid delusions started to take over. It's interesting to note how much fandom's hallucinated season twenty-three (let's call it the Fake Trial, shall we?) was influenced by the then popular views of the show's recent past, particularly of the Graham Williams era. We heard Michael Grade tell John Nathan-Turner to 'get the show back on the rails', and we were immediately put in mind of the instruction Williams was supposedly given in 1977 to tone down the horror content and increase the humour. A few voices recalled the 'corny, childish and badly acted' production that followed and thus fandom created its own monster; a corny, childish and badly acted twenty-third season. Because most fans didn't appreciate at the time that the Williams era was often genuinely funny, we imagined a season where any attempt at humour fell utterly and embarrassingly flat. And remembering the appalling mistakes of the notorious Key to Time season (sic) we quickly jumped to the conclusion that this would be just another contrived linking storyline between an otherwise incompatible set of serials. And yet, ironically, from the evidence we knew at the time and trace elements that made it through the haze into the Fake Trial, we can see that the Real Trial needn't have been, indeed wasn't, like that at all.

Take the umbrella theme idea, for a start. For such a turning point in the series' history, what better theme than the Doctor's intervention in Space and Time? And what better threat to present than the one that was actually lurking behind the scenes – that the errant Time Lord's travels would be halted forever by the Powers that Be? Of course the idea wasn't new and it had worked pretty well in 'The War Games', but inevitably the nature of the new Trial would be different. The Time Lords, in 1969 no more than a mere hint of a powerful race including the Doctor and the Monk, had now been revealed as a corrupt and hypocritical culture masked by a set of grand and archaic symbols and traditions to match the Great British Unwritten Constitution itself. Furthermore, they had not only rediscovered the Doctor but had sent him on numerous troubleshooting missions (arguably including his exile to Earth), used him to solve the Omega crisis and set back the Daleks' evolution, prevent the resurrection of Morbius and the Cybermen's plans to reverse the destruction of Mondas, amongst countless other desperate situations. 'Genesis' and 'Morbius' had made clear the Doctor's status as a wanderer on a long leash; as the Time Lord says in the former story, 'You enjoy the freedom we allow you: occasionally, we ask you to do something for us'. Despite breaking the Laws of Time in 'Frontios' and failing to take Romana home, there were broad hints in 'Attack of the Cybermen' that the Doctor's status remained the same, while 'The Two Doctors' had seen Robert Holmes imply that even before 'The War Games', the Doctor carried out missions for the Time Lords and that his TARDIS had carried a recall device.

So, the issue of the Doctor's intervention was now more complicated than it had been at the end of Troughton's reign. It now involved the question of Gallifrey's role in universal events as well. The Time Lords could no longer safely put the Doctor on trial for intervention without a countercharge of gross hypocrisy and we could expect the Real Trial to reflect this. For the Time Lords to pull back the Doctor from his leash and sacrifice his value to them something must have fundamentally changed: either a massive mistake on the Doctor's part, or a significant change in the Time Lords' policy for reasons of their own.

Not surprising, then, that the plots of Robert Holmes' 'The Mysterious Planet' and Philip Martin's 'Mindwarp' both include aspects relevant to both the Doctor's and the Time Lords' interference. Much of the plots of these two stories survived in their respective counterparts in the Fake Trial and it only takes a moment's thought to realise the relevance of each.

'The Mysterious Planet' centres on a potentially very dramatic idea: that the Time Lords, purely to protect their own privileged position in the Universe as keepers of the Matrix, would virtually destroy the planet in which the Doctor takes such a devoted interest.

The potential is there for a real dilemma for our hero; should he take the side of the Earth or that of Gallifrey? And as an extra twist, the evidence of a contemporary underground station being present in the ruins of the Earth strongly suggests that the Time Lords have even broken their own primary rule, destroying the planet in the twentieth century and wiping out millions of years' worth of history. As for the Doctor's intervention, it's as helpful and successful as ever but, as in the next story, his obsessive drive to uncover the mystery tends to ignore his companions' feelings a little more than we might expect. In 'Mindwarp' of course, that goes a stage further as the Doctor's recklessness gets him virtually knocked out by the Mentor's brain pacifier. Not only does he fail to stop Crozier's experiments, he is directly responsible for Peri's brain being the subject of Kiv's mind transfer. And again, the Time Lords are forced to intervene, this time not for their own sakes but because of the mistakes of the Doctor, whose mission just this once had ended in spectacular failure. Thus Peri is killed, the Doctor is taken out of time and a trial is arranged to determine where the fault lies and what should happen to him now.

This still leaves some questions unanswered. But before we go on, let's go back to the Fake Trial and see how it measures up so far. The plots of the first two stories are the same but the linking theme is dealt with very differently. When we imagined 'The Mysterious Planet', we evidently thought that Holmes' script would be dropped into the Trial format in a rather clumsy fashion, with no thought paid to the logic of the plot. Think back. In the Fake Trial, didn't the High Council use the Valeyard to alter the evidence of the Matrix and get the Doctor lynched because he'd found out about their secret plot to destroy the Earth? Does it therefore make any sense that they should then show a video of the evidence of the said plot in a public trial, making no discernible changes, censoring a couple of mentions of the word Matrix and apparently adding nothing to the Valeyard's case? If the story were to be shown as 'evidence' it would surely be part of the Doctor's defence; better still, it could be televised as a complete story, and not as 'evidence' at all.

As for 'Mindwarp', it was the plotline of the Valeyard's tampering with the evidence that negated that story's value as part of the Fake Trial. We didn't know whether the Doctor was acting strangely as a clever ploy, or because of the Brain Pacifier, or because the evidence had been altered and furthermore we didn't know what happened to Crozier's experiment in the end. Was the Inquisitor right to justify the

Time Lords' intervention, or did they ever intervene at all? We simply didn't know; but we do have a script that, minus the Trial scenes, would add a lot to the season's theme and doesn't lack credibility.

So my suggestion – take it on board if you will – is that the Real Trial didn't actually start until the ninth episode of the twenty-third season. 'The Mysterious Planet' and 'Mindwarp' were televised exactly as they would have been without the trial sequences (a few additions here and there, some subtle alterations in tone, but I'll come to those later); and with the plotline of the Valeyard's altering of evidence entirely absent.

This, of course, would make a lot more sense. It avoids the problems of what really happened in 'Mindwarp', the sickening gut-wrenching ('Peri lives?' 'She is a Queen!') scene from 'The Ultimate Foe', and the use by the Valeyard of a highly damaging, unaltered and entirely useless piece of evidence in his case for the prosecution. The lack of any need to go back to the Trial room every fifteen minutes to remind the viewer that this is a continuous story could also be a plus, allowing the stories to flow more freely and have some genuine dramatic impact; although there'd need to be a bit more work on the scripts, acting, lighting, music, costumes, you name it to turn 'The Mysterious Planet' into something dramatic. Remember, this was a story of a post-apocalyptic Earth, the setting being the ruins of London, its inhabitants reduced to barbarians and slaves. Good opportunity for a little black humour as well, of course, but that hardly excuses Humker and Tandrell. So let's assume the Real Trial had a little more style than its Fake equivalent as well.

This still leaves a problem or two of structure, which we might assume the Real Trial would have been able to overcome. We still have two essentially distinct stories and we still have a problem with 'The Mysterious Planet' in that a major plot element – namely the Time Lords' use of the Magnotron on Earth – has yet to be revealed. In any genuine television drama serial, the problems of sustaining a fourteen episode run in this manner would be dealt with by adding cohesive plot devices to a sequence of self-contained episodes (or in this case, three interlinked 'segments'), which enhance the story for those who are following the whole, but don't alienate those who are not. So, the Real Trial treated 'The Mysterious Planet' and 'Mindwarp' as separate stories, but with the secondary task of furthering the season's theme and leading up to the Doctor's trial in episode nine. The first story contains two 'external' plot devices, in the sense that they are not resolved in those four episodes but add to the umbrella theme. The question of who or what zapped Planet Earth light years across space is left hanging in the air, quite safely; the casual viewer doesn't need to know that in order to enjoy the story. The question of what was in Drathro's travelling case is answered to the viewer, but not to the Doctor; so that's only unresolved to the extent that we are left wondering when and if the Doctor will find out.

How do these enhance the story? They add a little intrigue; and as in any mystery, the hope that answers will be forthcoming keeps you hanging on. In the Fake Trial, there was absolutely no indication that anything in 'The Mysterious Planet' would later be explained; we simply went on to the next bit of evidence. In the Real Trial, things were different. Because we were watching a continuous stream of adventure, rather than two 'epistopic interfaces' (whatever that might mean), we could have the Doctor musing over Ravolox one week and tracing the origins of the alien Warlord's energy blaster the next. So, maybe the Doctor's only lead to find out anything about Ravolox is the guns that Glitz and Dibber use, that lead him to their suppliers on Thoros Beta. He tries to find out more but Crozier's experiments get in the way, and anyway the Mentors don't know very much. A broad hint from Kiv or Sil, that Glitz was recovering Matrix records, serves to keep the interest alive, and perhaps the suggestion that the source of the Secrets and the relocation of Earth might be connected leads us to suspect that the Time Lords might hold some answers. Therefore, the start of the trial has a double significance, linking the two stories of the season so far.

Which brings us on to the last six episodes. It should be clear by now that the story we remember as parts nine to twelve, 'Terror of the Vervoids', was nothing to do with the Trial at all. Not a bad story, perhaps; some pretty good cliffhangers too; but it would hardly be any use to the Trial storyline. Apart from the fact that it's nothing more than a standard *Doctor Who* story, the idea of it being the sole piece of evidence in the Doctor's defence is pretty damn comical. Would the Doctor be such a duffer at Gallifreyan law that he would fail to remember that genocide was a capital offence? Would it never occur to him to mention that he had helped the Time Lords on a thousand occasions and been used by them on a thousand more? There would also, of course, be the problem that if this were a story from the Doctor's future, that would conclusively prove that he would be let off by the Trial and allowed to go on travelling. It would also give the

47

Doctor precognisance of the story's events, which must be contrary to a law of time or two, and betray the very curious nature of a system of law in which someone sentences someone for a crime which they have not yet committed. Let's face it, if the object was to prevent the Doctor committing genocide, all they would have to do is order him not to answer the distress call from the Hyperion III and despatch an agent to make sure of his compliance. Automatic execution would seem a little excessive.

And in any case, we've already decided that the basic device of the Trial being a presenting of three *Doctor Who* stories as evidence – some of which has been altered by the Valeyard, some of which reveals Gallifrey's secrets, and all of which had been carefully videoed, edited, and had incidental music added by the Valeyard's henchmen in the Matrix projection room (presumably) – was such a bad idea that it can't really have happened. So including something like 'Terror of the Vervoids' looks like making very little sense. What was needed was something to conclude the season's themes and storylines dramatically and to the viewers' satisfaction. The Trial, the Valeyard, and the revelation of the Time Lords' destruction of the Earth, were all important. But a satisfactory resolution to a reasonably complex storyline need not itself be too complex, and is unlikely to work if it merely serves to complicate matters further. So the Real Trial contained nothing about the alteration of evidence, nothing about a Particle Disseminator hidden in the Matrix to assassinate members of the jury, and nothing about the Master taking control of Gallifrey in the midst of civil disorder. It's not as if these ideas would have worked anyway, and I'd be surprised if any of them – thought up as they were in spasmodic fits of *Who* fan delirium – could make the slightest bit of sense to any of you now. I mean, how could the Valeyard be planning to execute the Gallifreyan elite, while simultaneously relying on them to give him the Doctor's remaining regenerations? Why does Gallifrey suddenly erupt into civil war, and who wins? And where, precisely, does the Master fit in?

So, forget all that. What was really shown in parts nine and ten was a much simplified version of the Trial, incorporating some parts of 'The Ultimate Foe', and making maximum use of Michael Jayston as the villainous Valeyard. Part nine, in brief, is the Valeyard putting his case to the Inquisitor, with repeated clips from 'Mindwarp' and perhaps one or two other stories. Rather than a boring and static bunch of non-speaking parts in Time Lord fancy dress sitting watching a video, the fact that the Time Lords have the most sophisticated data retrieval system in the Universe might just allow for a more dramatic presentation with the Doctor, Inquisitor, and Valeyard actually being present (or apparently so) at the events in question, rather like the Holodeck in *Star Trek – The Next Generation.*

The events of 'Mindwarp' have left the Doctor shaken up and angry, and the atmosphere soon gets heated. Eventually, the Valeyard presents evidence of what he claims is a possible future of the Doctor – what will, or would, happen if he were allowed to leave the trial as a free man. It's a very short scene, unclear, and out of context, but it unmistakably shows the Doctor as a villain, siding with the Daleks in a plot to destroy Gallifrey. Shock horror, cue end titles.

The Inquisitor calls for a recess and the Doctor leaves the trial room. Elsewhere on the station, he meets up with the Master, who is loath to give him help but nevertheless unwilling to let the Time Lords get away with their plan. He tells the Doctor about the High Council's action against Earth, and suggests that if he threatens to reveal this, they might let him go. He reveals that it was he who paid Glitz and Dibber to recover the Matrix secrets, knowing he could use them as evidence either to bring down or to blackmail the High Council. He also tells the Doctor to keep a close eye on the Valeyard, inferring that he is something more than a mere prosecuting counsel but for now, saying nothing more.

The trial goes on after the recess, but this time the Doctor is giving as good as he gets, and the air buzzes with accusation and counter-accusation. Despite the Doctor's threats, the Inquisitor is unwilling to let the Doctor go, and he is taken prisoner. In time-honoured fashion, though, he escapes and once in the TARDIS sets the co-ordinates the Master has given him as the time and place to which he has sent Glitz, to have another go at taking the Matrix records. It is Earth, 1986, just before the Time Lords' Magnotron is to be used to displace the planet. He arrives there, but the episode ends with the news that the Valeyard has arrived there too.

The scene is then set for the final story of the season: a four-parter following directly on from the Trial and thus sharing the same production code; but written by the series' script editor, Eric Saward. The success of this story was crucial if the series was to continue: it had to be popular, to persuade the viewers that *Doctor Who* was still exciting and worth sticking with. Either as the climax of a crucial season, or possibly as the very last story ever, this segment had to stand out.

It could be that the main points of story 7C (2) are already coming back to you now, fitting into place like the last pieces of the jigsaw puzzle. The different elements of the story not only make sense of the context of the season but also in the light of later stories, and further-more had the necessary populist appeal to revive the series' fortunes. Bringing the story down to Earth in 1986, for instance, heightens the immediate dramatic effect, tallies with the contemporary tube sign on Ravolox, and allows for the introduction of Mel. The fact that this was a Dalek story also makes sense, not only for boosting ratings, but also for filling the obvious gap between 'Revelation' and 'Remembrance of the Daleks' in the otherwise continuous Davros/Dalek factions storyline. Making this a campaign by the Daleks to wrestle supremacy from the Time Lords not only fits in with the pattern of their campaigns in 'Resurrection' and 'Remembrance', but also chooses the ideal moment to try the classic fannish plot idea, Daleks versus Time Lords.

The Doctor's role is pivotal, his relationship with Gallifrey finally in stark opposition to his moral principles and his love for the Earth. The Valeyard, representing the Doctor's darker side, is on hand to make him side with the Daleks in order to save our planet. The fact that the Daleks are themselves taking on a judicial, pseudo-moral role in putting their creator on trial helps to blur the dividing line between good and evil. And the thrilling climax, showing once and for all that the Doctor is on our side, not Gallifrey's, has him break the laws of Time and prevent the Magnotron strike, using the Daleks to save the Earth and at the last moment frustrating their plans to take the Time Lords' place. In the process, the change in history means that the trial never happened, and the Valeyard – a creation of the High Council, using the creative powers of the Matrix – never existed.

Thus: no recurrence of the Valeyard; no return trips to Gallifrey (and *Blood Harvest* remains consistent, since the Trial did not actually take place); Mel joins, properly, and meets Glitz (she recognises him in 'Dragonfire'); Davros is shown to escape from the Renegades and acquire ambitions of conquering Time; and season twenty-three gets very good ratings. Needless to say, the figures are helped by the decision to broadcast the stories in the form of four stories rather than one, and both 'The Ultimate Foe' and 'Judgement of the Daleks' benefit from the publicity surrounding their respective first episodes.

The briefest of sketches, perhaps; but at least now you know the truth you can begin to forget the lie. Feel free to fill in the gaps for yourselves, but never lose sight of the central point; after all, what's the point in remembering a story that didn't make sense, wasn't any fun, and wouldn't, in the scheme of things, be sorely missed? I had thought of just declaring the damn thing non-canonical but that really isn't enough. We must face the fact that nothing of its sort could ever have happened, and adjust our memories accordingly.

Still no explanation for Colin Baker's departure of course, but then rewriting history can go too far. Baker was sacked, for no earthly reason, and it's probably better to remember that fact. We also, unfortunately, still have to contend with season twenty-four, but at least we can blame the ratings on *Coronation Street*, now we know that they were perfectly fine before the rescheduling.

Then again, if you want to forget season twenty-four . . . who am I to stop you? This selective approach to *Doctor Who* history has a lot to be said for it, after all; I dare say, in fact, that some of you are even beginning to hallucinate right now about Spielberg's production. The Doctor running from Gallifrey to save his kidnapped father, indeed! As if . . . You are gullible! At least now, after our little talk, you'll know when you see something that crap in the name of *Doctor Who*, that you must, after all, be dreaming it.

Tory Alpha: In Search of a Queer Nation
Matt Jones
(*Skaro* (New) #7)

'Well I couldn't believe my eyes. I almost spat out my cornflakes in shock. Homos in *Doctor Who*! Poufters in 'The Happiness Patrol'! Surely some mistake? But no, there it was – in black and white no less. Well really! Not that I've got anything against them you understand. If that's your bag . . . if that's what you're into . . . then fine. But there's a time and a place, Mr Loony-Lefty-GLC-Commie-Cornell Person. A time and a place! It's a kids' programme for heaven's sake! No, this is too much. It's time for decent people to stand up to this. Send in Mary Whitehouse. Send in the Marines. Brigadier, five rounds rapid if you please . . .'

There are more than just a few people in this country who would be a little worried, perhaps even a little outraged, if they thought that a children's programme contained references to homosexuality, or actually had homosexual characters portrayed in it. Mums, Dads, politicians, teachers, not to mention Mary Whitehouse and the 'silent majority' she claims to represent, would be up in arms. 'Disgusted from Tunbridge Wells' would sputter in rage and reach swiftly for her nib.

And yet this is exactly what Paul Cornell suggested a couple of *Skaros* ago. He commented that 'The Happiness Patrol' is 'an accurate assessment of the destruction of gay rights in the Thatcher years'. He claimed that the story is 'politically informed'. That beneath the veneer of science fiction it is actually debating a contemporary social issue.

Well, is it? Not according to Michael Stevens (*Skaro* #6). For Michael, there aren't enough gay themes in 'The Happiness Patrol' for it to be about gay rights. Unlike in 'Kinda', where we are constantly tripping over biblical symbols, 'The Happiness Patrol' simply doesn't have enough tangible signposts to lead him to the conclusion that it's about government homophobia.

If there is such a message in 'The Happiness Patrol' then it is a hidden one. For there was no uproar in 1988. Mary Whitehouse was not up in arms, and 'Disgusted from Tunbridge Wells' saw no reason to bother that nice Anne Robinson.

I was intrigued by what Paul Cornell wrote. So I dusted down my copy of Graeme Curry's novelisation and ploughed through the somewhat styleless text in search of this hidden meaning. I even borrowed a video copy and carefully rewatched the story searching for clues. But what would these clues look like? Certainly the story, and production, contain nothing that could be considered overtly gay. There are no 'out' gay characters, no mention of homosexuality. Further, I find it impossible to identify in the story a 'gay sensibility', or any images that resonate with gay subculture or gay life.

Let me take a moment to explain what I mean by a 'gay sensibility'. I'll give you an example. The other day, I was browsing through my ex-boyfriend's video collection. In amongst the *Doctor Who*, *Star Trek*, and *Blake's Seven* tapes I found the complete series of *The Golden Girls*. It reminded me of the time that Heaven, one of London's biggest gay night-clubs, used to turn off the music in one of their many bars, and tune the video monitors into that show. Everyone in the club used to dash into this bar in order to catch that week's instalment. It was almost a religious event.

Clearly *The Golden Girls* resonates with the experience of being a gay man. The preoccupations of the 'girls' are the same as the pre-occupations of many metropolitan queens. The humour of the show is based on the bitchy but loving relationship between the members of the cast, rather like the 'sisterly' way that fags often express our gay friendships.

Doctor Who clearly doesn't have a 'gay sensibility'. I would guess that for the most part, we are attracted to the programme because we still love the feeling of escapism and wonder it gave to us as children, as opposed to any resonance it may have with our sexual identities.

If the concept of *Doctor Who* doesn't lend itself to a gay interpretation, then all we are left with is the plot. I'm not completely sure what Paul Cornell means by 'gay rights', there have never have been – as far as I know – any to destroy. But I'll assume here that he's talking about Clause 28 of the Local Government Act, Section 31 of the Criminal Justice Act and the reluctance of the Conservative Administration to take the AIDS crisis seriously until heterosexual people started to die.

So what has 'The Happiness Patrol' got to do with the squashing of homosexuality? Well, after giving this some considerable thought, I have to say that I think 'The Happiness Patrol' has rather a lot to say on the matter. As the title suggests, 'The Happiness Patrol' is about policing. Both in its narrowest sense, and also the way in which desire has been policed and regulated by a hostile government. The simplest way to make a comparison between this story and Cornell's 'destruction of gay rights' comment is to replace the word 'happiness' with the word 'heterosexuality.'

Yes, those women in the fab wigs aren't really employed to make sure that the inhabitants are happy, they are there to make sure that they are straight. If you are 'unhappy'/gay then you will disappear. This is where the parallel with Section 28 comes in. Section 28 wanted to banish positive images of gay people leading ordinary lives from the shelves of libraries, from schools; basically from anywhere the public might see them.

The theme of invisibility is crucial both to an understanding of Section 28 and of 'The Happiness Patrol'. Where do people facing such oppression go? Underground, that's where. In the novel, Graeme Curry writes: 'Since the arrival of human life on Terra Alpha, the Alpidae (the Pipe People) had been forced underground.' The sentence can easily be rewritten: since the arrival of the Tory Administration, lesbians and gays have been driven underground. Whilst the second statement is undeniably an exaggeration, it is not wholly inaccurate. You just try doing basic things in this country as an out gay man, like get a mortgage, life insurance or a job at a Texaco garage (and with a whole host of other major employers). To do any of those things you now have to lie about your sexuality. You have to hide it. And this is where we find the second parallel between 'gay rights' and 'The Happiness Patrol'.

The second theme of the story is subhumanness. Helen A describes the starving Pipe People as Vermin, just as the Chief Constable of Greater Manchester described gay men dying of AIDS as 'wallowing in a cesspool of their own making'. In both 'The Happiness Patrol' and in the eighties, subhumanness is used as justification for making undesirable social groups invisible.

Why shouldn't homosexuality be promoted? Because gay people aren't as real, as natural, or basically as human as straight people. These are the beliefs behind the arguments that were used by back-bench MPs to stop Local Authorities spending (what was in reality a pittance) on Gay Teenage Groups, one awful book (*Jenny Lives With Eric and Martin*) and to prevent teachers telling gay kids about safer sex. Helen A describes the Pipe People as 'vermin' in a similar way in order to justify Fifi's vile sport and their persecution. Why do people want to do this? Because they have one vision of the way they think people should behave and they think their vision is the only valid one. And this vision centres around the family.

Helen A fears that her vision of the world is under threat. That the traditional family (and heterosexuality) is challenged by new images of 'pretended (gay) family life'. To some extent she is right, as the historian Jeffrey Weeks has argued. 'It is undoubtedly the case that the significant growth in the lesbian and gay community over the previous two decades had posed an implicit challenge to the hegemony of family values, or at least family values as endorsed by leading exponents of the New Right, the strongest advocates of Clause 28.'

It is no coincidence that Helen A says: 'families are important to people's happiness'. If there was ever any doubt that she was intended to be Thatcher, then this statement washes those doubts away. Helen A is fearful that 'unhappiness'/gay life will overrun 'happiness'/traditional family values and she attempts to correct the moral imbalance she perceives: 'They [the death squads/Clause 28] only came later,' she protests to the Doctor. 'I told them to be happy [to accept heterosexual values]. I gave them a chance. But they wouldn't listen.'

The justification she gives for the prisons, death squads and executions on Terra Alpha are exactly the same as the New Right gave for Clause 28. It is all, she claims: 'for the good of the majority'. And as for 'unhappiness'/gay life? Her views on this are clear: 'It's unnecessary. And those who persisted had to be punished.'

Thatcher herself didn't believe in the concept of society. On many occasions she stated that she saw Britain being made up of only individuals and families. And her definition of the family was an extremely narrow one. That's why those cool dykes invaded the BBC, that's why they abseiled into the House of Lords and that's why they brought Princess Di's speech to a halt at the Conference on the Family in Brighton. They were asserting the validity of their 'pretended families'; and as everyone knows, lesbian mothers aren't pretending.

'The Happiness Patrol' is an attack on the ethics of Thatcherism. The sweets symbolise consumerism and the numbers (Priscilla P, Joseph C etc.) symbolise the increasing emphasis on individual status which that consumerism encourages. The tactics of the Happiness Patrol themselves, using agent provocateurs to entrap unhappy people, mirrors the British Police's tactics of posing as gay men in order to arrest real gay men behaving, as Helen A might have put it, 'openly unhappily'. Not only is this form of gay sexual contact considered morally wrong and not as valid as heterosexual sexual contact, it is punishable by law, and zealously policed.

If 'unhappiness' symbolises gay life, then Helen A's vision of 'happiness' symbolises the Conservative view of heterosexual family life. I'm not putting the traditional nuclear family down here, rather I am attacking the notion that it is the best and only type of family. After all, only a minority of people in this country live in one.

At the end of 'The Happiness Patrol', Helen A's vision of a 'happy'/traditional nuclear family-orientated society is dismantled. It is revealed to be a sham. People just aren't like that. They are happy and sad. Just as Britain is made up of people who live in heterosexual nuclear families and other forms of 'family' (gay families, extended families, with friends, in old people's homes, etc.). It is no coincidence that Helen A's own nuclear family is dismantled at the end of episode three; Fifi is dead and Joseph C leaves her. And who does he run off with . . .?

If Norman Tebbit were perceptive enough, he would add 'The Happiness Patrol' to his arsenal when he goes on one of his frequent crusades against the BBC. Because the Doctor's role in the narrative clearly shows him siding against the New Right, not only is the Doctor on the side of liberation and equality, but the Time Lord is actually responsible for toppling the government, engaging in what can only be described as revolutionary behaviour.

'The Happiness Patrol' is a celebration of difference. A critique of the idea that any one way of living is inherently or naturally better than any other. It outlines the horrors that occur when one group in a society rams their vision of social life down the throats of all the others. It shows how distorted that vision becomes when it is used as propaganda. For Helen A's 'happiness' is as shallow as the Tories' 'cornflakes and washing powder' image of the nuclear family. And, it is just as dangerous. Because if you subscribe to an uncritical view of the nuclear family, if you see it as those mad backbenchers do, as a haven which should be protected from the prying eyes of social workers and 'do gooders', then it's not just fags and dykes who suffer because we are excluded from that vision, but also the battered wives and abused children who are included in it. As Ace said: 'Scratch Victorian veneer and something ugly comes crawling out.'

Can we be sure that this is what Graeme Curry meant? Can we ever know one hundred per cent that he was using the events that take place that fateful night on Terra Alpha to make a wider and stronger point? Well no, of course we can't. The answer to questions about meanings in *Doctor Who* can only ever be: it can mean whatever you want it to mean.

After all, this is only my view. Paul Cornell may have meant something completely different when he made that throwaway comment. And you may disagree with what I've written, and that's good. In fact, it's brilliant. Because if 'The Happiness Patrol' teaches us anything, it is the danger of there only being one view, one voice that shouts down all the others.

Happiness – true happiness – will prevail.

Love in a Cold Climate
Jackie Marshall
(Stock Footage #2)

Take a 'dishy' young man and an attractive, spirited young woman. Give them an obnoxious teenage boy, a noble, rather humourless young girl and a shifty, possibly untrustworthy youth as companions. Put the man and the woman into many dangerous situations where he not infrequently saves her life and/or civilisation as we know it. How will the woman feel towards this 'sexy' but vulnerable hero; this 'reckless innocent' who is her constant companion? What else could she do but fall in love with him?

What? Heresy, I hear you cry! The Doctor is 'above all that'; he is the 'pure, unsullied hero', beyond all earthly passion. Maybe, if you take the view that Susan's mother/father was brought by the stork or found under the Gallifreyan equivalent of a gooseberry bush. But what about the indisputably human Tegan? In the light of a recent extensive survey (complete with random sampling) I now feel qualified to hypothesise upon the likely reactions of human females to the presence of the fifth Doctor. The majority of the females questioned would quite definitely have fancied him (given his looks, charm, smile etc., etc.,) had they been in Tegan's position. The exceptions were those who found him so *un*appealing that, had they been Tegan, they couldn't have endured to travel with him at all. Now, whilst Tegan undoubtedly found the Doctor a pain in the neck at times, she obviously didn't actively dislike him: if she had, she'd never have bothered dashing off to rescue him in 'Frontios' for example. (She certainly didn't do it so he could return her to London; at that point all that was left of the TARDIS was the hatstand.) Clearly then, Tegan was fond of the Doctor and the survey results would seem to indicate that her fondness would go beyond mere friendship.

Moving into this sphere, there are two ways in which Tegan could have regarded the Doctor. She was a young woman and so her affections could have been entirely adult, based initially on physical attraction. However, Tegan frequently behaved in a rather less than adult way, reacting more like a confused, assertive adolescent. And adolescents are, of course, prone to crushes. The Doctor would have been the ideal object for a 'crush', his very inaccessibility only adding to his appeal – Tegan's virtue is quite assured. The Doctor does not flaunt his sexuality (by eyeing up every woman within range, for example). He is the model of decorum. Even when his female companions are reduced to running about in their undies, he remains the perfect gentleman. This lack of 'come hither' would ensure that Tegan kept her feelings under control, whether they were the daydreams of an adolescent girl for her knight in shining panama hat/beige frock coat trimmed with red/stripy trousers, or the frustrated longings of a young woman for a man who is totally oblivious to the fact that she *is* a young woman and not just a talkative part of the furniture.

It is certainly hinted in some stories that Tegan's feelings for the Doctor are more than platonic. Particularly illuminating in this respect is 'Enlightenment'. When Wrack comments that the image of the Doctor in Tegan's mind is 'quite intriguing', Tegan looks rather worried, as if she's given something away. Later on in the story Tegan's reaction when she thinks the Doctor has been expelled into the vacuum of space causes Marriner to remark in confusion: 'The sparkle has gone from your mind; there are only grey shadows.' Furthermore, whilst Tegan was fond of Nyssa she bore no

Andrew Martin's original artwork for this article.

such liking for Turlough. Given, then, that she spent a lot of time apparently fed-up with travelling through space and time, why was she so adamant about remaining on board the TARDIS at the end of 'The King's Demons'? Was it the attraction of the Doctor himself? In her farewell story, she seems to have worked herself up into a state in order to avoid him talking her out of her intention. The reasons she puts forward for leaving are quite convincing, if rather sudden. (Why didn't she stay in Little Hodcombe, for instance, bearing in mind all the death and destruction at Sea Base 4 in 'Warriors of the Deep'?) As to why, if she was attracted to him, she took the decision to leave, well, it was probably either brought on by the recognition that she was wasting her time and ought to cut her losses, or perhaps a sudden worry in case the Doctor decided to return her feelings and the sudden realisation that she couldn't cope with the implications of the age difference and his perilous mode of existence. Or then again, perhaps she just had a premonition of his forthcoming regeneration.

At this point I feel I ought to counter a possible objection which arises if one takes the viewpoint that Tegan's feelings were of an adult not adolescent nature – namely that the Doctor is an alien; that Tegan is quite aware of how alien he is (having witnessed his regeneration) and that she couldn't possibly fancy such a person. I don't see this as a barrier at all and in evidence I refer to the Spock Syndrome. Spock was found attractive precisely because he *was* an alien; well, he was only half human and determined to rise above it. Hordes of women (within the series and out of it) would have liked nothing better than to break down his distant reserve and draw him into a mad, passionate affair. It's a subtle attraction presented by Spock and the Doctor, something that the brash, beautiful Tegan might find impossible to resist.

So there you have it. Was Tegan secretly in love with the Doctor after all? Would it have mattered so much if this had definitely been shown to be the case? It wouldn't have amounted to hanky-panky and it certainly wouldn't have shattered the Doctor's essential enigma if one single, solitary female had found him fanciable; in fact, bearing in mind that the incarnation in question happened to be 'the youngest and sexiest Doctor yet', it seems very strange that no one noticed him in this way. As it is, we're left with Tegan's final words: 'Oh Doctor, I will miss you.' She'll miss, not Turlough, not the TARDIS, not travelling in time and space, but the Doctor himself. I rest my case.

William Keith's Ministry of Love
Guy Wigmore
(*Silver Carrier* #9)

Fellow fans, all hail the day
McGann appeared as Doctor Who,
Our new Doctor has led the way:
Girls and women, we want you!
No more will menky lives be grey.

Fans were once a sexless breed.
That changed with Paul McGann's first snog.
Our blood was stirred, we found the need
To love and live like our new god:
As love-doctors we would succeed.

We'll pull the birds, we'll not be sad.
We'll take our girlfriends home – and then
Let funky fanzines drive them mad.
Unmarried menks, be married men!
O, how our mothers will be glad.

2: Love Bits

Fandom isn't only about internecine warfare. Fans also love each other. Not only in the sense that it's easier to pair up with somebody who's not going to scream with laughter when they see your trading cards, as Alistair's poem below reveals, but in a warm, communal way as well. Ness's poem conveys the atmosphere of the convention hotel: eight to a room, people added to the gang after very brief aquaintance and a quick check of favourite stories, gossip as the currency of a community dispersed across the world and meeting half a dozen times a year. And Alec's poem fuses these mixed feelings: that one's childlike love for *Doctor Who*, or the fulfilled adolescent fantasy of sleeping in a pile of the big gang called fandom, are similar to romantic love.

That's the feeling that rushes through us when we hear the *Who* theme over the title sequence at a convention that our gang has organised, and we hug our partners. That we're surrounded by all the different sorts of love.

And we didn't even have to join a religion to get it.

Oh! To Be a Fanboy
Vanessa 'Ness' Bishop
(*Purple Haze* #2)

The 'phone goes for the umpteenth time,
'Hello, it's you . . . again.
Have you got some juicy gossip?
Really? Those two? Did what? When?
What about old fatty doo-da,

The Doctor and Cameca: love in a bloodthirsty culture. By Andrew Martin, from *Queen Bat* #5.

Have you heard from him of late?
Heck, your phone bill will be massive,
Right – who do we like and who do we hate?'

Oh! To be a Fanboy
Now the Cons. are here –
A pint of best, a chewed-up badge,
A Photo of my ear.
I've got a fanzine table
Just over by the loo.
'A darn good read, a bit of sex,
and a couple of things on Who.*'*

I'm feeling pretty dizzy,
It's only half-past ten.
Nicholas Courtney's doing
that old 'chopper' joke again.
Room 404 at midnight,
Bring your favourite tipple –
We'll trample food across the floor
And shout out words like 'nipple'!

I'm talking to a stranger
Who's into Season Eight.
I've eaten tons of peanuts
And half a paper plate.
Someone's trying to breakdance
And just kicked me in the head.
Cor, I fancy her, I fancy him,
Who's that beneath the bed?

Oh! To be a Fanboy
Dancing to The Clash.
A filthy joke, some underpants, a pimple and a rash.
'Hey, let's start a rumour –
I've got all of Season Five.
Colin Baker was a woman
And Hartnell's still alive!
Let's try and get in the monthly,
or phone DWB.
Let's give them the exclusive . . .
The new Doctor's Bobby Gee!'

That bloody video camera
Is pointing up my nose.
I'll flash a mouth of chewed-up crisps
In hoping that it goes.
'Oh . . . I haven't got a room tonight,
So could I use your floor,
Pinch that spare pillow
And sleep over by the door?'

Oh! To be a Fanboy
Down the local chippie.
Down the pub impersonating
Bungle, George and Zippy.

'Oh blimey, is it morning?
I think my head's caved in.
Whose foot's this inside my mouth?
Who's puked in the bin?'
'You missed a damn good night,' I say
To those who were elsewhere.
'Well I'm not sure what happened,
But I met a smashing chair!'

I've sold a couple of fanzines,
A Kleenex with each one.
I've only got a pound left
But I've had a lorra fun.
Post-convention blues are looming
As I sit slumped on the train.
Still, only one more month
Then I can do it all again.

Oh! To be a Fanboy
Now the phone bill's come . . .
I think I'll just leave home
With an apology to my Mum.

(Alistair McGown, of the long-running, sceptical and sharp Glasgow
fanzine *Paisley Pattern*, saw some photos of Ness and was moved.
To a regular column (!) of poetic praise . . .)

Together-Ness
Alistair McGown
(*Paisley Pattern #44*)

Ness,
I'm stuck inside the house tonight,
With a nice new shiny tin.
Why don't we watch some videos,
And share a nice night in?

Other girls that I have known,
Have liked my charm and style,
But when I put on Doctor Who,
They always run a mile.

They can't sit through 'The Krotons',
Or even 'Power of Kroll',
They say that 'Keys of Marinus',
Is rather slow and dull.

But you remember what it meant,
To sit behind the sofa,
Tonight we'll sit on my settee,
You're just the girl I go for.

'Cos you'd sit through 'The Krotons',
And even 'Power of Kroll',
In fact you wouldn't mind which tape,
You'd love to watch them all.

We'd watch some Troughton stories,
Say 'What a shame they junked 'em',
We'd watch 'Time and the Rani',
And shout 'What a load of bunkum*!'*

I've never done this kind of thing,
It's all so new to me,
Watched Doctor Who *all through the night,*
With lovely company.

At least that's how I see it,
A perfect evening planned,
You'll accept my invitation then?
. . . Oh, I knew you'd *understand.*

65

Show of Love
Alec Charles
(*Mayfield* #1)

Your smile's as bright and strange and new
as the title sequence for
an episode of Doctor Who –
though you last much longer than half an hour,
and your effects are far superior.

You've never had any scary monsters in you
nor even an electronic screwdriver
as far as I know.
You weren't a lot better twenty years ago.

You've never been bound to a TV studio
or at least haven't told me so.
You've never forced me behind the sofa,
although I wouldn't say no.
You've never given me a dreadful fright.

Yet you've kept me in on a Saturday night
when I could have been down at the pub instead,
and I love to watch you lying in bed
but not on video.

You sometimes end on a cliffhanger,
leaving me wanting more of the same;
but you don't come on after an afternoon of sport,
nor've been followed (thank God) by The Generation Game.
You've rarely been shy to cry your hero's name.

I can't imagine seeing you
as family viewing on one – you're more the sort
for Friday nights in French on BBC2
or even, if I'm in luck, on Channel 4.

3: Fanlife

So what do fans do? Make Fan Art, get pissed, take the piss, go to Olympiads (conventions with no guests), go to conventions (and stay in the bar), enjoy a unique cultural shorthand that can bond fanboys in seconds without even the need for a secret handshake. Infiltrate the BBC to the highest levels. Make proper television. Become MPs. (Hello, Tim Collins. Pity he's a Tory.) Shag. Fall in love. Hide. And the greatest of these is Hide, because while we know we're more *Trainspotting* than Trainspotter, the general public are still looking out for those scarves. At the Fitzroy Tavern the other day, the London pub where *Who* fans gather once a month to exchange addresses, gossip and contributors' copies, the crowd watched a boy in full Tom Baker costume enter, walk around the bar, and exit again, puzzled that he had not seen any more like him. Thinking he'd got the wrong night. That was a nice moment. In retrospect, perhaps someone should have run after him. At least he was out and proud in his fannishness.

This section is about what it's like to be a fan, from how to tell one person about your secret culture, to Tat Wood's point-scoring guide as to how to tell one's non-fan friends in general. There's an anonymous piece in this section, because his Mum doesn't know. The anonymous piece elsewhere in this book is that way because the author is a Professor of Eng. Lit. and doesn't want to 'come out of the TARDIS'. Weird how every angle of fanlife parallels gay life. But all despised cultures mimic each other. Rumour has it that staffers at a London listings magazine have recently started implying that somebody's gay by saying 'sounds like a bit of a *Doctor Who* fan'. Better than that last stereotype, anyway.

The first of our foreign selections is in here. Fandom in Australia flourishes, and culturally is much the same as Brit fandom, as this article, from the determinedly radical *Bog Off!* proves. (Like a lot of the New Fandom 'zines and the Queerzines, they've abandoned issue numbers. Some have done away with contributor credits, article titles, anything you could make a list of.) Liam Brison's *Pickled in Time* once ran a *Rocky Horror*-style audience-participation version of 'Dimensions in Time', and had lots of articles by people who fancied various people in various SF series. *Circus* is a modern A5 fanzine that aspires to be as definitive as the new *Skaro*, but is definitely post-*Haze*. They recently did the best guide to *Carry On* movies that I've seen in any format.

Oh, about the *Hounds of Love* thing. Alec Charles started the rumour that Kate Bush wrote 'Kinda'. Keith Topping developed it. I spread it. And, despite the fact that serious fanboys have 'disproved' it, it's our truth and we're sticking to it.

He's the man you love. You want to share everything with him but there's a big dark secret gnawing at your heart. Dare you share it?

Telling Your Boyfriend
(*United Colors of Cottage Under Siege*)

Despite the opinions and persistence of certain correspondents to *TV Zone*, *Who* fandom has a large gay element as is evident in the amount of 'camp' fanzines currently in circulation. Having been in fandom for ten years, and although many of my *Who* friends are gay, I've always kept that part of my life pretty much to myself. Similarly, my obsession with a dated, tacky sci-fi show has never been part of my chat-up lines. Nevertheless, the day came when I had to come out . . . to tell my boyfriend that I was a *Doctor Who* fan.

I'd always made sure we met in a pub or at his house for fear of being discovered with a collection of Target novelisations, BBC videos and *DWM*s. But it was on my birthday that he discovered the truth and all because my best friend goes and asks me for a copy of 'The Five Doctors'. In *public*. I knew from that moment on that our relationship was doomed. The realisation that someone he'd previously thought of as sane was, in fact, a totally sad bastard.

A month later we were in a gay pub in Liverpool where we spied a real saddo wearing a long multi-coloured scarf provoking a serious discussion along the lines of 'Why do you like something so tacky?' My attempts to fob him off with an argument promoting socio-political allegory and sharp intertextual parody fell on deaf ears and, sadly, my insecurities were fuelled. Our discussions degenerated into a state of petty name-calling and jibes about rubber and plastic (we got a few funny looks from the other customers).

It took twelve months of coercion and pleading before he finally consented to sit through four selected gems. 'Ark in Space' was dismissed as an '*Alien* rip-off' despite the difference in transmission dates. 'Terror of the Zygons' showed promise right up to episode two where the Skarasen lurched into view, its terrifying roar drowned out by wickedly cruel laughter and howls of derision. The first few seconds of 'The Pirate Planet' were similarly ruined by 'Isn't she on *Brookie*?' before he left the room in search of an ABBA track he'd just remembered, returning in time for 'Ghostlight'. Bad choice! 'What's he doing? Which one's the Doctor? Size of her tits,' etc.

Dejected and humiliated, I packed my videos and left. The realisation that as a gay man I was an outcast in a minority was too much to bear. I solemnly vowed never to mix passion with entertainment ever again. It's a typical Aquarian trait, I'm told, always feeling that life has to be segregated. In my case, whovers in one closet, lovers in the other . . .

Crimson Joy
Tat Wood
(*Frontios* #9)

For many of you this will be familiar. I can't pretend to have the entire situation sussed, mine's just one account. Like most fans-turned-students, I've found that watching the programme in mixed company highlights how odd fandom is. Aspects of the programme and its associated gameplaying suddenly seem weird, sometimes a bit silly or desperately important to your sense of who you are. If you're just starting out on being a student fan in the company of other, non-fan, students, then it may be in order for me to offer some hard-won advice in the form of rules for a game. The object of the game is to get your new friends and acquaintances to play without realising the game is in progress. The prize is their undying admiration and the ability to function in everyday society without becoming tainted by their mundane, quotidian ideals, but without becoming known as a sad case.

1. The Disclosure. Whilst it is possible to recover from a bad opening, the inexperienced player may prefer some tried-and-tested gambits.

1.1 The Feint. This method is to be deployed in circumstances where an outright admission could cost you the game and where suspicion may lead to distrust. Those studying engineering or other such carnivorous and macho subjects may, for instance, prefer down-playing this aspect of their lives to being called a poof and having fire-extinguishers aimed into their faces. Similarly, those hoping to get off with anyone at the Freshers' hop (or indeed ever at all) should opt for this. The key element is to create a less embarrassing smoke-screen. Pederasty, American football or a deep and abiding love for Gilbert O'Sullivan have proved popular in the past. In all but the last case these will also provide you with a 'posse' with whom you can become identified until sufficiently emboldened to 'Come out of the Police Box' as the current jargon has it.

1.2 The Feint (Slight Return). In this the choice of smoke-screen is so outrageous and unpleasant that being a *Doctor Who* fan seems comparatively innocuous. See *Pink Flamingos* for further details.

1.3 The Brazen. Long term this has proven spectacularly successful in some cases, but takes bravura, stamina and a willingness to be in solitary company for up to eighteen months. One simply flounces in and says 'I'm ———————— and my life revolves around *Doctor Who*. So sue me.' People invariably do.

1.4 The Emo Philips. Like 1.2 the object is to redefine the context in which the activity is considered. If you seem to be at a remove from the rest of the planet then watching any television programme '. . . would be so wonderfully normal . . .'

These ploys may be combined by more experienced players, generally in 1, 2, 4, 3 order.

2. The Capture. Unless independently wealthy, the player will be forced to share a house with people by at least the second year. This means the cessation, at least within domestic situations, of any feints played in round one. Early development of 1.3 or 1.4 will ensure cohabitation with more tolerant individuals. Henceforth these will be considered the only pieces still on the board.

2.1 The Missionary Position. In selected conditions and with certain combatants it may appear that your duty to this person is to tell them everything and broaden their horizons, by force if necessary. Few tries lead to conversions, but the exercise in considering fandom as if exploring uncharted territory and relating travellers' tales in a bar on the Belgian Congo may prove salutary. NB: Never, *never* fall into the trap of 'did you know ...' for its own sake. Have it handy if they bring it up but don't become spoddy by initiating conversations with cast-lists. If you do, that's GAME OVER.

2.2 The Striptease. Tantalise your opponent with hints of another world and a host of secrets you daren't tell. Those in the Home Counties or wealthy can add to this mystique by cancelling any social engagements on the first Thursday of the month (it is not strictly necessary to frequent the Fitzroy Tavern, but to appear as if you have). Long phone calls in – apparently – coded messages ('Liberty Hall'), posters of Kristian Schmid or Jeremy Bentham and whoops of delight at spotting John Scott Martin in a video on *The Chart Show* are good starts; for Grand Master status try giggling inexplicably at the phrase 'Twix Fits'. (No, I don't understand that one either.)

2.3 Baby Oil. Given that the public think of the series in terms of childhood and nostalgia give it to them in the context of *Pogles' Wood* and *Dougal and the Blue Cat*. This leads, however, to the notion that the past was one big drugs orgy and that somehow Hammy the Hamster was a coded message from Ken Kesey. Resisting the temptation to hurl this week's hit Kindergarten Rave Anthem on the bonfire of the inanities, refresh their memories. This leads inexorably into ...

3. TV Heaven. Either they want to watch or they don't. If they don't but they let you get on with it you've broken even. Game Over. If they don't and resent you doing so go back to the beginning. If they want to watch ...

3.1 Home Box Office. Let them make up their own minds, rummage around in your video library and compare notes afterwards. This requires nerve.

3.2 The *Mr Benn* Gambit. Over endless late-night conversations find out what they remember (if anything. You may get a virgin *Who*-viewer which, being an away win, scores double). On wet afternoons with nothing on (on telly, fool) select, apparently at random, a tape to put on. Special rules apply here which will be considered in section four. Your opponent should, if this move is executed adequately, be impressed by your selection of exactly what he/she would enjoy by an apparent display of telepathy.

3.3 'Oh, this old thing. I've had it for yonks.' Nonchalantly put on something for your own amusement and hope they wander in and get involved. If the telly is in sight of, or indeed in, the kitchen, culinary background *Who* rules come into play. See next section.

4. Story Selection: received opinion within fandom is no guide to the impact a given story will have on the opponents. 'Talons' bombs almost without fail, 'Earthshock', 'Ark in Space' and all but one Hartnell are watched without response. Three orthogonal elements have to be considered.

A. Size of audience. Large audiences tend to be pissed and need something less sophisticated so they can talk all through it without missing anything. Sod it, put the *Clangers* on instead. Non-pissed (morning after party?) audiences tend to go for Williams era irony and, after a few minutes of derision at the start, will watch raptly. 'Androids of Tara', 'Ribos Operation' and 'Greatest Show' (not in front of drug-bores though) work well.

Two to three players are needed for anything involving concentration or the maintenance of atmosphere and mood. If any explanation is required a small gathering is necessary or else it gets didactic and pompous.

B. Need for kitsch. The one Hartnell mentioned above is, of course, 'The Web Planet'. Along with Pertwee and the Pip 'n' Jane era this is a story that could have been made for students (and no one else, surely). Now, many people go into the game believing that the Pertwee stories are as good as it ever got. To this end it may be necessary to play dirty and begin with 'Claws of Axos' and 'The Time Monster'. If nothing else, this will afford endless fun with wine-bottles after parties. Then hit 'em with 'Remembrance' to really disrupt the 'new stuff's crap' mythology. If the viewer is prepared to watch a story on its own terms give them something atypical fairly early on to set boundaries ('Mind Robber' and 'Revelation' are fairly handy for this).

C. Experience of players. If you've got a hardcore who want to watch it long-term it might pay to show them in some semblance of chronological order. Seasons 13–15 work well. If the viewer dimly remembers 'Horns of Nimon' show season 17 after Hinchcliffe and Pertwee highlights in order that clichés are in place before they see the parodies. Generally, arts students or those with a bit of irony respond better to seeing season 17 when grown up than grebo engineers (such generalisations are crass but, alas, nearly true. Although Dostoevski was an engineering student as were Pynchon and Thomas Hardy, there seems to be a herd instinct which stifles any attempt to avoid the caricature). Continuity overall matters less than continuity within eras. Some recent converts of my acquaintance, unaware of the programme's history but exposed to what's left of seasons 5 and 6 were generally concerned at episode 9 of 'The War Games' even though the phrase 'Time Lord' was vaguely familiar.

Part of the fun of letting them into your dark secret is the looks on their faces. Scoring for this round, therefore, is roughly as follows:

	They Enjoy It	They Don't
You enjoy their reaction	+2	−1
You're too anxious	+1	−2

5. End-Game. Now's the time to tot up scores and prepare to take the next big step. Do the people with whom you've been living get lumped in with your fan-pals after the degree? Do you introduce them to each other? Your score will decide.

For each person you have inveigled into watching one of your videos score 2 points. Score 3 if they buy a fanzine off you (5 if they helped you write or produce it). Add two if they were unfamiliar with the programme except as a name (e.g. parents wouldn't let them watch, grew up abroad etc.). Multiply each player's score by the number of episodes watched voluntarily. Any player (player now means your former opponent) scoring over 100 deserves to be told about some of the more questionable aspects of fandom, and can be introduced to selected friends from this world one at time (playing two sets of rules at once is difficult). Add the scores from each of your 'proselytes' to produce your final score. Anything over 1,000 and you've probably been name-checked in a Cornell 'novel'.

Frocks, Coats and Dress (Non)Sense
Sarah J Groenewegen
(*Bog Off!* #pi (2))

'Followers and glorifiers of the fantastic tale like to think that they are different, that they represent something new on the face of the Earth; mutants born with an intelligence and a sense of farseeing appreciation just a bit higher than the norm. They like to believe that their counterpart has never before existed, that they have no predecessors.'

Sam Moskowitz, *The Immortal Storm: A History of SF Fandom*, 1954.

I've been reading a fascinating tome on cross-dressing (*Vested Interests*, Marjorie Garber, Penguin 1992) where the question of real versus artifice is raised continually. The question of clothing – those external garments we have to wear in public and like to wear in private – is examined at great length. Time and time again, the paucity of the English language is raised. We only have two words for male and female, and the latter is defined as lack of what the other has (i.e., a penis. Men are almost never defined in terms of not having a vagina. Women, however, are often defined as lacking a penis, especially according to Freud and his ilk). But, what of the people who are outside the realms of male/female? And what really defines sex anyway? Is it just a matter of who has a dick, and who doesn't; and what about surgical 'rectifications'? And those people who have successfully cross-dressed so that even their spouses haven't realised?

And sexuality? The cause of homosexuality has been in the news a bit, with all the attendant fuss. In my case I feel very strongly that I was born a [aah . . . a problem with writing and editing; you will only read the word that I finally chose to identify myself, without the thought I've gone through to determine it! Just so you know, the terms I prefer are dyke, queer (I love queerfan), gay, Sapphist and what I'll slot in . . .] lesbian and that people who say their queerness is through choice are bisexual. It's a feeling that I won't label as an opinion as I haven't made up my mind yet on the question.

Clothes are again important here. Some friends of mine have real difficulty with gay men who 'act gay' (i.e., the stereotype seen in TV shows still being shown – cf. *Are You Being Served?*).

But, really, it is all a question of perception.

Fans have dealt extensively with perceptions of fans. It's a topical subject, and one that rears its ugly head all the time. At the beginning of December 1993 a group of us were debating this very point at a party. The very next day the good ol' *Sydney Morning Herald* highlighted the SF-Fans-are-dorks line one more time. Again, it was *Star Trek* that copped the flak. It was the usual story, backed up by quotes from fans (so it must be true): 'Yes, there are those who take it too seriously, but not me . . .' It might be true (and I know it is), but don't tell the media that because that's *all* they will use! Stereotypes feed stereotypes . . . and people who think the media are interested in disseminating truth really are living in a fantasy world.

The biggest problem that the media seems to have with SF fans is our cross-dressing. Double-take on my choice of words: we don't cross-dress, we dress as our favourite characters. Well, that is precisely what drag acts, female-to-male cross-dressers, and transvestites generally (though not transsexuals) do. The difference is that their (to create a false dichotomy) characters are internal fantasies about themselves as the 'opposite' sex, and we dress as recognisable characters from a TV series or something purely for fun. (Note that I use 'we' deliberately. Most fans have donned some sort of costume at some stage of their fannish lives; be it just the long scarf, or a full-fledged costume for a play!)

I don't have a problem with the idea of 'cross-dressing'. It's not through political correctness, but experience. Nearly all my life I have had battles with my mother over external appearance. I prefer not to wear make-up (I find it simply uncomfortable), or frocks of any type (for the same reason). I like my shoes comfortable (and I only came out in 1993?! Talk about slow on the uptake) and I love men's hats. By definition, I cross-dress, at least to a certain extent. I also used to (and still do, on occasion) dress up for conventions, normally as a male character. I know some guys who also have cross-dressed.

One or two guys I know have complained that for me to wear my standard trousers, boots, and shirt is acceptable on the street where for them to contemplate a frock isn't. They've used that to argue that being a woman isn't all that bad, but actually that cross-dressing quandary has its roots in the patriarchy too. Women dressing in men's clothes are, so the argument goes, exhibiting their desire for what they lack. They are aspiring to be the cultural norm, and as such it is understandable and therefore tolerated. Men, however, when they dress in women's clothes, etc., are trying to be the 'minority' sex. They are threatening the hegemonic status of masculinity. Of course it would be frowned upon, which doesn't mean that it should be.

But, why should the idea of fans dressing up as favourite characters be so disturbing?

Human beings are at once social beings and private beings. At least, this is true in our 'Western' society and at this late twentieth century time. Many fans (myself included) are shy. Some hide this by being outrageously extrovert at fan functions; or put on characters complete with their own costumes (sometimes borrowed from the media, other times self-created and a facet of their actual personality – the ones you'd never guess were in costume/character unless you knew the private person); and others hide in their insecurity, coming across as a bit of a dweeb when someone does talk to them. Just to show how unique this is, I've encountered the same thing at uni and at work. We all dress up (or down, well or badly – clothes are a costume dependent on their context) and we all act when we're in public and even in private. Our actions can be misread easily, our speech misinterpreted. What others think has an effect on you, an effect that cannot be predicted.

Kate Orman has said that it takes chutzpah to wear costumes in public. It sure does – you will be called a host of things, not many complimentary. And you may get in the papers or on TV, accompanied by some oh-so-witty comment.

I think that the anxiety people have about other people dressing up in an extreme way (either cross-sex or as characters) is not so much about the actual action, but has more to do with the perception of the costumiers. The costumier is doing something that 'society' says is bad. The costumier is being whom they want to be, and to hell with what society says. And they're doing it for their own reasons!

Need a better definition of anarchy?

'The reader has turned the page and arrived in the future.'
(Sidney Abbott and Barbara Love,
Sappho Was a Right on Woman, 1972.)

My Noddy Holder Badge
Ness Bishop
(*Skaro* (New) #3)

I was vegetating in front of *Blue Peter* when the new Doctor was announced. Suddenly this funny little man who I'd never even heard of appeared in front of my eyes, and I just about managed to take in his name before rushing to telephone the boyfriend with the news:

'*Who* did you say?' came the voice down the phone.

'Sylvester something. I can't remember his surname. He's just been on *Blue Peter*. After the recipe.' There was a long silence. It was long enough to be worrying and I wondered why. 'Hello? Are you still there?' A funny squeaking noise echoed down the receiver.

'Um, this . . . Sylvester chap . . . is he short with sort of funny dark wavy hair? And does he wear glasses?'

'Possibly. Why? Do you know him?' The rest of my conversation was drowned amidst a gurgling mixture of laughter and crying . . .

Little did I know that this was to be my first taste of a Doctor who would catapult me into the world of *Doctor Who*.

Not that this was my first experience of *Doctor Who* – no indeed. As with many households, our very own black, PVC and exceptionally gross sofa was put to good use in the seventies, with my brother, as well as myself, battling to hide behind it. The Doctor was part of our Saturday evening's entertainment along with *Basil Brush* and jammy toast, and the whole family crowded round the TV to witness the departure of Tom Baker and the excitement of a regeneration. After all that build-up, I never did hit it off with the Fifth Doctor, and we only kept it on for a few weeks to indulge my Mum in her 'adolescent' fantasies over the faceless vet (she even kissed my Peter Davison autograph received from a pestering letter to the *All Creatures* office a few years earlier!).

This brings me up to 1986 and meeting the boyfriend, 'a fan since nappies'. I must have seemed like a lost cause at the time – I didn't watch *Doctor Who*, my memories of the Tom Baker stories were now dim, nay pathetic, and I'd certainly never heard of Terrance Dicks, God forbid! Still, there was no intention of turning me into a 'fan', and I was eased gently back into the programme with the occasional video. For example, on one particular occasion, he hired out 'Day of the Daleks' from the local video shop. Now I should have been alright here – I'd heard of Daleks and yes, I'd even heard of Jon Pertwee! Nevertheless, five minutes into the story and my eyelids went limp . . . the next thing I remember is waking up to a loud explosion, watching the credits come up, then turning round with the words 'Well, that *was* good, wasn't it?'!

And so to McCoy, the little man who took me by the scarf and led me smack bang into *Doctor Who*. Season 24 was still a long way off, but it wasn't long before I knew every snippet of banal trivia there was to know about Sylvester McCoy . . . the ten-inch nails, the baked beans and yes, those ferrets. I felt like second cousin to Ken Campbell and you'd think *Vision On* had finished only yesterday . . . it all came flooding back. Season 24 began, and they all came out of the closet like an onslaught of whingeing Mavis Rileys, with their 'Ooh, I don't know about that title sequence, do you?' and 'No, I don't like what Keff's done there.' Pip and Jane Baker were both for the rack, and as for Sylvester – well, nothing short of a firing squad for him, according to the so-called 'fans'. I was oblivious to all this. Shameless to say that I sat in front of 'Time and the Rani' dressed as the Doctor (!) and was riveted. I was hooked. The Doctor (and he *was* the Doctor) was wonderful. It was like starting my Whodom all over again, and being naively under the impression that being a fan meant that you *liked* the programme, I wanted to talk to people about how good it was. I went to college and ranted on about the show to the first person I encountered in the refectory, regardless of the fact that they hadn't watched it for at least twelve years. As the weeks went on, I became more and more enthusiastic, having discovered three or four people at college who also watched the programme regularly. I began to talk about nothing else but *Doctor Who*. I even started wearing badges to lectures with *Doctor Who* emblazoned all over them. One day, I got on a bus wearing one, and the bus driver, noticing it, commented that 'they were a good group in their day, they were' (!?). On another occasion a girl in my English group, who had spent the last hour staring in fascination at my Tom Baker badge, came up to me after the lecture and asked 'Why are you wearing a badge with Noddy Holder on?'!!

Then I decided to start a club with the other people from college. We called ourselves the 'PolyWho's' – 'Poly' from Bristol Polytechnic (this name took up a whole lunchtime of deep thought and no doubt it shows). We met up at lunchtimes and talked about Who, even running our own magazine called *Who Watch* – edited by me with info from the latest *DWM* (!), photocopied by my Dad and with a colour card cover. It was free of charge (I must've been mad) and we lasted three issues . . . there was the yellow Sylvester, the blue Sylvester and, maybe quite aptly, the green Tom. By this time we had about thirty members. We also held some rather interesting (and slightly dubious) events at my house, on the rare occasions that I managed to get my Mum to go out for the afternoon. My personal favourite was the 'Paradise Towers'-inspired 'Cookie 'n' Crumpet Afternoon', where we all dressed up as Tabby and Tilda clones (regardless of sex), ate giant cookies and crumpets, and watched selected *Who* stories with occasional backing music provided by 'Samba with Ross' and Keff McCulloch.

It was not long after this that I experienced my very first *Doctor Who* convention . . . 'Falcon' in Bath. Having been obliged to attend someone's wedding on the Saturday, we had booked up for Sunday only, and I was so excited! What do people wear to these events, I asked myself, and Heaven only knows where I got my answer from, but I spent the early hours of Sunday morning putting the finishing touches to a Sixth Doctor costume in front of *Logan's Run* of all things. Sunday came and in I marched, trying to look incon-spicuous in my Colin cozzie (no chance!). All eyes were on me as I stomped around wearing my one-size-too-large bright green plimsolls . . . everyone else strolled around in jeans and T-shirts.

'Oh dear,' sympathised a woman, 'you should've come yesterday for the Fancy Dress, you would've walked it!'

Yet another highlight of the day was a short photographic session with John Levene.

'Who's John Levene?' I hissed, as his arm tightened around my waist.

'Sergeant Benton – you know!'

'Oh . . . yes . . . of course.'

Convention fever had gripped me by the PanoptiCons . . . and appropriately, this was next on the agenda. I wore my *Doctor Who* T-shirt this time, but it was so hot that I had BO all weekend. Nevertheless, I still wore those stupid green plimsolls, and spent a lot of time tripping over my feet. I was overwhelmed at the sheer size of this convention, by the number of attendees, but it was quite a thrill to know that these were all *Doctor Who* fans, and some of the conversations overheard were amusing, not to say enlightening.

I had spent the whole summer of 1988 dabbling my toes into the world of fandom, and I knew that I liked it.

So now I'm a fan. Prepared to defend 'my programme' (as it has become) against any kind of verbal abuse from short-sighted old Joe Public, who thinks that *Strike It Lucky* is Heaven-sent, and that nothing is of more primary importance than the latest carryings-on between Ken and Deirdre Barlow. Prepared to take on the BBC by dusting off my Colin Baker costume and standing in the centre of Bath for two hours with a petition, a BBC camera crew and a silly grin. Willing to spend my money on any badge, book or photo that takes my fancy. In effect, I'm hooked . . .

I've laid my arm around Colin Baker's ample waist. I've got JNT's autograph. I have a slightly unnatural fetish for Lalla Ward, hence my bedroom (well, half a wall) is a shrine to her face. I love everything about Tom Baker down to the cilia of his nostrils, and he occasionally appears in Freudian dreams. I've given one of my poems to Sylvester McCoy and he told me that he liked it (yehhhh!!). I've stared at Jon Pertwee as he slurped his soup at PanoptiCon X but I still can't sit through 'Day of the Daleks'. I've touched Lis Sladen. I co-edit this magazine (and use the college word-processor to type it up on!). I could go on. And on. Oh, and most importantly . . .

I now know who Terrance Dicks is.

Adric's Nose
Jac Rayner
(*Pickled In Time* #3)

When I was asked to write an article about Adric, the first problem I faced was deciding which aspect of the character to examine. What stood out most in my memories of the early eighties? After all, Adric was an extremely complex character: a genius; a loner who longed for acceptance but never quite seemed to find it; an idealistic adolescent – he was all these things and more. So which of these aspects had the greatest influence on my formative years? Well, none of them actually. To tell you the truth, it was his nose.

Adric had the most gorgeous nose I've ever seen in my life. It was definitely worth tuning in for every week. (By a lucky chance, a lot of the stories were quite enjoyable too.) This wasn't a sex thing at all (lucky really) – well, I was only eight when 'Full Circle' aired and I wasn't that precocious – just plain adoration. I don't remember writing 'Adric' enclosed in hearts on my school books, but I wouldn't be surprised if I had done.

I really do think that the production team didn't appreciate what a valuable asset they had at their disposal. References to (and close-ups of) Adric's nose would have added an extra dimension to many stories. I'm sure Camilla is looking at Adric's nose when she murmurs her opinion of his looks in 'State of Decay', and, sod his computations, I think that the main reason the Master stuck Adric in a web was so that he could gaze upon the boy's nose whenever he wanted. (I've heard other stories – Ed.)

Of course, the character of Adric fitted in best with the 'family' of the fourth Doctor (who had a rather impressive nose) as the father figure, Romana (who had a very sweet nose) as a sort of big sister, and K9 (who stunned people with his nose) as the family pet. In my opinion this was one of the best (albeit short-lived and underused) combinations in the show's history. Tom and Lalla were so obviously in love that it is just brilliant to see them together and Adric, being so much younger, just fitted in perfectly and was not a gooseberry as an older companion may well have been. As more or less sole companion for two stories he was also a success – he looked up to the Doctor, and the Doctor obviously felt paternally affectionate towards the boy.

It was unfortunate for Adric that the TARDIS crew underwent such a dramatic change. The combination of the fifth Doctor, Tegan and Nyssa (none of whom had particularly outstanding noses) together with Adric was interesting but they acted more like a group of flatmates than a happy family. One almost expected to see them arguing about whose turn it was to wash up, who ran up the huge phone bill, or who should buy the next lot of loo rolls. Perhaps it is as well that Adric was the first of these to leave.

There is obviously a direct correlation between the gorgeousness of a companion's nose and the impressiveness of their departure. Basically, virtually every companion: boring nose – boring departure, e.g. getting married (20% of departures), getting back to old time/place (48% of departures). Following this rule it should have been obvious to everyone that Peri wasn't really dead as her nose is nowhere near interesting enough to earn such a brilliant ending as the one shown in 'Mindwarp'.

Adric, of course, had the loveliest nose and the most effective departure of any companion in the show's history. To prove my point I asked five randomly chosen (i.e. nearby) non-*Who*-fans of approximately the same age as me this question: 'The departure of which *Doctor Who* companion stands out the most in your memory?' expecting the unanimous answer, 'Adric'. What they actually said was: 'None'; 'Romana – because I liked her hair'; 'K9'; 'K9'; 'I can't remember any of them – oh, K9'. Oh well, c'est la vie.

I suppose that I should be pleased that he left in such a memorable way. Well, I wasn't at the time. No more nose. The thought of Adric being *dead*, not there any more, never to be seen again (except as an occasional visitation) was almost too much to bear. The idea of that nose being scattered about the atmosphere in a million tiny pieces was so horrific that I'm surprised it didn't blight my entire childhood. Perhaps it did. If so, 'Earthshock' made me what I am today. All I can say is, thank goodness he didn't die in 'Timeflight'.

Things You've Done . . .
Colin Brockhurst
(*Circus* #2)

– Said '*Doctor Who* is just the name of the *series!*'
– Begged Granny not to cut the price out of your annual.
– Spread your Target books out into an attractive mosaic on your living room floor, then taken photos of them.

- Argued with an 'older and wiser' about how many Doctors there've been and which order they came in.
- Reckoned Terrance Dicks is the best novelist ever.
- Wished they'd have *Who* books on GC(S)E reading lists.
- Collected John Fitton catalogues.
- Bought a 'not by the original artists' LP, just for the unrecognisable *Who* theme.
- Revamped your video labels/inlays half a dozen times.
- Written a multiple Doctor 'reunion' story.
- Worn *Hounds of Love* to nothing trying to find the *Kinda* dialogue.
- Tried to novelise missing stories using *DWM*'s archive.
- Taped *Who* using an audio recorder and lots of cushions.
- Had your exciting Longleat/Blackpool photos come back completely blank.
- Decided Peter Davison is undrawable.
- Looked up 'Dalek' in the *OED* while pretending to look for swearwords.
- Tried to build a Dalek and not got past the base.
- Fallen in love with Nicola Bryant.
- Typed/written out a dozen lists of *Who* stories so you can 'annotate' them.
- Been vexed with the 'Mutants' book because it has 'Dr Who' on the spine.
- Written something called a 'Merchandise List'.
- Panicked sweatily at a convention when you've had to share a lift with a celeb.
- Stayed at home the whole day *Who*'s on. Just in case.
- Mispronounced 'Sontarans', 'Krynoid', 'Logopolis' and 'Mandragora'.
- Bought *T.V. Zone* . . . sorry, that's sick.
- Suddenly realised that *Doctor Who* is silly after all.
- Looked at the names kids have scribbled in felt-tip in old Target books, and thought dark thoughts.
- Re-arranged *Who* videos/books into order in a shop.
- Told the 'Doctor who?' knock knock joke, and *thought it was funny*.
- Been asked when you'll grow out of *Doctor Who*.
- Become a junkie to the smell of brand new Target books.
- Had an inexplicable urge to go to the toilet just as the end credits of *Basil Brush* or *Final Score* came up.

    . . . Or was it just me?

4: Rude Bits

John Molyneux is: renowned for his video mixes; subject of a form letter to the Pope nominating him for sainthood in the last issue of *Anti-matter Chicken*; was every one of the five 'Fanboys Best Avoided' in *Pickled In Time*; and in that same fanzine was declared to have been 'detourned', transformed from a human being into a cartoon character by fandom's great love for him. He's a *bricoleur*, an artist who makes art out of bits of other people's texts. That's what a video mix is, basically. Bits of videoed *Doctor Who* cut up, re-edited, and either put to music (for comic or dramatic effect), or resequenced to make cheap jokes. For instance, the cast of *Jurassic Park* are seen to be gazing in awe at the (considerably less convincing) dinosaurs from 'Invasion of the Dinosaurs', whose gentle rubbery battles are, bizarrely, accompanied by the seductive tones of 'Je T'Aime'. Video mixes often play on those shared jokes that fandom creates, myths of what we think we know about the 'stars': everybody in UNIT is a camp old thing, the Doctor is shagging his companions, the First Doctor is very confused and averse to any suspiciously liberal behaviour. Molyneux once edited together every 'what?' Tom Baker ever said as the Doctor, with a rhythm that elicited rolling laughter. Such Fan Art could never be commercially released. The copyright fee on that clip alone would be torturous, and as for the libel laws . . .

The short collection that follows begins with Molyneux's spoof invitation letter to a prospective guest from a convention's guest liaison officer. It indicates several things about fandom: the way that awe swiftly gives over to a commercial decision concerning how many bums a particular 'celebrity' can put on how many seats; the way that fandom loves to catch a companion sneaking out of another companion's hotel bedroom; the fact that we haven't got a quarter of the respect for such folk that we should have, especially if they haven't managed to get a career outside of *Doctor Who*, because, as we correctly assume, then *they* belong to *us*.

The Black and White Guardian was the first 'zine to start enjoying fandom for its own sake (then) alongside and equally to the programme. In the following case, this was by wondering at the prose style adopted by a major contributor to *DWM* . . .

Ian Berriman is: scabrous, anguished, fiercely intellectual and passionate about everything. He can be seen, naked from the waist up, climbing on stage to embrace Morrissey in a Smiths video. The work he did for *Five Hundred Eyes* (David Gibbs's bi-yearly intellectual 'zine that was so infrequent that it belongs to every era and may in some sense still be going) was some of his best.

The DIY Guide to Convention Invitations
John Molyneux
(hiding behind the pseudonym Lenny X. Hoojum!)
(*Cottage Under Siege* #2)

Nowadays, everyone, not just the DWAS, is organising crap conventions. The most important aspect of conventions is, as we all know, sitting around in the bar all day, bitching about the guests. On this basis, the next important thing is to actually get those guests; sad old hasbeens who need a vast, subsidised ego-trip to help prop up their tired careers. To this end, here's a foolproof guide to inviting your favourite convention object of ridicule. Just follow the instructions and select the appropriate phrase.

Dear (insert name of artiste),

I'm one of the guest liaison team for the forthcoming convention (insert name of convention), *and I'd like to ask if you can spare the time from your schedule, which has been empty ever since you left the programme/were sacked from BBC Enterprises* (delete whichever is not applicable). *The event takes place on* (insert any bank holiday or religious festival) *as we are cheapskates and can get the* (hotel/town hall/public lavatories) *for several hundred pounds less on those dates. All the profits go to* (name some charity your biggest guest supports) *as we're more likely to get you if we employ moral blackmail.* (Here, take the opportunity to slag off any recent DWAS events that the prospective guest might have attended.) *We'd be delighted if you'd be able to come along because:*

a: we couldn't get your namesake.

b: tarts like you always go down well.

c: there must be some people who haven't heard the eyepatch story.

d: there will always be a few heterosexuals among the attendees and other guests for you to shag so that we can all bitch about your nymphomania at cliquey Olympiads.

e: we agree that the programme's patriarchal structure represses the possibility of positive female role-models.

f: a camp old twat like you is always useful for the cabaret/toilet duty.

g: we're so desperate to get your client that we're prepared to risk a crap panel with an old luvvie from the sixties who no one remembers.

h: there are always some tossers in the audience interested in a lot of old wank about Cybermen.

i: your widely reported near bankruptcy means that we can probably get you cheap.

j: everyone who saw 'Dimensions in Time' wants to shag you.

We're offering full expenses (as long as you don't drink the bar dry or take your friends out for a curry), accommodation and:

a: a complete set of Dickens and a tour around all the local cemeteries.

b: The fanzine editor of your choice gagged and bound up in a maggot pit during your panel, plus the script editor of your choice's head stuffed with garlic in a mushroom sauce served up at the celebrity banquet.

c: a vat of gin and tonic and the services of a hash supplier.

d: a condom dispenser in your bathroom and a ticket service outside your hotel bedroom door.

e: a new wardrobe and the opportunity to sell your photos to an audience who'll buy any old tat if it was done by somebody from the programme.

f: we promise not to mention Israeli agents or arms sales to the Middle East.

g: a completely uncynical donation to Romanian orphans charities.

h: a beautician to show you how to apply your make-up properly so as to disguise your sever l layers of Polyfilla.

I see that your spouse/ x-spouse was also in the programme:

a: but 'Terminus' was shite so we're not sending her an invitation.

b: however, she never does conventions as you might be there.

c: but we can't invite her as her appearance always causes several hundred fanboys to ejaculate spontaneously over the stage.

d: but who's interested in 'The Celestial Toymaker'? (And as for 'Arc of Infinity' . . .)

e: and he's over eighteen years your junior.

f: so bring her along as she'd be a crowd puller unlike a boring old Dalek panel.

If you don't feel you can make the event and can live with yourself for disappointing five hundred fanboys and ruining the chances of our making anything at all for charity then:

a: can we at least have an autographed photo of yourself (if applicable, insert 'preferably from before the menopause') for our auction?

b: we'll be telling all the tabloids that you couldn't give a toss about the sick and underprivileged.

I hope all's well and look forward to hearing from you soon. I enclose an SAE, so if you don't write back you must really be a miserable, selfish old sod/bitch.

Yours sincerely,

Guest Liaison

Trendy, politically right-on New Adventures author (if applicable)

Favourite *ODWM* Boobs Nos. 78 and 79
Selected by Justin Richards and David Richardson
(*Black and White Guardian* #4)

78: ' "The Smugglers" actually started off the fourth season of *Doctor Who* somewhat strangely, a peculiar story to open a season with.' (That was Gary Russell in issue 94 winning the *BAWG* prize for mindless repetition in a blatant attempt at getting twice as much money.)

79: 'Certainly with the state of technology today, one imagines that a great deal of colour could be used to create the world of magic.' (Gary Russell in an article on 'The Celestial Toymaker', expounding his Earth-shattering view that if the story had been made today, the BBC would have made it in colour. Bless him.)

Ian Berriman's 1001 Things more Enjoyable than watching 'Time and the Rani'
(*Five Hundred Eyes* #5)

1 Sweating.
2 Styling Arthur Scargill's hair.
3 Teaching mathematics.
4 *Star Begotten*.
5 Talking to Stewart McLaren about existential philosophy.
6 Having your nipples pierced.
7 Watching a certain fan trying to mime *Lesbian Lavatory Lust*.
8 Trying to 'transport yourself to another dimension' by injecting yourself with *Doctor Who* Bubble Bath.
9 Trying to write down what is actually said in a speech by Paddy Ashdown.
10 Eating a pillow.
11 Limbo.
12 Being a spot of dandruff on a *Doctor Who* writer's head.
13 Editing *The Key*.
14 Curling up in a foetal ball in the corner and rocking slowly backwards and forwards.
15 Swallowing.
16 Tying Matthew Waterhouse's underpants on to your head and jumping up and down shouting 'sploing sploing'.

17 Being taught how to act by a former Doctor.

18 Pretending to be a melon.

19 Sharing a flat with Mary Whitehouse.

20 Doing an Olympic gymnastic routine in the back of a Mini Metro.

21 Sucking a razor blade.

22 Hanging from the ceiling by two feet of piano wire.

23 Insulting a Muslim prophet.

24 Seducing Su Pollard.

25 Farting loudly in a public place.

27 Sleeping in a wickerwork chair.

28 Having a child and calling it Sharon out of sheer spite.

29 Wondering why there is no number 26.

30 Looking for a paperclip.

31 Trying to sell the Nazis underarm deodorant.

32 Being Welsh.

33 Getting into the lotus position in the bath.

34 Arson.

35 Laughing at old *Doctor Who* stars who are reduced to tiny bit parts on *Casualty*.

36 Taking an Irwin Allen series seriously.

37 Snorting Domestos.

38 Listening to a K-Tel album.

39 Monday mornings in Darlington.

40 Watching your rectum prolapse.

41 Being locked in a room for a week with all your best friends.

41 Eating boil in the bag food and wondering why it's a totally different colour and shape to the appetising repast in the pack photograph.

41 Shaving your legs with the Remington Fuzz-Away.

42 Wondering what weird fixation the typist has with the number 41.

43 Making a home-movie version of *Hellraiser* using a box of cocktail sticks.

44 Rubbing shampoo into your eyes.

45 Actually playing 'Doctor Who and the Planet of Monsters'.

46 Reading *The Wasp Factory* aloud to your grandmother.

47 Playing chess with an amoeba.

48 Cutting your toenails with shears.

49 Napalming Cheltenham.

50 Meeting a presenter of Breakfast Television.

51 Jumping naked onto a giant donner kebab spike.

52 Setting fire to your belly button.
53 Pretending to be surprised by *Tales of the Unexpected*.
54 A 'Youth Programme'.
55 Drinking a pint of rancid spit.
56 Having an appendectomy carried out using a curly straw and a lot of suck. (This one is overrated – DJG.)
57 Designing a new fascistic logo for a privatised industry.
58 Reading Shakespeare without the notes.
59 Bending over at –

to be continued . . .

5: Tom and Graham

The series producer Graham Williams hasn't quite got to the point where he died for fandom's sins, but he's getting close. It really is a pity that, in his lifetime, his work never got to be as adored as it is now. The following mock call to arms championing a video release for 'The Androids of Tara' appeared on the back of the first issue of *Cottage*. At the same time, a petition on the subject was organised at the Fitzroy Tavern. The Williams stories, and 'Tara' particularly, represent the dividing line between Old and New Fandom: they're silly to some, sublime to others. Quite a few people refused to sign that petition. Of course, there was no actual march. The petition was never delivered. To call for things is cool. To show up for the protest, to be photographed and categorised, would be menky in the extreme.

As this book goes to press, a fan group is trying to organise a coordinated campaign of protest about the BBC's failure to produce new *Doctor Who*. It won't work, because the BBC still see fans as basically mad, and protesting about the demise of a TV show is a mad thing to do. The fans involved will look like anoraks, to use that bullying word. But in creating that protest, those fans are organising, learning about politics and the media, making Fan Art. The protest itself is much more important than what they're protesting about.

Tom Baker, in his performances both on and off screen, encourages us in the thought that one can and should be above categorisation. He could wear an anorak like a raiment. Ness, in the interview below, gets more out of Tom than anybody else ever has. Ian Berriman's piece is another evangelical rant (pity it's at the expense of the Cartmel era, another lovely oasis for a different group of radical fans – but remember what I said about war poetry?) and

Paul Griffin's serious Tom and Lalla from *Cloister Bell* #1.

we also hear a voice from down under, saying yet again, as fan crit keeps saying, that the critical consensus is wrong.

As Tom says: 'Fans . . . are really responding to their own youth, to their own vitality.'

That should be the slogan on the back of our anorak.

March From Leeds Castle
to
BBC Enterprises
Demanding the release of
The Androids of Tara
Tom Baker will be leading the march from Leeds Castle
2pm. Sunday November 31st
Sponsored by the Doctor Who Liberation Fund

(Roberts/Corry. *Cottage Under Siege* #1)

The Lovers
Why I like Tom Baker and Lalla Ward and other people
like Sylvester McCoy and Sophie Aldred
Ian Berriman
(*Purple Haze* #1)

I think the psychological reason why I think Tom Baker and Lalla Ward are wonderful is much the same reason why Hamlet, Prince of Denmark, is such a popular literary figure. If you can identify with a character, you understand it, and you'll gradually develop a fondness for it. Hamlet is loved because you read *The Tragedy of Hamlet* as a student, and as a student you are more likely than not to be a pseud, and Hamlet is one of the great pseudo-intellectual icons. Probably more people read *The Reader's Digest* every month than read *Hamlet*, because *Reader's Digest* is shit, and shit is, generally, popular. So if you read *Hamlet* you're likely to have some special reason for it, the most likely one being that you're a bent-backed myopic knowledge-junky who finds solace, stimulation, and perhaps even a smug sense of superiority in books. As such you're likely to be an admirer of thinkers, sensitives, aesthetes and poets (because body-people scare the shit out of you). So you'll love *The Tragedy of Hamlet* because

Hamlet writes terrible, pretentious love poetry, wallows in beautiful indulgent grief, confounds people with witty remarks, and rather than *getting on with it* wastes all his time pondering on the morality of revenge.

'the language of flowers'

Tom Baker and Lalla Ward are *Doctor Who*'s great intellectual icons. Whereas McCoy's Doctor has omniscience, and the super-heroic ability to zap people with his little finger, all Tom and Lalla have to defend themselves with is their super-wit (Oscar Wilde in a long scarf), super-sarcasm, and their studenty super-silliness (relying on K9, tripping people with long scarves, etc.). They flew around the universe in the TARDIS, transforming it into The World's Biggest Blue Student Rag Week Float . . .

'everyone thinks he looks daft'

. . . Tom spending his spare time drinking alcohol, quoting Shakespeare ('Dusty death . . . out, out . . .', 'and jocund day stands tiptoe on the misty mountain tops . . .') and Isaac Newton, being very clever, shouting the word 'arse' in art galleries, leaping out of chairs like a doped-up Jeremy Brett Sherlock Holmes, whispering 'The Mona Lisa', going to Cambridge and punting up and down the river, dressing like a character from one of those horribly drab Toulouse-Lautrec posters, sewing patches on the elbows of perfectly good jackets, identifying antique chairs, reading *Peter Rabbit*, popping his eyes out like some weird neurotic from a Russian novel, and on the way bashing anyone who wasn't a decent Radio Four Englishman (nasty ethnic-type Movellans, shifty Krauts like Tryst, Cockney pickpockets from the planet Tythonus, and smarmy, neck-tied, white-suited, greasy Kenneth Clarke-esque creeps like Skagra and Skaroth) or at least someone that a decent Radio Four Englishman would like and collecting dictionaries so that he could say 'my word's longer than your word' . . .

'sugar spun sister'

. . . Lalla nostalgically yearning for yet more knowledge by dressing as a schoolgirl, supping wine, painting pictures of cute animals, reading books in boats dressed in a big white virginal girly frock from a Thomas Hardy novel, pointing out that the Mona Lisa had no eyebrows because she'd read books about it and she knew that sort of thing, pointing out that she definitely *had* eyebrows by waving them about elegantly to emphasise her intellectual point-scoring, talking about psychology, and other trendy sciences, and leaving to fight injustice and dogma in another universe. They both knew the secret of life: become an adult, then take all the good bits from your childhood and relive them, with the same childish sense of wonder. Up above the streets and houses, they flew . . .

'true coming dream'

. . . and as they flew, they took other people with them who also yearned to fly about the universe propelled only by their intellect, wit and aesthetic judgement. And instead of discarding trivial *Doctor Who* when they grew up, these people clung onto it, safe in the sense that they didn't really take it all that seriously, and turned the writing of crap articles on *Doctor Who* into a sort of intellectual sport. And how good it was/is for fanzines.

'dreams burn down'

For modern fans (which I too am/was) I sometimes think the fannishness is the thing. I have a fear that people are fans of the idea of being a fan, and desperately need an overwhelming obsession, the obsession being the aim rather than any true appreciation of and affection for the series. It all gets out of proportion. For some the obsession becomes bigger than the love of the series. Having said this, if it weren't for obsession, *Doctor Who* would have died years ago (you can argue about whether that's a good or bad thing in the comfort of your own home). Modern *Doctor Who* only exists (existed) because of the merchandising possibilities, which provide (provided) enough money for the BBC to produce the programme, with a few million pounds change. Fans are the life support for the ailing programme. Sadly, it's not much of a life when you're being kept alive artificially on life-support.

'born to be sold'

Sylvester McCoy's Doctor and Sophie Aldred's Ace are definite products of the fin-de-siècle 1989 zeitgeist, where Theme Parks, Supermarkets, Crap Alcohol, Charlton Athletic, Holiday Camps, Freezer Centres, Coach Tours, Milkshakes, the *Daily Mirror*, Cheap Circuses, BMXes, Tacky Post-Modernist Architecture, Tacky Post-Modernist Telephone Boxes, Television and Crap Pop Music (all of which appear in Cartmel's *Doctor Who*) do not just *exist*, they are embraced and *loved* – and used as comforting images in *Doctor Who* to fix the idea of 'Earth'.

And that's part of why *The Happiness Patrol* didn't really work, because it itself was a product of the society it was mocking, and was surrounded by three other products of this society. How could someone who loved *Silver Nemesis* appreciate *The Happiness Patrol*, a story that took the piss out of the plastic culture that *produced Silver Nemesis*?

'the key to the attic door'

Doctor Four and Romana Two, on the other hand, were the products of four fertile imaginations – Adams, Williams, Baker and Ward – not a definite zeitgeist. They were unfettered by popular culture, adrift in a time-warped world that was a liberal intellectual's wet dream, a weird wonderland formed from bits of the 1890s, 1960s, the future, a higher plane, a secondhand bookshop, an ivory tower, and the anti-bourgeois underground, where pretentious people could talk about symbolism in pubs without getting glassed. It was a butterfly world, destined to be as transient as it was beautiful.

'it's what you want that matters'

But wake up, Kiddo, it's the 1990s now, and laid-out, freaked-out, art-terrorists like Lalla and Tom, fighting the good fight with inky quill pens and copies of *The Tragedy of Macbeth* are no longer fashionable. What the public wants and gets are characters cribbed from 'graphic novels' (proper name: comics). What they get is a Doctor with a brain like a huge database and cartoonish false eccentricity.

'pretty girls make graves'

. . . What they get is a girl who's a post-post-post-punk feminist anarchist arsonist urban guerrilla, with a baseball bat, suspenders and Doc Martens, who burns down houses, jumps out of windows, and doesn't give a toss. A companion who lulls the monsters into a false sense of security by flashing her thighs at them and talking about sex . . . before kicking the shit out of the tin horrors and stamping on their bollocks. If only Ace shaved her head and flashed a bit more flesh, she'd be cult heroine 'Tank Girl' from the comic *Deadline*.

'Lazyitis'

Part of the current dynamic duo's popularity with 'the fans' surely lies in the fact that Doctor Seven and Ace *are* also 'fans'. So, these overtly fannish fans (post-modernist fans? There's a stupid concept . . .), these 1980s Thatcherist Zeitgeist fans can *identify* with them. Ace is a fan of Charlton Athletic, Courtney Pine (she even asks for his autograph), Rock Music, *Blue Peter* and Fanderson. Sophie is a fan of Gerry Anderson and Tintin. The Doctor is a fan of jazz, the blues and tacky circuses: he sings songs, he plays the spoons, he juggles, he does tricks, he behaves like someone desperate for a bit of TV stardom auditioning for *Opportunity Knocks*. The only book he ever reads is one on juggling. In between saving universes, the two of them swan about the universe on nostalgic trips to the forties, fifties and sixties meeting famous TV and film stars and Enjoying Themselves in a populist manner. They do what Mr and Mrs Ugly Ordinary Person people would do if they won the TARDIS in a *Daily Mirror* bingo game . . . They sell photographs of themselves in sunglasses. They're known as TV stars rather than the Doctor and Ace because they have appeared/ appear in dozens of other plasticky television series, whereas Tom and Lalla arrived virtual unknowns and for the most part, before and afterwards, only appeared in poncy 'proper acting' parts. Because of this, and a lot of bad scripts, it took three seasons (and latterly, pages, dedicated to Ace to try and make up for her terrible start) to even *suggest* that either of them was a *real* character, something Tom and Lalla both managed in a couple of episodes.

'getting nowhere fast'

If this sort of Doctor and companion continue, fandom will die, because Doctor-Seven-Ace could attract and encourage fans who are consumers rather than creators, who buy Dapol toys and every single other item of merchandise regardless of its value (modern merchandise doesn't even have the cute kitsch value or nostalgia value of sixties/seventies merchandise to commend it), who masturbate over glossy photographs of Sophie Aldred, who buy glossy crapzines like *The Frame* and who will not (unless the old freaks jump on them and freak them out with Tom Baker videos and drugs) write pretentious dissertations on the series. And most of them will like the new rather than the old *Doctor Who* whatever they're shown, because they were attracted by *Shit Doctor Who* and hence cannot understand something that is not *shit*. Shame.

'paint a vulgar picture'

Modern *Doctor Who* is a product of eighties culture, which fed upon itself, eating up the past, spewing it out, and eating up the vomit . . . and so on, on and on.

Any minute now, *Doctor Who* Will Eat Itself. It will implode.

Our only hope is vested in British Satellite Broadcasting, and the next generation.

'love in the emptiness'

All of this is why when a story like 'Ghostlight' appears, written by the bastard son of Tom Baker, 'City Of Death', Black Comedy, and Symbolism, fandom gets split down the middle: the pseudo-intellectuals love it, and understand it (and, if they don't, try until they DO understand it, and can write very long articles about it) whereas *DWM* readers show their contempt for it by voting 'The Curse Of Fenric' (*shit!*) as best story of the year instead, and the more down-to-earth, sensible majority of fandom points out that it doesn't make sense and is a load of pretentious old tosh.

As, indeed, is this article. Forgive me. I'm an art student and you shouldn't take any notice of anything I say. I only wrote this so I would have a legitimate excuse not to write an essay about a damn awful Thomas Hardy book . . .

Note from editor Stephen O'Brien: He's so modest, Ian. Don't take any notice of that cop-out finish above. Ian shies away from controversy all the time by claiming that he writes everything on a foolish whim and that we shouldn't believe a word of what we've read. Crap. He means all of it. And that excuse about the Hardy book . . . He's not even doing English. I mean, well . . .

Tom Baker Interview
Ness Bishop
(*Skaro* (New) #6)

The Royal Bath and West Show 1992 . . . At one end of the huge Shepton Mallet showground, a collection of prize-winning cows and sheep. At the other, relaxing in a hospitality tent in that well-worn pinstriped suit, sat Tom Baker, there to promote the imminent release of *Shada* in the BBC exhibition marquee. Amidst the sounds of accordion music and stall-holders touting for business, Tom Baker drank coffee and ate flapjacks. Hardly the place Ness would have expected to find him. But then again . . .

'Just Who in Shepton Mallet is Tom Baker?'

Television, like *Doctor Who*, seems to be going through something of a Tom renaissance at the moment. Not even an agricultural show was safe from the man! At present, there seems little attempt to distance himself from *Doctor Who*; in fact, he appears to rather enjoy it.

'I think it's something to do with *Medics*. You see, Granada's a big organisation and I accidentally met some of the girls who were doing the PR. And because I liked them and they also seemed vastly amused by me, they actually took me out on lots of publicity jaunts and the whole thing snowballed. (I'm terribly vulnerable to girls who find me wildly funny. It's interesting that they can manipulate me so very easily.) So, in the last six months, there has been an inordinate amount of publicity, mainly because I was in good form and happy. And when I'm happy, like anyone who's happy, one can do anything. Anyone can be cheerful when you're happy. So it's because of those girls, and it always leads to more things. I'm doing more schools' radio, etc. I thought *Chocolate* was very interesting, and I helped work on the script of the narrative, and it turned out to be quite good. Somebody in my village – the ironmonger – loved it! And *Doctor Who*? . . . Well, there's no escape from it, is there? Every now and again, the appetite, the interest, comes up and people ask if I'm still alive? "Well, yes he is," they say. "Oh, that's funny – we thought he was dead." As you know, when you're involved with any of the mediums – television or press – if you fall out of them, people think you're dead; or at the very least retired. That's why there's a certain group of anxious people who are constantly in the public eye – they don't believe they're actually alive unless they're mentioned in the press, or unless they're doing quizzes or panel games. I don't do that. But every now and then, people do rediscover me and say "Is he still alive?" And so I am.

'If there were a current *Doctor Who*, I don't think people would necessarily be so interested in me. If they ever brought it back, whoever got it would take the interest of the fans, and quite rightly.

But obviously, when a thing is suspended, of course the fans remain very very interested. So because there is nowhere for them to focus in a new sense, they've got to focus on the past . . . So here comes today and the release of 'Shada', and 'Shada' is something with which I was involved. So I'm here. It isn't particularly because I want to pursue old stories, but obviously people like you drive me back into my Garden of Remembrance, wherein lies *Doctor Who*, my one great triumph. Now they're finally laying to rest all my work at the BBC with the release of 'Shada', so there's that added little thing that brings me a little closer to it. John (Nathan-Turner) asked me to come down here, and actually, it's quite nice to come to an agricultural show. I used to come to these shows years ago – I used to be very interested in flowers . . .

'The 'Shada' video was very strange, I enjoyed it, but it was also quite painful having to watch oneself as I don't do it very much at all. Even recently, I heard my wife chortling with laughter because she was watching *Cluedo* in the other room; she loves me I suppose. It turns out that the only people who watched *Cluedo* were the people who love me, and I can't blame them for that . . . Recently I did a compilation where I comment spontaneously on clips from my *Doctor Who* (John thought the fans would like that). When I saw myself, I still had that recurring regret, which is painful because I always wanted to do everything again. Actually, it was quite painful doing the compilation because the cameras were rolling on me all day – even when I was very fatigued they didn't give up! Ever seen yourself in an amateur video? If you have, you must have thought "Christ! I could do that again and better!" And in that sense, it's painful for me, because I never had the power to say "Let's do another take," whereas in commentary, you can do ten takes and say "Great – let's use number three," and feel comfortable with it.

'At times, I did become agitated and argumentative with the work, but I believe I'm very commonplace in that – everyone thrives on arguments, don't they? Nowadays, thank goodness, in most areas, certainly in my job, everyone's at equals, and now if I'm anxious or bad-tempered, I will trim my emotions as it will get in the way of the work; but that's the way I express myself because I'm very nervous. Other people express it in different ways, like being very taciturn or something like that. So sometimes I get my way, and sometimes I have to give way to other people. But I would never express my anxiety or impatience by attempting to bully anyone. I couldn't bully my equals because people wouldn't put up with it. I certainly wouldn't bully younger or more timid, less experienced people that I happened to be working with. Never. But I am very anxious. I desperately want to make things work all the time.

'In all honesty, I don't think I've mellowed at all! Whatever I get to do, I work obsessively at it. Like anyone else, I come alive doing what I do best, so when I'm acting, I feel more alive, and I have a greater sense of fun and identity. In other words, it's that shagged-out old paradox: "I feel most real when I'm most fictional," which is what most performers do – one is seeking to come alive . . . I might be slightly more tactful with directors than I was. I didn't realise when people said to me afterwards that I'd been insufferably rude or unkind – it wasn't because I meant to be! So I think I may have softened in that way. But my enthusiasm hasn't diminished at all. I'm still anxious to "solve" what I do.

'Sometimes the press still make me a bit niggly. Here, for instance, I wouldn't mind being photographed with an old cow or bull or something. But the idea of being photographed in front of a time machine (a SWEB Electricity display!) . . . I find terrible. I've done all those clichés. I mean, what they really want is my old ruddy costume, with an ex-wife or an old lover or something. That's what photographers like, poor sods! I feel sorry for photographers, that they find me so uninteresting that they have to make me do peculiar things in order to get their picture published. They make me very uneasy, although I have been photographed four or five million times!

'You know, I still am very surprised that people are interested in a dear old thing like me! But I'm surprised that it is *me*, I'm not surprised at the *Doctor Who* phenomenon itself because obviously everyone's a fan of something. When I see a famous old cricketer, or footballer, or an artist that I admire, it doesn't matter to me that he or she is old . . . I simply respond. Fans, you see, are really responding to their own youth, to their own vitality. I think you will obviously go on to do lots of things – you're young. But you'll probably always have a soft spot for *Doctor Who* because it will remind you of this lovely magazine that you're heroically producing, and in turn, it will remind you of your youth. And later on, if you finish up in West Africa or Australia, being a hard-nosed investigative journalist, one day you may overhear a conversation: "Yeah, he died actually!" and you'll say "Who died?" "Tom Baker died" – and you'll think "Gosh – I met him once in Shepton Mallet, and we sat in a windy tent eating flapjacks!"

and so it'll come back. And that's the lovely thing about being a fan of something.

'I saw a chap this morning, about my age, train-spotting, and there he was, in his drab little anorak and drab little sandals and dark socks. And I looked at him and I thought "How marvellous, he's still enthusiastic about a number on a train. It's only a number on a train to me, it's a whole world to him!" It's the same with people who say "Apparently he's a *Doctor Who* fan – is he odd in the head?!" and the reply will sometimes be "Well, yes, he is a bit really." But it's because they don't understand. It's that old analogy – "For people who don't understand, no explanation is possible, and for people who do, no explanation is necessary."

'When I left, I never personally felt immediately cut off from *Doctor Who*. I left because I was beginning to feel someone else could do it better, but because it was still current and I was still getting lots of publicity, *Doctor Who* followed me for quite some time. And because I still had my hair very long and always dressed in an old Burberry tweed coat, people still associated me with it, so it was a very chastening experience. Then I was asked to play *Hedda Gabler* by Donald McQuinney, who was a very famous director, now dead. Most of the people I've worked with are now dead. They all die soon after they've worked with me – this might be why I don't work very often . . . people are generally afraid of dying. Anyway, I was to be in *Hedda Gabler* and I thought, naturally, that I was going to play Hedda, which I thought was inspired casting, but it turned out that Susannah York wanted to play that part, so they gave me Judge Brack, and to play him, I had to have my hair cut short. So I went to a very expensive hairdressers, paid for by the company. When I walked in, I was famous – I bought them champagne and vodka, and whatever the young people wanted; then I was taken for a discussion about my hair. They cut it and I walked out completely unknown . . . in the space of an hour and a half! The girls who made such a fuss of me at the front of the shop didn't recognise me as I left. And so I was gone. My identity, rather like Samson, was my hair. So that was the end of me. Mostly, I've kept my hair short, but at the time of *Cluedo* it grew rather long and I was recognised everywhere as "that old *Doctor Who*". It's short again now, and about an hour ago, I walked around this ground and nobody recognised me – isn't that incredible?

'It's a delicious anonymity! You know, I used to know a very famous actor who, when his self-esteem was low and he was feeling

101

depressed, used to adore going on long tube journeys up the District Line, just so he could be recognised all the time. That reassured him that he existed. I don't feel it that acutely. I do have a capacity to be absolutely alone, to sit in my house all day and read, and then, occasionally, I go down to the pub and buy everyone drinks, in the hope that they will listen to my stories. And if they don't, I won't blame them either. But I don't actually thirst to be recognised in public, although I thirst continuously to be noticed by producers and directors. It's actually very, very wearisome to be looked at all the time – it's very tiring. That's why some people get very hysterical about it. It's terrible to feel those eyes upon you – awful! There were times when I was so tense from being looked at that my body didn't work properly. I'd go all day without going to the lavatory and obviously I couldn't drink lots of beer, as I would have been embarrassed by that. And you know, it's terribly humiliating to be standing in the lavatory having a pee as someone jogs your elbow and says "Didn't you used to be Doctor Who?"

'No-one is qualified to be able to say that you are playing a character like the Doctor, an alien, inadequately, and as long as you don't go in and try to subvert it, which you wouldn't be allowed to do, no-one can fail. How can I not believe it? I still hold onto that. You can't deny that, can you? No-one has failed, have they? I mean, obviously there are preferences and tastes change, but never mind. You might say the same about two or three formulas. This has been demonstrated with James Bond par excellence and, of sorts, with *Star Trek*. Take James Bond – the genuine sadists and the ones who hate women love Sean Connery's interpretation because he appeared to be so genuinely sadistic. Now, myself, I cannot grasp – maybe because I'm a bit short of humour – why on earth Bond is so popular. I find him utterly, utterly repulsive. Everything that he stands for makes me sick, he's the absolute antithesis of everything that's decent. But not the way Roger Moore played it, because Roger is so utterly decent himself, and it's interesting that he was a success in spite of his inherent decency. But the idea that someone who treats women so badly, who's so overwhelmingly arrogant, who is constantly violent . . . that repulses me. But nevertheless, the formula survives.

'You can't go into happy things, as *Doctor Who* was, creative things, entertainment – you can go into wars, but even then it doesn't work – full of all sorts of exact preconceptions about how you're going to do it. The thing about life and in plays is one only gets the outline of a script. Then you have to go in there and respond to other people. If I were asked to do *Doctor Who* again – which is inconceivable – I would just simply respond. (Mind you, I wouldn't mind playing a monster or a villain if they ever get round to making that film!) The real key to having a lot of fun, it seems to me, is actually responding to what is happening instead of wheeling out the stock responses, like when grumpy people are always grumpy, or selfish people always selfish. The trick is to make something of it. The real thing is performers – it's very sad, isn't it? – have this kind of need. It's motivated often, not only by inadequacy, but also by generosity. Performers really want to be alchemists. Dickens' novels are full of alchemists. An alchemist is obviously someone who, in a sense, makes the best, who turns the dross and the whippet shit of disappointment into the alchemy, into the gold of being positive. Otherwise, the alternative to that is despair, and so performers want to make something more of what's going, to tell a good story . . . The marvellous thing about actors is they never seem to learn! They become very experienced, but never learn. A little earlier, I was talking to Hugh Lloyd, and I knew instantly how wonderful he was, and I've seen him be wonderful. But if he and I were together in a play, it would be as if we were drama students. We would sit down over a script and we would babble, lost and excitable, and I think when that evaporates, then we're nothing. It's like that within relationships. If we begin to respond the same way all the time, then the magic has gone. Admittedly it's the hardest thing in the world to keep it going, because inevitably, repetition dulls the sense of excitement.

'There is a character in Dickens' *Martin Chuzzlewit* (not one of his most popular novels, but I think it's particularly brilliant) called Mark Tatby, and Tatby is one of these alchemists. He's ordinary, not educated and he's working at a pub called The Blue Horn. He's met in the day by a man called Tom Hinge, who asks "What are you doing, Mark?" and he replies "I'm leaving The Blue Horn." And Tom says "Leaving it, Mark? But you were so happy there." "Yes sir – but where's the merit in that? Anyone can be happy at The Blue Horn. Now I'm going to take up something else in life, sir – something more difficult. Then I'll really have some merit." You see, he deliberately tests his capacity for merit. The story moves to America, and it's the marvellous Mark Tatby, the *ultimate* alchemist, who lifts everyone. And later, when he's dying, it's almost unbearably poignant. Chuzzlewit asks "How are you, dear Mark?" and he says "Oh, jolly, sir. It's ever so dark, but I'm jolly." What an alchemist! Mother Teresa's an alchemist; in your way, you're an alchemist, against all the odds, producing this magazine to cheer people up, which will make a contribution to the sum total of human enjoyment . . . which is good, isn't it?!!! That's what I tried to do all those years ago.

'Once I'd signed the contract I was very relaxed about it, and again, I just responded. And of course, I was playing an alien, and what are the rules for aliens, except of course that they might be constantly surprised, like a child. It's a lovely thing when you see a child over its mother's shoulder, and you wink or pull a face when you see the child look round. That's wonderful. Maybe that's the first time that child has seen another face from that angle, through its mother's hair blowing, as he's seeing you. Some people have the capacity to remember that and to recall and respond like that.

'I'm very interested in aliens. Not just benevolent aliens, 'cause that's easy – any bloody fool can do that – but in people who feel alienated. And of course, we live in a society, as we always have, that produces such people. I'm fascinated now by so many young people who feel alienated. If you're young, it must be terrible, as that's the beginning of your life. It makes me feel sad and inadequate, because one doesn't have the ability to comfort them with ordinary rhetoric – it's sad, it paralyses me sometimes. I think "How can I think of something to say that might comfort them? Will a pound do?" If I'm on my way to Soho I think, "I'll give him a pound!" Then I remember "I'm getting near Waldorf Street – I'll give him two pounds!" I feel chosen by the beggars! I think perhaps sometime I should found an agency where I can take on all the clients who are disenchanted, the alienated poor young, and I could actually write their scripts and become a kind of benevolent Peacham from the *Threepenny Opera* – Peacham used to organise all the criminals. Well, I would gather all the beggars together and improvise scenes, so that when they went out, they wouldn't depress people. You see, when beggars come up to you and say "Excuse me – have you got any small change?" that really is a downer, isn't it? Now, if they said "Oh! I don't believe it! You! You have been chosen to help me – I'm desperately trying to get a bottle of Scotch together," then everyone would be a lot happier. So we would improvise, like Fagin teaching the Artful Dodger, but in a positive way – teaching people how to be a really valuable beggar. So the beggars could teach us something and we could learn from them. You could turn the whole world upside-down. You'd hear very posh people over dinner saying

"Darling – I met the most fascinating beggar today, I really learnt something!" . . . Do you want another flapjack?

'I want a postbox with a bell on it . . . I get rather a lot of mail and it would make life easier for my postman. Or perhaps I should tip my postman – he would prefer that! You see, one of the boring things about progress is that it disenfranchises people. For example, if someone actually invents a machine that does the work of 300 girls, what's the point of this machine if it only makes 300 girls sad and unhappy and out of work? So that machine can't be good. In some ways, I'd prefer us not to progress so quickly, and to have more activities for people to do. I was trying to explain this to some students whilst filming *Cluedo* in Cheshire. It was about 100 yards to where the make-up caravan was and I was being zipped backwards and forwards for all sorts of reasons, because the continuity was very crucial. The students kept seeing me in a big stretch limousine with a chauffeur called Frank, who would drive up, jump out and open the door for me. I'd get in and he'd drive away . . . but he'd only back it up to the tent, and then I would get out. What the students didn't know was that my relationship with Frank was quite understood, as that was Frank's job, and because I was earning good money, every night I gave him a tip of ten pounds – so at the end of a twelve-day shoot, he'd done quite reasonably . . . he liked that. But the students were looking at me with a jaundiced eye, shaking their heads. So when I got talking to them, they told me they disapproved of it: "You don't need a car to go 100 yards; neither do you need a man opening the door for you." So I explained to them: "What do you want me to do? He's got a family – do you want me to sack him and say I don't need him? . . . Of course, if I say 'Don't worry – I'll get in and out,' I'm stopping him at his job – that's what he does, that's what he's good at. He's a brilliant chauffeur, and at the moment, I'm the reason for his existence." Then the students were more sympathetic. I don't want to imply that anyone could be inferior in any way, but I do believe in keeping things going, and him doing his wonderful job allows me to tip him out of my own pocket. Over here, we're a bit touchy about this kind of thing, for reasons which are very complicated, involving services, snobbery and class systems. In America, it's different. But I see nothing wrong in being a brilliant chauffeur or a dazzling waitress and making a lot of money by being terrific at your job . . .

'Ever since M.O.M.I., people have started making allusions to possible *Evenings With Tom Baker*. I don't know really. The thing is, while it's funny for half an hour, spinning it into 90 minutes or so . . . well, there are few people who can do it; Dave Allen, Peter Ustinov . . . I suppose I could do it – for the fans. Maybe I will. Sometimes I'm asked to do after-dinner speeches, but they're mostly for all fellahs, and I'm not interested in that. I really am not. I'm not into jokes either. You know – "There was this girl with tits out here . . ." . . . *Oh Christ No!* I'm interested in stories. Those jokes are routed in prejudice, racist and sexist, and so tired and shagged-out – I think we've come on a bit since then.

'I like that funny, reassuring kind of humour – melancholy. *One Foot In The Grave* with Richard Wilson and Annette Crosbie is extremely well done. I'd love to do something like that. In fact, at the BBC many years ago, I was asked if I would like to do something else and I said I'd love to be in a comedy with Miriam Margoyles. "But Tom," they said, "she's big and fat," which I found quite an incomprehensible response, so I stopped right there. An awful lot of sit-com is paralysingly predictable, it really is. There's a bitter line in *Man Of The Moment* by Alan Ayckbourn, which I saw last year, starring Michael Gambon simply being dazzling. It's a terrifying line when someone in television is trying to interview Michael's character, and he kept saying how happy he was. And this girl who was making the documentary says "Listen, Mr Willis, middle-aged happiness is death at the ratings," and this terrible, cynical line just hung in the air, making you shiver. I thought "Really? Is that true?" And unfortunately, it appears to be so. People really are only into young happiness or misery, but middle-aged happiness . . . So my idea of being terribly in love with Miriam, *terribly* in love – you know, lots of bed scenes with lots of laughter – would not have been popular. We could have been two shagged-out old actors running this school for people who are uncertain of themselves. We'd have this awful thing in a garden, in a villa, where it says *Yvonne's School of Self-Assurance*. We would welcome people in, then act out situations to them, and then we'd put them back into real situations. And then people would come back for more lessons, but a few would flower because of us and our lessons in self-assurance, and how to make yourself alluring and witty and sexy. In other words, it would be a kind of rapid and upbeat psychotherapy. Of course, sometimes it would be agonising because we would fail. Yes – the plot's just occurred to me, and things that just occur often take my fancy. You know, it's a terrible thing not to know what one thinks until you hear yourself saying it. I think "Good

Heavens – is that really my opinion? I didn't know I believed that!"
Maybe that's the next thing. It sounds terribly original!

'I suppose *Cluedo* was a step in that direction, although what
attracted me to that was that it wasn't going to take too long, and they
were going to pay very well. I was also acquainted with many of the
people. I absolutely adore Ruth Madoc . . . she's wonderful. And
Christopher Biggins, who is so amusing and utterly shameless. And
then there was Pam Ferris, who I didn't know beforehand. She's
extraordinarily nice, and nearly always tells the truth – it's quite
amazing! So I got on quite well with her. Really it was just so jolly!
You see, sometimes it doesn't matter what the job's like. You know
when someone rings you up at night and asks you to a party, but
you're feeling shagged out and you decline pleasantly? They often say
"Oh, come on! Frank'll be there, and Mary, and Bill, and Pippa's just
come back from Spain and she's got sunburnt." And you think "Sod
it!" and you go out to the party. It's a bit like that with jobs. I don't
really need lots and lots of jobs, but if people ask me at the right
moment or in the right way, I'll do it. Like John saying "Do you want
to come down here?" and then I meet you, and it's marvellous, isn't
it? . . .

'I wouldn't say I was an obvious choice to play anything. I certainly
wasn't for Sherlock Holmes. As for the Doctor . . . I remember I met
Jonathan Miller when I'd just got the part but before it had been
announced, and he said "Hello Tom, what are you doing?" and I
gabbled, still in disbelief at my luck, "Jonathan – I've just been given
Doctor Who!" He paused for a moment – "Oh," he said, "that's very
good casting." And in those days, of course, we were often mistaken
for each other. I do remember one time going to a play that he directed
– *Three Sisters* at the Cambridge Theatre. It was in the afternoon and
it wasn't very full, but there were lots of earnest Americans there. I
was standing in the bar having a drink in the interval, and suddenly an
American led over twenty of his graduate students. "Doctor Miller,"
he said, "I'd just like to shake your hand please, and introduce you."
So I shook hands with twenty-one Americans, and they all kept asking
me what it's like to be a genius. And I kept shrugging modestly
thinking, "What would Jonathan say?" Of course, it was no use me
saying "I'm sorry, but you've mistaken me," because that would have
embarrassed them, so I thought quickly and decided Jonathan would
want me to give an impression of him. So I did, because I knew him.
So I said how difficult it was being considered a genius, and used

some of his anecdotes. They asked about my patients, and knowing he was a pathologist, I said "Well, most of them are dead, so I don't really have a great bedside manner," which they all thought was wonderful. So they went away thinking how nice Jonathan was, and they're quite right too – he is!

'Was I obvious casting? No, not obvious, but it was good casting. Yes, it was a good move. I'll allow myself to say that. It was a good move.'

Why the Nimon Should be our Friends
Storytelling and Stylistic Change in *Doctor Who*
Phillip J. Gray
(*TSV* Vol. 8, #5)

FACT! 'The Horns of Nimon' is a truly dreadful example of *Doctor Who*. After all, the story is dominated by over-acting, a silly script, poor production values . . . you can probably recite the generalised fan criticisms yourself. 'The Horns of Nimon' issue of *InVision* opens with a preachy diatribe on the story's financial problems and states that it would attempt to 'find out what went wrong . . . and account for the story's ultimate failure despite the straightforward narrative and care of production'. (*InVision* #43, 'The Horns of Nimon', p2.) The assumption that a *Doctor Who* story could be counted as a 'failure' despite straightforward storytelling disturbs me deeply. What I intend to argue is that 'The Horns of Nimon' is one of the last *Doctor Who* stories which concentrates on telling a story. It is notable for being the final story before *Doctor Who* became obsessed stylistically with shadow factors, primarily a focus on glossy production values. These were fatal to the series' central tenet: that the primary function of *Doctor Who* is to tell a story successfully.

Presently *Doctor Who* fans are rushing disingenuously to praise the series in the years 1977 to 1979. Fandom has been retreating from its once near-hysterical adulation of the early Nathan-Turner period, but after concentrating on the Hinchcliffe era is only now beginning to re-examine the late 1970s as a potential area of quality. Something which I strongly suspect will be evident in the fan reception of the recent BBC Video release of 'Destiny of the Daleks'. *The Fourth Doctor Handbook* interprets the Williams period more generously than might have been expected five years ago, commenting that the comedic/camp aspects of these stories 'often disguised the fact that the scripts were, on the whole, highly literate and intelligent. They exhibited a knowing, postmodern playfulness with the traditional conventions and clichés of *Doctor Who* and of TV drama in general.' (*The Fourth Doctor Handbook*, p167.) I intend to examine this statement in relation to 'The Horns of Nimon' and the importance of its relationship with the stylistic changes which took place in 1980.

Storytelling is the central feature of 'The Horns of Nimon'. The plot is unlaid carefully at an even pace throughout the story. The initial exchange between the pilot and the co-pilot set the scene immediately with a single line of dialogue: 'The second Skonnon empire will be born.' The audience is immediately aware of several things: the decayed setting, that Skonnos is a militaristic but declining society, that it has plans to revive itself and that the Doctor will somehow become involved. The motivation for the Nimon's machinations on Skonnos is revealed in episode three, although the audience has known of the Skonnons' ambitions since the first episode and has received hints about the 'Great Journey of Life'. The grotesqueness of the Nimon's ambitions is painted in broad strokes. They are 'swarming like a plague of locusts' across the galaxy, creatures that strip the 'binding energy' from the universe. In other words they are a variation on the vampire motif. *InVision* concedes that Anthony Read's understanding of *Doctor Who* was spot-on: 'His script was near enough text book *Doctor Who* in terms of affordability, practicality, casting and structure.' (*InVision* #43 'The Horns of Nimon', p4.) The in-jokes to the Greek legend of Theseus and the Minotaur which culminate in the Doctor's recognition of the maze-like structure of the Power Complex are satisfying textually because they are an overt confirmation of what many viewers would have recognised. The stylised costumes and sets reflect elements of the plot. The elaborate shoulder pads of the Skonnons assist the story's scriptual description of a militaristic, self-important society. Romana's red hunting costume suggested by Lalla Ward refers to the hunting of the bull. The production reinforces the nature of the storyline, supporting the story as told by the script rather than dominating it. Moreover, occasionally the production actually aids the humorous subtext. When landing on Skonnos, the Doctor remarks to K9 that they should land 'somewhere unobtrusive' – and because of the nature of the central Skonnon set, the TARDIS appears in the very centre of the agora. When Seth tells the Doctor inside the maze 'all these corridors look the same', this is an effective postmodern statement on the nature of the programme and a knowing nod to the audience. Presumably the writer Anthony Read had a fairly good idea of the capabilities of the BBC set designers. As a final example, in episode two the Doctor is in the maze attempting to mark his way by affixing stars to the walls. Not only is this a reference to Theseus' ball of string, it is also a knowing in-joke on the science fiction nature of *Doctor Who* itself.

In terms of characterisation, the Doctor is a straightforward investigator of events and the programme's liberal/moral imperatives are in full force. Because of the Doctor's stated determination that the Nimon must be stopped the anti-imperialism of this story is much more succinct than the next tale to deal with the subject. Christopher Bailey's Buddhist references and the production's obsession with a visual display of the symbols of the Raj, rather than a coherent storyline, confuse and distort 'Kinda'. Unlike the moral indecision of the Fifth Doctor, there is no hesitation by the Fourth Doctor on behalf of the Anethans. Romana too is determined to stop the parasitic Nimon, something confirmed by her encounter with the dying Sezom on Crinoth.

The relationship between Tom Baker's Doctor and Lalla Ward's Romana is an interesting one. Although Ward fulfils all the criteria of the traditional companion as the channel for explanation for the audience, because of her nature as a Time Lady and Ward's rapport with Tom Baker, Romana is something quite different. She seems more of an equal despite the Doctor being quite clearly in charge of the situation. It is Romana who points out the radioactivity of the Hymetusite and who suggests using the mineral to power the spaceship back to Skonnos. The 'switched sonic screwdriver' scene demonstrates Romana's technical prowess, yet Ward is careful never to overstate this (probably recognising Tom Baker's position as the programme's acknowledged star). Romana's behaviour is startlingly varied in 'The Horns of Nimon'. In episode one she is capable of demanding that the co-pilot turns back for the Doctor, labelling him a 'despicable worm'. In other scenes, Romana is the traditional line-feed for the Doctor, enhanced by the sly wittiness which is Ward's characterisation ('Oh, you will Doctor! You will!' she replies to the Doctor's wondering why he hadn't thought of the solution when she had). Such subtlety of performance adds layers to the traditional companion role without falling into the stereotypes of later companions: 'gentle' Nyssa, 'aggressive' Tegan.

'Horns' has been criticised severely for its guest performances. David Owen claims that the nature of the performances betray the nature of previous *Doctor Who* style, which used 'credible performers and dialogue to outline the unfolding of the incredible'. (David Owen, 'Just Seventeen', *InVision* #45 Season Seventeen, p13.) Justin Richards also argues that the performances are largely inappropriate to this story, citing inevitably the notorious Crowden maniacal death-laugh. (Justin Richards, 'Simple Nimon', *InVision* #45 Season Seventeen, p12.) Graham Crowden's performance is a good deal more subtle than he has been given credit for, fans concentrating generally on the infamous 'laughing' at the death scene which has been labelled illogically 'pantomime'. Yet the death scene is not uncharacteristic considering Soldeed's reversal of fortune and the character's realisation that the Nimon has deceived him. When Romana forces Soldeed to perceive that there are three Nimon in front of him the Skonnon tips over into insanity, although the viewers have been aware that the character has been unstable since his first appearance. Despite *Doctor Who* fans' po-faced expectation that the programme should be terribly serious drama, Read's writing and Crowden's performance demonstrate that the actor and the production team were aware of the mixture the general audience were expecting. Analyses like those of *InVision*, which attempt to reconcile on-screen dislikes with back-stage and production 'faults', betray the intended nature of the trans-mitted story. The fan appraisal of 'Horns' as a 'failure' because of 'inside information' on production represents a basic failure to realise that production information was not supposed to affect one's recep-tion of the story. The vast majority of the 12.4 million viewers who watched episode four of 'The Horns of Nimon' would not have known about the effect of the studio strike, and it is an illogical inheritance of the 1980s that fandom would judge a story on such grounds. Justin Richards acknowledges that the audience reaction to the story was favourable and that the memories of many of the personnel who worked on the story were generally not favourable. But he places great emphasis on the fact that the curtailed 'Shada' had been allocated much more effort and money and was to be the climax to the season. Apparently 'Horns' is incapable of being a story in its own right apart from the 'cheaply made filler story which should never have ended the season'. In plotting terms Richards admits that the story is more than adequate and that the Nimon have a credible motivation but in his summation he returns to the production theme.

Although thought-provoking, the article's return to fan stereotypes is unsatisfying because it uses the purportedly 'inadequate' production as a basis for judging the end product. Inferences such as these illustrate one of the greatest faults in fan appreciation of *Doctor Who* stories, a trait which was fuelled by the production-obsession of the Nathan-Turner era. When confronted by something mythologically bad fans grasp for some aspect of the production which can 'explain away' the supposed faults. In any case, a concentration on the 'production faults' of 'The Horns of Nimon' does not successfully explain the disparities in viewer ratings between Seasons 17 and 18. *Who* fandom has major problems coming to terms with the fact that in the late 1970s *Doctor Who* was a popular, and a populist, teatime programme designed to appeal to the general public rather than to a small group of viewers. Many fans found (and still find) it difficult to accept that the 'serious drama' of Season 18 could be less popular than the 'pantomime' of its predecessor (the prime offender supposedly being 'Horns'). Despite a disparaging fan reception at the time 'The Horns of Nimon' was very well received by the general viewing public at Christmas 1979. It peaked with ratings of over ten million viewers in January 1980. Of course ratings should never be regarded as an adequate judgement of a television programme. Season 17's popularity had undoubtedly been boosted by the ITV strike, although this had been resolved by October 1979. Probably 'Horns' shared in the consistent viewing patterns initiated by the BBC Saturday evening monopoly earlier in the year. But even taking this into account in the context of the audience for whom it was created 'The Horns of Nimon' was an undoubted success.

The stylistic differences between 'The Horns of Nimon' and its successors are illustrative of the flaws in the programme's post-1980 format. Telefantasy always pays homage to its stylistic ancestry. The Hinchcliffe era did this often in a very contrived and obvious fashion with references to *Forbidden Planet*, *Frankenstein* and the B movie genre as a whole. It strikes me as extremely odd that fandom is prepared to accept intertextual spoofing in the elaborate costume dramas and space operas of 1974–77 ('Planet of Evil', 'The Brain of Morbius' to name but two), yet are not prepared to do so in Season 17. The Nathan-Turner era is often characterised as being a return to the 'serious drama' of the mid-1970s over 'pantomime', but such analysis fails to recognise the humorous subtexts of Seasons 13 and 14. In an interview for *InVision* on the script editing of Season 17, Douglas

Adams argues that comedy should always underscore but never undercut drama in *Doctor Who*, working best when 'in tandem with the drama, reinforcing it at certain key moments'. (Douglas Adams, 'Adams Appeal', *InVision* #45 Season Seventeen, p11.) The Seth/ Teka double-act in 'Horns' accurately reflects this essential stylistic device. The dramatic peaks of the story are accompanied inevitably by Teka's confident appeals that Seth will defeat the Nimon. At one point Teka is expounding the virtues of Seth, followed immediately by Romana's realisation that they are trapped in a cell as she has left her sonic screwdriver on the flight desk. In fact there are a variety of storytelling pairings in 'The Horns of Nimon'. As well as the Doctor and Romana, there are Seth and Teka, who act as a conduit for explanations from the Doctor in the Power Complex during Romana's absence on Crinoth. Sorak and Soldeed also act as an expository duo, especially in the scenes in Soldeed's laboratory where the audience learns of Soldeed's bargain with the Nimon and the scientist's plans for the future. Soldeed's characterisation to Sorak of the Nimon as simple and under his control is an effective contrast to viewer aware-ness of the Nimon's technological superiority which has baffled even the Doctor and Romana.

Stories like 'Horns' are full of references to the literary genre (rather than the Hinchcliffe emphasis on filmic referencing), but although this literary inter-referencing was a new direction it still operated within the series' central emphasis on storytelling. Under Graham Williams the story had been raised even above the previous norm to a post-modern emphasis on the telling of the narrative as much as on plot itself. In 1980 the previous stylistic similarity (regardless of purported 'gothic' or 'pantomime' elements) of focus-ing on telling stories successfully was discarded in favour of present-ing a strong visual picture. What Christopher Bidmead and John Nathan-Turner failed to recognise was that *Doctor Who* was success-ful because of its textual balance between humour and drama, regard-less of which was more overt. The dichotomy was all. Removing the humour (with vague promises of providing 'wit') distorted the nar-rative and corrupted the essence of the programme. *The Fourth Doctor Handbook* describes the programme's new direction as a 'noticeable change in [the scripts'] basic approach to storytelling, with less emphasis being placed on detailed, straightforward plotting and more on concepts, style and imagery.' (*The Fourth Doctor Handbook*, p248.) The Nathan-Turner/Bidmead Season 18 is the beginning of *Doctor Who*'s inability to tell stories successfully to a general audience. Pseudo-science takes precedence over straightforward narration.

During Season 18 glossy production values were supposed to hold together stories that were convoluted at best ('Full Circle') or incestuous and generally incomprehensible ('Logopolis'). 'The Leisure Hive' ('something of a triumph of style over content' – *The Fourth Doctor Handbook*, p130) and its early seasonal compatriots are told adequately, probably in large part because of the initial consistency of leads from the previous season. But even in stories like 'The Leisure Hive' there are glaring inadequacies in the plot for which visual effects were supposed to compensate. How can Romana and the Doctor know about the faked tachyonics experiments when they enter the room after the hologram has finished? The emphasis on production values degrades the credibility of the script. There would have been fewer problems if the script had been given priority over the visual nature of the story (in this case the hologram effect). In my belief, this is why on repeated viewing many eighties stories are reduced to inadequately-scripted visual ciphers. Too often after Season 17 *Doctor Who* is a programme consisting of visual effects with a script instead of a story with visual effects. 'The Horns of Nimon' is the final *Doctor Who* story where the script comes indisputably ahead of the production.

The fact that *Doctor Who* was cruder visually than flashy American series or big-budget cinema films is fantastically irrelevant. The programme's success had not been built on special effects but on solid storytelling. John Nathan-Turner's statement that *Who* had to attempt to keep up with *Star Wars* and that ilk illustrates his almost complete lack of understanding of what made the programme so unique, and ultimately so successful. American series such as *Battlestar Galactica* and *Buck Rogers* were unsuccessful because they emphasised the visual rather than story-based nature of their format. Neither lasted more than two seasons, and both had major structural changes for the second.

In *Doctor Who* the stylistic emphasis on a visual nature predominated by Seasons 18–21, and the arrival of Eric Saward as script editor contributed further to the decay: as well as abandoning its traditional focus on storytelling *Doctor Who* also abandoned its traditional liberal/moral imperatives. Violence and threats of violence in 'Horns' are understated, or at least treated humorously. When the Nimon tells the Doctor that he will be 'questioned, tortured and killed', our eponymous hero replies that he hopes that they'll get them in the right order. When Romana, Teka and Seth come across the hulk of a previous Anethan tribute in the Power Complex and guess what happened, the reprisal of the Seth/Teka double-act underscores the situation without denying the graphic nature of the Nimon's feeding habits. This vital underscoring was virtually abandoned after 1980, especially after the arrival of Eric Saward as script editor. As Graham Howard's excellent article in *TSV* 40 illustrates, the violence of a story like 'Vengeance on Varos' and the lack of any supporting and diffusing humour is disturbing evidence of the moral uncertainty which had captured *Doctor Who* by the mid-1980s.

Instead of regarding 'The Horns of Nimon' as a 'somewhat unsatisfactory conclusion to [Williams'] tenure as producer' (*The Fourth Doctor Handbook*, p170), I believe it should be regarded as the final *Doctor Who* story which has strong and consistent storytelling as its central aim. 'Had [the fans] known that in years to come this degree of knowing wit, a deliberately self-conscious nod to the more sophisticated viewer would be rudely knocked out of the series to be replaced by a less-stagey, but also less self-aware form of presentation, they might have relaxed a little bit more, and settled back to watch a type of *Doctor Who* flourish that has not been seen since.' (David Owen, 'Just Seventeen', *InVision* #45 Season Seventeen, p12.)

(Thanks to Graham Muir for the loan of the *InVision* issues.)

Paul Griffin's unserious Tom and Lalla from *Alien Corn* #1.

6: Oddly Fond But Also Mocking Bits

Lee Binding is one of those multitalented individuals that fandom consistently produces. His *Anti-Matter Chicken* is hilariously and gleefully full of stuff like the following interrogation of the character played by Honor Blackman in 'Terror of the Vervoids'. Neil Corry's solo effort, *Sarah Jane*, attempts to be a little more traditional, but is just as funny. Gareth's piece from that 'zine is based on a series of features that ran in Terry Nation's Dalek Annuals, where breathless 'facts' about the Daleks were revealed. Beside these two postmodern pieces we have Andy Lane writing in *BAWG*, with his tongue so far in his cheek that it, erm, comes out the other side and makes some valid points. (Fan Crit does this a lot. I've never been able to decide if Ian Berriman's Freudian analysis of penetration imagery in 'Inferno' (from *Peladon*) was deeply insightful or hilarious. Both, perhaps.) From those heady years also comes the former *Celestial Toyroom* editor Dominic May's 'zine-long homage to a *Doctor Who* guest actor, Christopher Robbie, who played two parts in the show, one of which (the Cyberleader in 'Revenge of the Cybermen') was a speaking one. This collection wouldn't be complete without some sort of letters page. The thing all these pieces have in common is a very complicated relationship with their subject matter, that typical fandom stance of loving something so much that we can take the piss, both fondly and even cruelly, because we own it. Christopher Robbie was interviewed for *Christopher Robbie: A Celebration*, and probably presented with a copy. He may not have noticed the deep irony involved, partly because nobody expects fans to adore someone publicly and then go and snigger at them behind their backs (the fools!), but most certainly because May was both taking the piss and expressing genuine appreciation. Simultaneously. That, again, is another of those things that only fandom really does. But in a fractured world where opinion is being overwhelmed by information, it's a mindset that's catching on. Witness the entire career of Jonathan Ross.

'Explain This!'
Professor Sarah Lasky interviewed by Lee Binding
(*Anti-Matter Chicken* #1)

In these special interviews, we ask people to justify their actions that we feel were simply irrational. This edition: Sarah Lasky tries to explain the Vervoids.

PROFESSOR, ABOUT THE VERVOIDS. PUTTING IT SIMPLY: WHY?

'Couldn't you tell? I'm a thremmatologist, darlink! Doesn't that mean anything to you?'

WELL, WE ALL THOUGHT THAT THE WRITERS LOOKED UP BOTANY IN THE THESAURUS AND FOUND THE LONGEST ASSOCIATED WORD.

'No, no, no! It means that I was breeding them as house plants!'

WHAT?!

'House plants. What's wrong with that? Geraniums used to be wild too, you know.'

I DON'T THINK A GERANIUM EVER KILLED ANYONE.

'No, come to think of it, neither do I. But they would have made excellent man, er, plant servants. I was breeding them with the idea of slavery in mind.'

THE MULTIPURPOSE SLAVE, EH? I CAN JUST SEE AN INTEL-LIGENT, MOBILE PLANT WITH AN APRON ON, DOING THE IRONING.

'Exactly!'

PROFESSOR, I WAS BEING CYNICAL.

'Oh. But they were designed to be brought into the home to do those sort of jobs, darlink.'

THEN WHY WERE THEY EQUIPPED WITH VENOMOUS STINGS?

'Burglar alarm! If anyone tries to break into my house, I'm glad to know that they're turned into fertiliser while I'm out.'

WHAT HAPPENS IF YOU GET UP IN THE NIGHT FOR A GLASS OF WATER?

'Be very, very, quiet.'

I'M SORRY, PROFESSOR, I'M STILL NOT CONVINCED. I SERIOUSLY DOUBT THAT THEY WOULD MAKE GOOD HOUSE PLANTS.

'I think they'll catch on. I mean, most people talk to their houseplants, don't they? What if they talked back?'

WHAT IF IT WAS A BORING CONVERSATIONALIST? I FEEL THAT YOU CAN ONLY GET SO MUCH MILEAGE OUT OF FERTILISER.

'But you could treat it like a pet! Imagine that – a slave that could answer the door to the Avon Vervoid and still have time to play with the kids!'

PERSONALLY, I DON'T THINK THERE'S AN OPENING AT CRUFTS FOR 'BEST PRUNED VERVOID', DO YOU?

'Well, no. But this is one pet that doesn't need to go into kennels when you go on holidays. No need to send someone in to look after it – it just runs itself under the tap!'

IT'D PROBABLY DO WHAT MOST KIDS DO WHEN THEIR PARENTS GO ON HOLIDAY. YOU'D COME BACK TO FIND THE HOUSE A TIP WITH IT SITTING ON YOUR SUNBED, PISSED ON 'BABY BIO'.

'Well, maybe. But it'd clean up later, I hope.'

AND WHAT EXACTLY WAS THE MARSH GAS FOR?

'Ah, now, that was a side-effect from crossing them with beans. But it was useful.'

REALLY? FOR WHAT?

'Putting the cat out.'

THANK YOU, PROFESSOR LASKY, BUT I DON'T THINK YOUR ACTIONS WERE JUSTIFIED. BE OFF WITH YOU.

Dalek Boasts!
Gareth Roberts
(*Sarah Jane* #1)

The Daleks regularly broadcast propaganda messages to terrify the populations of planets neighbouring their mighty empire. Here are a collection of their claims, as transcribed by anti-Dalek agent Gareth Roberts.

The electricity generated by one half-second blast from a Dalek gun-stick could power the Blackpool illuminations for seventy-three years.

Every Dalek is constructed of special Skaro metal that's so tough that if you dropped a Dalek from the moon it would land safely on Earth the right way up.

Inside a Dalek casing is a special unit for summoning aid from other Daleks. However, this has never been used because no Dalek has ever needed help.

Daleks don't drink halves and they never go home before midnight.

The Daleks are so bastard hard that they're not afraid to take anyone outside.

One Dalek could pleasure every woman on Earth for a week.

The Daleks' Mum is bigger than your Mum.

Mike Teague's Doctor Schmoe in 'Hack of the Cybermen' from *Opera of Doom* #2.

The Symbolic Uses of Hot Beverages in *Doctor Who*
Andy Lane
(*Black and White Guardian* #1)

I find it difficult to overstress the importance of hot beverages in *Doctor Who*. In the twenty-year history of the programme we have been given a continuous presentation of the many facets of hot beverages, and yet scant attention has been paid to the vital role of boiled leaves and beans. This article is a meagre attempt to restore the balance.

Out of the main purveyors of warm liquid refreshment, cocoa (or hot chocolate) has been used the least. This in turn means that less ambiguity surrounds it than in the presentation of tea or coffee. Cocoa, in fact, has only appeared twice on screen, during the eras of Hartnell and Pertwee. The first 'brew' was of course during the 1964 story 'The Aztecs'. The Aztec lady Cameca accepted a cup of hot chocolate from the Doctor whilst they were both in the Garden of the Aged. What the Doctor did not know was that to the Aztecs a cup of hot chocolate was the equivalent to a proposal of marriage. He soon found out, when Cameca accepted, saying 'Oh sweet favoured man! You have declared your love for me, and I acknowledge and accept your gentle proposal.' Cameca fell in love with the Doctor, and judging by their farewell, he with her.

The second brew-up of cocoa occurs during 'Terror of the Autons', again with two people with a bond between them. It is Mike Yates who offers a cup to Jo Grant, an action which later leads to the accidental reactivation of the Nestene doll. So we can see clearly that cocoa in *Doctor Who* appears in a purely sexual context. The action of making a cup of hot chocolate is a symbolic expression of affection, as theorised by Freud in his classic paper: *Cocoa Products and the Repressed Sexual Urge* (Univ. of Vienna, 1890).

Coffee, however, appears in ambiguous terms. On the one hand we have 'The Moonbase', in which Polly makes coffee for the Gravitron crew, unaware that the sugar is poisoned. Many fall prey to its effects, and we are left to ponder the point. Is Kit Pedlar trying to make us aware of the unhealthiness of sugar, or is he trying to counterpoint Polly's *offer* to make coffee with the *lack* of free will shown by the men controlled by the Cybermen? This connection with consciousness is explored further in 'Planet of the Spiders', where it is a cup of coffee that revives the Doctor from his trance. After awakening, he compliments Sergeant Benton on making the finest cup of coffee since

Mrs Samuel Pepys, wife of the infamous diarist who set down his life in infinite and tedious detail, fortified, no doubt, by many reviving cups of coffee from his long-suffering wife. Thus we may see that it is the *reviving* qualities of coffee which are extolled in the programme. The Doctor is woken up by it, whilst Samuel Pepys and the Moonbase crew are kept awake by it.

Tea is possibly the most complicated beverage, not only in literature, but in life itself. Due to the range of effects it produces, it may crop up in virtually any situation, garnished in the unlikeliest manner. Many people have tried to examine its effect qualitatively, from Sigmund Freud (*The Significance of Lemon Tea in the Treatment of Long Term Repression*, Univ. of Vienna, 1901) and Carl Jung (*Teapots – A Myth Archetype?* Univ. of Vienna, 1917) to C.S. Lewis (*Tea Drinkers – A Christian Standpoint*, OUP, 1942). The uses of tea in *Doctor Who* are equally intricate, and cannot be drawn under a single unifying umbrella.

There is, however, a 'main theme' to the making of tea. For want of a better word, this may be termed 'civilisation'. In 'The Talons of Weng-Chiang', the Doctor and Professor Litefoot feel that Leela's education would not be complete without a course in advanced tea-making. In 'Genesis of the Daleks' the Doctor tests the level of Kaled civilisation by asking for a cup of tea when he and Harry are imprisoned. As he guessed, a thousand years of war has reduced them to semi-barbarism, and the secret of tea has been lost. Indeed, when Ronson comes to release them, Harry is far more interested in whether he has brought any tea. Walker, the ultra-civilised politician in 'The Sea Devils', forces two cups of tea from Captain Hart's secretary Jane Blythe. Even amidst the squalid trenches of the Great War, the English troops have time for a brew-up in 'The War Games'.

A subsection of 'civilisation' might well be 'competence'. In 'The Ribos Operation' the Doctor couldn't give a fig biscuit for Romana's qualifications. He wants to know if she can make tea. A similar scene in 'The Time Warrior' proves that tea, and by implication, civilisation, represent the domesticity and conformity of the female – although Sarah does later comment 'I could murder a cup of tea'. In rejecting the Doctor's request for a cuppa, she also rejects male-dominated society, hence the inherent irony of her later remark. Again, in 'The Sea Devils', the otherwise useless Jo Grant can at least try to make tea for the shocked Clark, until interrupted by a marauding reptile with no interest in the finer points of hot beverages. This link with 'alien-ness' can also be seen in 'Shada', where Professor Chronotis demonstrates his alien origins by asking his visitors if they wanted tea. A typical exchange might be: 'Tea?' – 'Yes please.' – 'Milk?' – 'Please.' – 'One lump or two?' – 'Two please.' – 'Sugar?' – 'Er, what?!' The Doctor and Romana, both from the same civilisation, are not confused. They both describe themselves as 'Two lumps, no sugar'. An interesting sideline on this story is that while Romana is fetching a fresh bottle of milk from the TARDIS, Skagra enters Chronotis' study, declines tea, and steals his mind. When Romana returns, a rapidly cooling cuppa acts as a metaphor for Chronotis' condition – which is none too hot.

Tea can be linked with coffee in that certain stories use it as a symbol for a free mind. During 'Image of the Fendahl' it is partly the promise of a cup of tea which induces Gran Tyler from her hypnotic trance, echoing similar scenes in both 'Mawdryn Undead' and 'Planet of the Spiders.' Also, during 'The Invasion', UNIT troops who have not fallen under the influence of the Cyber-signal keep themselves going on cups of tea. The connection is made clear in 'The Invasion of Time'. In a pivotal conversation, Chancellor Borusa replies that he cannot shield his mind from the telepathic Vardan invaders. 'Tea', replies the Doctor. Borusa cannot see the link, this being precisely the Doctor's point. It is the logical working of Borusa's mind which renders him helpless. A mind which can suddenly think (and drink) tea for no apparent reason cannot be pinned down long enough to control.

We have seen tea as symbol and as metaphor, but what of tea as an actual physical reality? The only time that it has become an integral part of the plot is during 'The Time Monster'. Trying to interfere with the Master's TARDIS, the Doctor constructed an odd device from a wine bottle and various kitchen implements. This culinary lash-up fails to work until the addition of *tea leaves*, and a proud Doctor explains that he and the Master used to do the same thing to each other in their Academy days. This implies that a plant similar to genus Camellia grows on Gallifrey, and it is interesting to speculate that the effects of so many cups of tea over a near immortal Time Lord lifespan might account for their apparently decaying society.

This has of course only been a limited overview of hot beverages in *Doctor Who*. There are so many avenues left unexplored. Digestive biscuits – why are there none in the programme? Is the cucumber sandwich really a viable alternative to jelly babies? Why *are* chicken vol-au-vents so inoffensive? These questions are beyond the scope of this article, but they must be answered.

Perhaps a nice, hot cup of tea might help . . .

Robbie Ramblings
edited by Dominic May
(*Christopher Robbie: A Celebration*)

In my pre-publicity drive for this magazine, I invited potential readers to sum up in about 25 words what Christopher Robbie means to them. Here is the response.

First off, we have that Queen Bat, Jackie Marshall, from Sheringham, Norfolk.

'Where would *Doctor Who* have been without Christopher Robbie? Who can ever forget the memorable Karkus being tossed about by Zoe? Or the Cyberleader apparently about to do the pelvic thrust? Magic moments indeed!'

Okay, that's not a bad starter. Now who's this? Guy Clapperton from Tooting, London.

'No kidding? There really is somebody called Christopher Robbie? Well, well, and I thought the big D made him up for his Padding, sorry, People column in *DWM*.'

Cruel, Guy. Very cruel. Now a pseudonym. Tiger Lilly, lately from Norwich and now entrenched in Edinburgh (see, I know who you are) writes:

'Christopher Robbie is one of *Doctor Who*'s great supporting characters, rated alongside Gaunt and Gable. What hips, what shoulders, what a carcass! But why does he have to drag that moth-eaten bear around with him?'

I knew that would come up sooner or later. Keep taking the tablets, Tiger. One David Howe from New Malden had to get his ten pence worth in, didn't he? Here come his three contributions. I'll wake you up when it's over:

> *There once was a man called Chris Robbie*
> *Who had an unusual hobby.*
> *A superhero was he*
> *And a Cybe with much glee*
> *And a friend of the hand on hip lobby.'*

'I used to be frightened of the Cybermen until I saw Christopher Robbie's sterling performance as their leader. Now I know that inside every Cybersuit is a superhero dying to get out! It changed my life!'

'CHRISTOPHER ROBBIE is an anagram of BORIS THE BIRCH ROPE – was our Chris a multiple murderer in another existence?'

WAKE UP! Actually, for David Howe, that wasn't bad! One artist (of sorts), Phil Bevan, from the Borehamwood environs (well, he would bore 'em!) says:

'You can tell Chris Robbie that I've always had a thing about Zoe's bum too! Maybe one day I'll draw it if she'll pose for me!'

Well, of all the cheek! Finally, we have Richard Mills from Vauxhall, and it's just about what you might expect from someone who lives in that area:

'Ahh! The shed at Stamford Bridge, "Blue is the Colour", Peter Osgood scoring a brilliant goal from one of Ian Hutchinson's extralong windmill throw-ins. That's what comes to mind when I think of Bobby Tambling. What? Oh. Robbie who?'

7: Analysis

Thomas Noonan was the first New Fanboy. He appeared way back before the A5 era, and started agitating in the Dwas and in the pages of the old *Skaro*. He was one of the first fans to take litcrit techniques and terminology, ally them to a sense of theatre, and throw them at the wall of conventional fandom. The reaction to his work at the time was explosive. He was called 'pretentious' a lot, which is still a word used quite randomly by those fans for whom the joy of *Doctor Who* is that they don't have to think about it. These days it seems to mean 'anything I don't immediately understand'. Noonan was also declared to be a troublemaker, for his critique, and for writing about the then taboo subject of fan politics. Again, this was because fandom does, unfortunately, tend towards a herd instinct. Certain phrases in our culture are used almost as creeds, touchstones to our childhoods (which is when Terrance Dicks invented most of them for his *Making of Doctor Who* book): 'Yartek, leader of the alien Voord'; 'Broton, warlord of the Zygons'; 'UNIT family'; 'Cosmic hobo'; 'Man of action'. You see them repeated, along with the standard critical viewpoints that accompany them, in many ordinary fanzine articles, and many ordinary convention con-versations, like a kind of catechism. As long as Yartek's Voord are still alien, then all's right with the world. To the new generation of fans, these phrases have become satirical icons, the subject of ridicule, but still great fondness, because we get a secret rush from them too.

This chapter, then, is about fandom thinking for itself, post-Noonan, and applying critical techniques to the thing it loves. Even the new *Skaro*, which started on a populist 'isn't it all fun?' ticket, has started to run Fan Crit. *Matrix*, from which we present the twin *enfants terribles* Daniel O'Mahony (once editor of the groovy *Club Tropicana*) and Lance Parkin, revels in it. Also in this section is another piece from one of the earliest proponents of Fan Crit, my anonymous author who's now resident in academia. Finally, we have Val Douglas and the mystical, a whole area of experience that's nurtured by the women of multimedia fandom, but rather scorned by the SF boys of *Who*dom.

This would, of course, be the place for more Tat Wood. But I've put a limit on how much of each writer you get.

Television, Technique and Convention
Thomas Noonan
(*Gallifrey* #14)

One aspect of the eighteenth season which has provoked discussion is its innovation in television technique. I want to indicate here what I take to be some of the principles which should govern such discussions.

Doctor Who is, I think, essentially television, and television is a medium between stage-drama and film. Stage-drama and film are contrasted in that, in the latter we are told the story by the camera, whereas in the former it is by the actors' speech and movements. This is a matter of the spatial relations of presentation: the film camera can view its subjects from any angle or distance with complete freedom, whereas the member of the theatre audience has a fixed point of view on the stage. This means that film can control very precisely the direction of the viewer's attention, whereas the theatre spectator has a relatively free choice as to where to focus his attention, being guided only loosely by the actors' speech and movements (and perhaps by lighting). Again, film is more illusionist. The fact that the subject can be inspected from any viewpoint tends to give it a convincing, three-dimensional reality, whereas in the theatre this may not be so. Also in the theatre it needs only a small movement of the spectator's gaze to take him outside the area of illusion altogether (so that he finds himself looking at the wall of the theatre or rows of heads etc.). In the cinema that's less easy.

Television, I think, is between the two and nearer to the stage-play, particularly in *Doctor Who*. (Actual film sequences in the programme are usually, at least often, dreary attempts at suspense or pictorial values.) But I suspect that the drive behind what are noticeable as innovations in technique, often effects of video-tape editing (e.g. the frenzy of images at the end of 'The Leisure Hive' episode 3), is the effort to make the programme more like film. This is misguided. One of the virtues of the programme is that it allows a free play of the viewer's attention, calls for decisions on his part for the relative weighting of what he's shown – as in the opening of 'Warriors' Gate' episode 1 the view of Aldo and Royce playing cards and cheating, a joke, was offered in the midst of the suspenseful, slow camera tracking, and at the same time as the commencement of the countdown, which was starting. We had to balance these to decide on tone. Again, *Doctor Who*, I think, can never be successfully illusionist, so it shouldn't seem to be trying.

But some kind of innovation in technique can be positively interesting. I'll illustrate the kinds from 'Warriors' Gate' episode 2. The most striking effect there, was the use of the camera to represent the Tharil's point of view towards the end. That's been done before with monsters but it was already clear that the Tharil wasn't quite simply a monster – his boots were too interesting (i.e. if he had been simply a monster there would have been no point in distracting us by making them noticeable in close-up as he straightened off the trolley). It was more striking still when the camera adopted Romana's point of view, swinging across her lap looking down at her hands straining the bonds on her chair. And then there were those extraordinarily close close-ups of her towards the end. Their effect was not merely a visual matter. Earlier, we had been given a shot of her in a sudden shift from the scene where Aldo and Royce were bungling the revival of the Tharil; it showed her reacting to his scream. But it seemed to me that the scream sounded just as loud when it accompanied the picture of Romana as when we were down with Aldo and Royce, although since the two places were supposedly separated it ought to have sounded less loud from her position. The effect of this is, immediately, of unreality, then the questioning of a convention. Usually in *Doctor Who*, we have a 'fly on the wall' convention: the viewer is as if positioned in the room where the scene occurs, invisible but otherwise observing in the normal way with eyes and ears. The example here departed from that convention by suggesting a dissociation between the channels of sound and vision. And partly because of this the later close-ups with their accompanying sound of her gasping breathing seemed extraordinarily close: I felt at the time that, if there were a little more of this it would not be surprising to find ourselves moving right into her mind by an inner monologue, a soliloquy giving her unspoken thoughts, as in the 60s' television Shakespeares where the actor would often give a soliloquy with the camera looking deep into his eyes. (Similar effects in the BBC's *All's Well* the week before probably helped stimulate that thought.) That, I think, would be a truly interesting innovation in technique (because 'technique' here is equivalent to 'convention').

We Meet Again, Doctor ...
Daniel O'Mahony
(*Matrix* #48)

When it came to voting in *DWB*'s 30th Anniversary Poll in 1993, I found myself doing what seemed, with hindsight, a very strange thing. I voted for 'The Master' as the series' all-time worst villain without a second thought.

When I looked back at my answers I was a bit fazed by this. What was wrong with the Master? Though the idea of the character had never really grabbed me as such, I had to admit that there were many more *Doctor Who* villains who were more ridiculously conceived, with even less plausible schemes and motivations. Similarly, while Roger Delgado and Anthony Ainley were capable of poor performances, there have been other villains whose turns have been diabolical. So why pick on the Master? After a little thought, I found the answer: the Master, as a concept, just doesn't work in the context of *Doctor Who*.

Consider who he is. The Master is a semi-regular adversary for the Doctor. He *recurs*. He's not Moriarty – who appears in one Sherlock Holmes story specifically to destroy the great detective. He's not, therefore, the Doctor's *nemesis*. He's an arch-enemy – in the mould of the Joker or Blofeld – and it is the nature of such characters to pop up regularly to pester the protagonist. Theirs is a mutually defining and potentially endless loop of hero–villain antics.

So by his very nature, the Master is bound by convention, and we can characterise Master stories by their common routines. The Master must wear a patently unconvincing disguise in the early parts of the story, only to appear grinning from behind the mask at the end of Part One. He hypnotises some people, shrinks others to death, argues with his henchmen. He captures the Doctor and/or his companion, but passes up the opportunity to kill them easily. His plans fall apart in Part Four, but his escape is assured. Even the temporary confinement of 'Terror of the Autons' and 'The Daemons', or his unseemly physical condition at the end of 'The Deadly Assassin' and 'Survival' are just interesting variations on this theme, which more often than not adheres to the most nauseating of comic book clichés: 'if you can't see the body, he isn't dead'.

The Master, in other words, is a creature of formula. He's more of a plot function than a real character. He exists to serve the series' formula, and this is the problem, as *Doctor Who* hasn't got one. It may dabble in the same sort of areas from story to story (and increasingly so as repetition solidifies into orthodoxy) but it doesn't need to. While on television there was rarely any startling diversity, the potential to go anywhere, to be anything, is inherently part of the series and can't be bucked by lazy production teams alone. The Master doesn't fit easily into this lack of design. Of course, if *Doctor Who* does have the potential to do anything, then it also has the potential to have an on-going semi-regular villain, but this doesn't obscure the fact that the series doesn't *need* such a concept. There are plausible exceptions. The Doctor needs a nemesis to despatch his fourth incarnation and so the Master's presence in the 'regeneration trilogy' is highly logical. On other occasions, that logic is absent and the series' credibility suffers.

The problem becomes blatantly obvious during Eric Saward's script-editorship, when the Master becomes a genuinely semi-regular fixture for the second time. Just about all the post-'Castrovalva' Master stories are rickety structures that collapse on close inspection. For the Doctor and the Master to clash time and again suggests that the Master must be actively seeking our hero out – which he isn't – and Anthony Ainley's turn in the role just doesn't conjure the malignant hatred for his old enemy that such an approach would require. Instead the Doctor accidentally and implausibly stumbles upon the Master's latest scheme time after time. Yet the Saward-era Master stories are contrived vehicles for the character with no logical coherence or outcome beyond the need for hero–villain conflict. What does the Master want the Xeraphin for? Why does he plan to wreck Magna Carta? What are his aims in nineteenth-century England? These things are never properly rationalised, and the stabs at adhering to the arch-enemy format – such as the Master's disguises – were ridiculed by fans at the time of transmission.

To be fair, the production team seemed to become aware of this problem, but neither John Nathan-Turner nor Saward seem to have possessed the necessary insight to generate an imaginative response. Instead they took pains to create new semi-regular Time Lord villains who were, to all intents and purposes, the Master by a different name. Most were abortive. Only the Rani seems to have caught on to any extent (almost certainly due to the casting of Kate O'Mara rather than any depth of conception or characterisation). Once we reach 'Time and the Rani' it's clear that she's the Master with breasts but no beard, implicating a production team that is rapidly running out of ideas.

The Master's early appearances obscured the problem to some extent. The Master, a creature of formula, was created as part of *Doctor Who* at the time when it was most formulaic. The UNIT/exile years were the only extended period in *Doctor Who*'s history when the viewer could be certain that things weren't going to change wildly between stories. The original Master was not only born out of that but also defined it.

During these years the series stood still for much longer than it had ever done before, or ever would do again, and when *Doctor Who* stands still it tends to become flabby, feeding on the success of the immediately preceding period. During the Pertwee years it had a good fictional reason for formula – the exile – but clung to it long after that rationale was done away with. The Master is not a product of the lean, dynamic, and fresh season seven, but the cosy, familiar and parochial season eight. The Master, as portrayed by Delgado, embodies that safeness. He may be a ruthless murderer – he kills hundreds of innocent people in his debut story – but he is a part of the UNIT family, and carries their warm (though slightly dysfunctional) glow with them. The end of 'The Daemons' says it best. The village children boo as he's carted off to jail (in the first take they cheered). It's a pantomime end for a pantomime villain.

Speculation time. Things might have worked differently had Delgado not been cast. This is not to knock the actor, whose performance is generally impressive despite the first-night nerves of 'Terror of the Autons' and his sheer disbelief with the script of 'The Time Monster'. But his Master is too safe. He is altogether too suave and too charming – usually at his best when impersonating authority figures or dealing with top people who've come to rely on him – and nowhere near dangerous enough. If an equally experienced but less obviously charismatic actor had been cast, we might have ended up with a Master with more of an edge. I'm thinking specifically of John Dearth here, given that Lupton, and to some extent, BOSS, were the Master substitutes of their day. Dearth's Master would have had none of the hypnotic appeal of Delgado's but would have brought to the part the vicious obsession that Delgado lacked. The writing would have to change to suit the tone of the acting. There would no longer be any room for the hints of friendly rivalry with the Doctor, the elaborate Doctor-killing devices, the plot exposition to the tied-down companion or the 'you must be humiliated before you die' clichés. A Master in this mould would be perfectly prepared to shoot the Doctor in the back of the head. Dearth's Master would be dangerously unpredictable and could have revitalised the stale Pertwee formula with the ever-present fear that the Doctor might just wind up dead on a grassy knoll somewhere before the end credits roll.

Interestingly, this is exactly the path Robert Holmes takes with 'The Deadly Assassin', a story that demonstrates exactly why the Master *can't* work on full throttle. It may be argued that this story was written in response to 'Terror of the Autons', an attempt to get the Master 'right' now that Holmes had control of the series. It doesn't quite work, although Peter Pratt does bring to the Master a malignant hatred of the Doctor that no other actor has conveyed in the role. His performance is a kind of criticism of Delgado's, one that honours his memory far more effectively than a straight homage.

Everything is perfect until the Master's feigned suicide in Part Four. Then things start to fall apart as the story is wrapped up in fifteen minutes of cliché from which the Master plunges to his 'death' like any good arch-enemy, with sequel rights. It might be that Holmes didn't have the skill or the inclination to carry his ideas through to their logical conclusion, which isn't likely given what we know about Holmes from elsewhere. More probably, he realised at the last minute that if the Master was to be done 'properly', he would have to win! The Master would become what he has always been promoted as: the Doctor's Moriarty. Chris Bidmead seems to have understood this: 'Logopolis'' Master is, at least, a nemesis, and the Doctor does indeed wind up dead on the aforementioned grassy knoll before the end credits. This explains why the latterday Master seems so embarrassing: an arch-enemy who's already killed off the hero is a bit redundant.

The Master becomes neglected after the mid-eighties. He pops up in

'Survival', though his involvement in the proceedings is a little pointless and distracts from the rather nice story going on around him. There is nothing distinct in the character here – he is just the agent of corruption in a plot which clearly does not require a villain with a face. There is a slight change in tenor from Saward's script-editorship. Andrew Cartmel, I'm convinced, was following the same basic path as Saward, particularly in the use of the dusty warehouse of *Doctor Who* back characters. Yet where Saward used the Master – and the Cybermen, Daleks, et al – because he could, Cartmel doesn't seem interested in the mythology of the series except in so far as he could use it to legitimate his own ideas. In 'Survival', the Master is roped in as a part of this process. He's there specifically to *not recognise* the Doctor in an ending which, famously, got cut so as to end the twenty-sixth season on a happy note.

In the wake of that season, *Doctor Who* spent six and a half years poised between death and radicalism with the Master suiting neither state. He was, with the Daleks, an obvious omission from 'Dimensions in Time', the funeral celebration of everything else that was tacky about the series. At the same time, he didn't seem to interest the writers of the more constructive fictional responses to the series' cancellation. When *Doctor Who* returned for the 1996 TV movie, however, the Master was suddenly, if briefly, thrust back to the centre of the series.

The TV movie boils the hero–villain conflict down to its essence. Fox Television's blurb for the film summed it up, saying something like *two powerful aliens crashland in San Francisco and only one will leave alive!* The cliché of the arch-enemy has suddenly become valuable, its familiarity being used to sell an old product to a new audience, and in this instance the paucity of imagination is perhaps forgivable. Unfortunately, the script constantly undercuts this, alluding to the morality of the conflict without bothering to explain even its own content. The movie has clearly sampled the visuals of Tim Burton's *Batman* (amongst others), but that film almost wholly divests a long-standing pop culture hero–villain relationship of its traditional 'moral' content and recasts it as a cycle of destructive urban psychosis. By comparison the TV movie seems almost archaic in its presentation of its hero–villain dynamic, but the lack of any coherent conflict between the two, overbalances the production away from Paul McGann's colourless-hero Doctor and towards Eric Roberts' self-confident Master (who gives the movie some desperately-needed irony). The viewer is left with fragments, hints at the Master's fear of death, even an unpleasant homophobic subtext (the Master orally rapes a man, has designs on Chang Lee and acts like a camp stereotype once inside the TARDIS – a theme made even more disturbing by the Doctor's newly acquired virile interest in girls). The new production team has nothing to say about the Doctor–Master conflict, which is at the heart of their film.

In its failure to portray the Master with conviction, the movie exposes the problem with the character more completely than any previous production. The Master is simply not supposed to be a villain of stature, but has had that status imposed on him by fan expectations and the production teams that have fed them. He was created simply as an all-purpose plot device that could carry the principal villainy of a *Doctor Who* story. He was less a character with plausible motivations of his own than a structural device that could be chopped and changed to order from story to story. In portraying the Doctor–Master conflict without conviction, the TV movie is only failing to do anything new with an already exhausted palimpsest.

The problem with the Master is not simply that his effectiveness varies from writer to writer, but that he is a symptom of a production-line approach to making *Doctor Who* for which recurrence and repetition are obligatory. The Master was designed to facilitate this *formatting* of *Doctor Who*. Out of context he is only a weak villain: in context he is the antithesis of a series that aspires to individuality and diversity. And that's why I rank the Master as the worst villain in *Doctor Who*'s history.

Past Lives
Lance Parkin
(*Matrix* #51)

Virtually every *Doctor Who* fan knows that the Doctor, like every other Time Lord, potentially has thirteen incarnations, that William Hartnell played the first of these and that the character has regenerated six times. This is accepted without question, but the facts as presented in the series are by no means as clear cut. The orthodoxy, of course, is expressed on a number of occasions, but these are surprisingly few: in 'The Three Doctors' the Time Lords claim that the Hartnell Doctor is the 'earliest'; we learn that the Time Lords are limited to twelve regenerations in 'The Deadly Assassin', this is reinforced in 'The Keeper of Traken', 'Logopolis', 'The Twin Dilemma' and 'The Trial of a Time Lord'; in 'Mawdryn Undead' the Doctor claims to have regenerated four times and to have eight regenerations remaining; in 'The Five Doctors' the Hurndall Doctor sees the Davison Doctor and concludes 'so there are five of me now', he also talks of himself as 'the original'; finally, in 'Time and the Rani', the Doctor talks of his 'seventh persona'. No unfamiliar early incarnations come to light when previous Doctors are lifted out of their timestreams in 'The Three Doctors', 'The Five Doctors' or, heaven help us, 'Dimensions in Time'. However, there have been a number of hints that the Hartnell Doctor was not the first. In the script for 'The Destiny of Doctor Who', the new Troughton Doctor confides to his astonished companions that he has 'renewed himself' before. Of course, in the transmitted version of the story, 'The Power of the Daleks', the line does not appear, but neither is it contradicted. In Part Four of 'The Brain of Morbius', Morbius succeeds in mentally regressing the Doctor back from his Baker incarnation, through Pertwee, Troughton and Hartnell, and the process does not stop there, we go on to see a further eight incarnations of the Doctor prior to Hartnell. This is indisputable: however we might want this scene to fit into the continuity of the series as established elsewhere or rationalise it away, here, as the sequence of mysterious faces appear on the scanner, Morbius shouts 'How far, Doctor? How long have you lived? Your puny mind is powerless against the strength of Morbius! Back! Back to your beginning! Back!' These are certainly not the faces of Morbius, as has occasionally been suggested, or the Doctor's ancestors, or his family. Morbius is not deluding himself. The Doctor does not 'go on to win' the fight, he almost dies, only surviving because of the Elixir, it just happens that Morbius' brain casing can't withstand the pressure either. The production team at the time (who bear a remarkable resemblance to the earlier Doctors, probably because they posed for the photographs used in the sequence) definitely intended the faces to be those of earlier Doctors. Producer Phillip Hinchcliffe said: 'We tried to get famous actors for the faces of the Doctor. But because no-one would volunteer, we had to use "backroom boys". And it is true to say that I attempted to imply that William Hartnell was not the first Doctor.' In another Hinchcliffe story, 'The Masque of Mandragora', the Doctor and Sarah Jane discover the secondary control room, and one of the Doctor's old costumes. The Doctor says that this 'used to be the old control room', and as we have never seen the room or the costume before, the implication is that an unseen incarnation (presumably prior to Hartnell) used it.

Elsewhere, facts about the Doctor's past are more ambiguous: the Doctor seems vague about his age throughout his life, the figure varying wildly from story to story and incarnation to incarnation. The Pertwee Doctor twice states that he is 'thousands of years old', the Master of the Land of Fiction describes him as 'ageless'. Tom Baker's Doctor is 750, then 760, then 750 again. In 'The Deadly Assassin' Runcible remarks that the Doctor has had a facelift and the Doctor replies that he has had 'several so far', although in the original script he had done so a more specific 'three times'. In 'Silver Nemesis' it is hinted that the Doctor might have been a contemporary of Rassilon, millions of years before, and various other hints in the Cartmel era (most of which were edited out of the broadcast versions), suggested that the Doctor was no longer even a Time Lord.

If there were eight Doctors before Hartnell, and Time Lords are limited to thirteen incarnations, then that would mean that Davison was the last . . . he does say that his regeneration 'feels different this time' – is this because he's just started a second regenerative cycle? This would explain why the Colin Baker Doctor's incarnation was 'unstable' and why the McCoy Doctor claimed to be 'more than just a mere Time Lord'. It would also mean that the Watcher existed between the Doctor's twelfth and thirteenth incarnations. This, of course, is the same position that the Valeyard occupies. Could the Watcher and the Valeyard be created at the same time, one a distillation of good, the other a distillation of evil? On television we are never actually told that the Valeyard is from the Doctor's future (obviously it is the implication, and it's explicitly stated in the novelisation), all we are told is that the Valeyard wants his remaining incarnations . . . what if he was a potential past of the Doctor? It would explain a number of anomalies: why the Valeyard doesn't know he'll lose the Trial, why he tries to kill his former self, why he survives the Trial after the Doctor has promised to mend his ways.

Are Time Lords really limited to twelve regenerations, anyway? We were originally told that the Time Lords could 'live forever, barring accidents' ('The War Games'). Only later, in 'The Deadly Assassin', was it revealed that Time Lords just regenerate twelve times, but even in that same story the Master proves that it is possible to prolong life beyond this, and in 'The Five Doctors' the Time Lords officially offer

Paul Ferry and Ben Hudson's 'Unseen Stories!' from *Fan Mail #3*, a fanzine that was particularly strong on comic strips, featuring, as it did, Quatermouse and Abslom Dukk: Dalegg Killer!

the Master a new regenerative cycle. Additionally, we know that Time Lords are able to survive death by sheer force of will (Omega, Morbius and the Master all do so), and that it is possible to divert energy from other Time Lords to gain a new lease of life (Mawdryn, the Master and the Valeyard all planned to do this). Rassilon, we learn, has the secret of Perpetual Regeneration, so is truly immortal. The Time Lords appear to have given the Minyans the same gift – rejuvenation, rather than regeneration, but immortality nonetheless. In 'The Creature from the Pit', the Doctor jokingly states that Time Lords have ninety lives – and that he's used one hundred and thirty. All this opens the possibility that the Doctor might have more than thirteen incarnations up his sleeve.

Time for some speculation. Perhaps the Gallifreyan Time Lords aren't limited to thirteen incarnations. They possess a whole array of equipment that could keep them alive: we know of the Symbiotic Metamorphosis Generator ('Mawdryn Undead'), the Elixir ('The Brain of Morbius'), the Rejuvenator ('Underworld'). Renegade Time Lords like the Doctor or the Master have no such luxury; they are limited to one regenerative cycle unless they return to their homeworld. This would explain a number of anomalies: why the High Council can offer the Master and the Valeyard more lives, why Romana seems unaware that she has a limited number of regenerations in 'The Creature from the Pit' and so on. It would also mean that the Doctor had heroically forsaken immortality in order to wander space and time. Time Lords can still die in accidents, natural disasters and perhaps out of choice, so Borusa has an incentive to seek true immortality in 'The Five Doctors'. Death is not terribly disadvantageous for a Time Lord anyway: thanks to the reflex link and the APC Net, their memories and experience live on.

We can piece together a great deal about the Doctor's early life, but much of it is contradictory and it is impossible to say outright that William Hartnell played the very first incarnation of the Doctor. We don't even know that it was Hartnell who left Gallifrey. The Monk might recognise Hartnell when they meet, but the War Chief, Runcible and Drax all recognise the Doctor after he has regenerated. We have also found out that the Doctor travelled the cosmos for the Time Lords while still an official member of Gallifreyan society ('The Two Doctors'), but we don't know how often he did this or what he looked like at the time (again, Dastari recognises the Doctor when they meet again, despite the fact that he has regenerated since). Presumably while acting in an official capacity the Doctor used a state-of-the-art TARDIS, or a Time Ring, not the antique model he would later steal. It is unclear whether the Doctor left Gallifrey because he was exiled or of his own free will.

The Doctor suggested in a couple of early stories that one day he might return to his home planet, but had he already done so? We discover in 'The Time Meddler' that the Doctor left home at least fifty years before 'An Unearthly Child', but Susan is only fifteen – did the Doctor go back home after thirty-five years travelling the universe only to leave again, this time with his grandchild? If we take everything said in the series at face value, then the Doctor left Gallifrey when he was 236 years old, but was 309 when he attended a Tech Course with Drax – this would seem to suggest that the Hartnell incarnation also returned to Gallifrey, but after the television series had started. It's certainly simpler to suggest that the Doctor was simply being vague about his age, but would it be right? In 'The Two Doctors' we learn that the Doctor maintained contact with the Time Lords in his Troughton incarnation – was he ever really out of touch with Gallifrey?

If the Doctor did regenerate several times before the series started, it might explain the contradictions in his early life – one incarnation could have been the mischievous, late-developing student, a second the serious young man who studied under K'Anpo near the family house and learned the myths of Ancient Gallifrey, a third the brilliant pioneer, a fourth a family man and father, another the respected Time Lord ambassador, yet another the political agitator who campaigned to ban Miniscopes. When the Pertwee Doctor is exiled to Earth he already knows Venusian Aikido – can we really picture Hartnell or Troughton acquiring fighting skills under a Venusian sensei? We know that the Doctor and Susan visited Venus before 'An Unearthly Child', but perhaps the Doctor wore a younger, more agile body at the time. The Time Lords might think that Hartnell was the earliest incarnation, but they have a very poor record of keeping track of renegade members of their species – the Master, Salyavin, Rani, Morbius, and Valeyard all manage to remain undetected. Perhaps 'the Doctor' is an alias for a Time Lord who has secretly transgressed a number of Gallifreyan laws, in a number of incarnations. The Time Lord we know as the Doctor might have only adopted that name in his Hartnell incarnation – Hartnell would be 'the first Doctor', the 'original' runaway, but the ninth (or more) incarnation of that Time Lord.

There are a number of other solutions that might explain away the contradictions. Several of the New Adventures have suggested that a leading Time Lord from the time of Rassilon has infiltrated the Doctor's subconscious, but haven't revealed yet when this happened. If it was before 'The Brain of Morbius', then the faces might be those of The Other, rather than the Doctor. The faces might be 'potential Doctors' like the Valeyard or the ones we see in Episode Ten of 'The War Games'. The costume in the secondary control room might belong to the original owner of the TARDIS (another mysterious figure). Unlike the 'past lives' theory, though, there is no evidence whatsoever on television that would support such speculation.

The Doctor is a mysterious figure, and every time we learn a new fact about his past, it raises more questions than it answers. Although more than one New Adventure has had scenes set before the Doctor leaves Gallifrey, Missing Adventures authors are forbidden to set their novels before 'An Unearthly Child'. There is no chance whatsoever that we'll see a Missing Adventure featuring the Hinchcliffe Doctor and Susan, a story in which the Gallacio Doctor visits Dastari or the Camfield Doctor gets Miniscopes banned. Phew. The Amblin/Fox/Segal Pilot is rumoured to depict the Doctor leaving Gallifrey, but this will be the start of a new continuity, not a continuation of the BBC series. Last September, though, Philip Segal did suggest that 'his' Doctor might be a 'pre-Hartnell' one, stating 'Brain of Morbius' as evidence. We will probably never know the whole truth about the Doctor's past. Just remember that we have actually seen incarnations of the Doctor's before the Hartnell incarnation.

Creating A Role: The Doctor Who Girl
(*Queen Bat* #6)

Characters fill holes: the holes come first. Take the TARDIS crew. Their presence is dictated not by the arbitrary chance which the dramatic fiction claims, but by basic structural patterns that make space for a particular number of characters of particular types. During Seasons 1 and 2 the pattern was a kind of oblong – two distinct pairs, but with each individual relating to all the others. There was room, that is, for four characters, two with a fantastical basis (the Doctor and Susan/Vicki) and two with more 'realistic' origins. With the departure of the latter this changed to a triangular arrangement, creating an apex: there was a more central Doctor, with two companions, who, according to their paired position in the structure, are male and female; this helps explain why there was such a problem fitting in Jamie for his first few stories.

The next major change came with Peter Bryant's format for Season 7. With Patrick Troughton's underdog portrayal, the Doctor had seemed increasingly not to be on top, 'deposed' either by the cynical Jamie, or Zoë, who delighted in telling him he had 'got it all wrong'. Bryant made this a fixture: although the group of characters remained tripartite, the top man was now the Brigadier, the Doctor's employer. The long-term effect of this was to forge a much closer relationship between the Doctor and a single female companion, so that in later seasons when Barry Letts took him back out to space, it was only Jo who tagged along. 'The *Doctor Who* Girl' was born – and has predominated since then, with only some rather unsuccessful experiments under John Nathan-Turner departing from the binary structural norm.

So, the space exists for a female character to accompany the Doctor. How is it to be filled? To some extent, 'the *Doctor Who* girl' has certain associations to start with, associations which will delimit the character material that is superimposed; Miriam Margolyes, Tom Baker's suggested replacement for Mary Tamm, would have been a very round peg to fit into a rigidly square hole. The press are on the right track in the analogy they like to draw between 'the *Doctor Who* girl' and her counterpart in James Bond. (Words to that effect were put into Mary Tamm's mouth, and most recently Nicola Bryant was introduced through comparison with Ursula Andress in *Doctor No* – more of which later.) 'The James Bond Girl' would be better termed 'girlfriend', the object of Bond's sexual athletics. While that may be a bit strong for *Doctor Who*, the girl is nonetheless required to be a more than usually attractive woman; Graham Williams has mentioned this as a major conscious factor in the casting of Mary Tamm.

It's not simply a matter of physical attributes however: it's important in the presentation of the character too. She must usually dress well, to be construed as either fashionable (Jo/Sarah) or glamorous (Romana) – Lis Sladen has commented on the need to costume the only girl in the cast 'for what she's worth'. Alternatively, she may become the focus of adolescent sexuality, as did Leela and Peri. If such qualities aren't already there, they are likely to develop, even with Nyssa and Tegan, neither of whom were 'the *Doctor Who* girl' in the strictest sense: that's why one took her skirt off and the other ended up dressed like a prostitute. No wonder the press made such a meal of Matthew Waterhouse taking over the job!

Other than that, and of course certain dramatic functions too well-known to need repeating, 'the *Doctor Who* girl' doesn't have a generic existence; for the producer developing a new character, anything goes. Or does it? It's often said that each new girl is deliberately crafted as the antithesis of her predecessor, and to some extent this is true. The companions of the 70s swung a pendulum back and forth between a succession of gradually mutating attributes: intelligence and independence (Jo, who by and large didn't have those qualities, to Sarah, who did) turn into education (Sarah to Leela), and then to civilised sophistication (Leela to Romana). One can extend this tentatively to the change from the upper-class cultivation of Lalla Ward's Romana to the colonial brashness of Janet Fielding's Tegan, planned as a '*Doctor Who* girl' but cramped in practice by the eleventh-hour introduction of Nyssa.

A principle of difference, then, seems to dictate the character format at its most fundamental level. The temptation is there nevertheless to attempt to transfer one girl's following direct to her successor rather than allow the latter to build up her own – something which came closest to execution in the creation of the original Romana. Graham Williams had been desperate to keep Louise Jameson for Season 16, and had put a great deal of effort and wine into persuading her to stay. The new character precipitated by his failure had elements of Leela mingled in with the basic 'ice maiden' stereotype up to a very late stage indeed; Mary Tamm remembers discussion about karate and even archery (after Leela in 'The Invasion of Time'). More revealing, in more ways than one, was the idea that the Doctor should criticise her long white dress, causing her to hack off the skirt and spend the rest of the season dressed in the resultant ragged mini – an obvious and thankfully abortive attempt to reproduce the 'thigh-flashing' side to Leela which the press found so fascinating.

Another change from Williams' original conception of this character indicates the more abstruse nature of the third element in creating a new girl – casting an actress. Romana was supposed to be blonde. It's easy to see why: Williams obviously wanted a Nordic quality for his ice maiden; he cast around for fair-haired actresses accordingly. That's what you'd expect: the character format was dictating the casting process. What's surprising is that ultimately it didn't, and Mary Tamm got the part.

Appearance was also important in the original conception of Leela – Louise Jameson may be exaggerating when she says that all they had to start with was the name and the costume, but she had a point. Part of that appearance was skin colour: the earliest photographs of Leela show that she was to be a rather more than nut-brown maid, though this was toned down by the time 'The Face of Evil' was recorded. (Perhaps this also explains the much-complained-of contact lenses to make Louise Jameson's blue eyes brown.) Yet neither the actress who got the job nor others considered for it were black; maybe Hinchcliffe was afraid of being thought racist.

So beyond acting ability, what precisely is the dominant factor in a casting decision? John Tulloch and Manuel Alvarado have argued (in their book *Dr Who: The Unfolding Text*) that Peter Davison had prior associations for the audience, derived from his previous television roles, which tallied with the demands which Nathan-Turner was making of the character; but this manipulation of typecasting can't apply in the case of the girl, since for the actress involved it is usually her first major appearance on the small screen – Nicola Bryant, indeed, had never acted professionally before.

Association of ideas did secure the part of Sarah for Elisabeth Sladen, but the associations were the producer's and not the public's. It's not difficult to deduce the brief for the character: the scripting for her first season shows that she was first and foremost to be 'real'. She is made a journalist, a profession from and concerned with the outside world, in contrast with the 'unreality' of Katy Manning's position as a UNIT employee. There is a deliberately plebeian tendency in her dialogue beyond the ad-libbed Scouse 'geroff' of 'The Time Warrior': 'That's what put the mockers on the TARDIS' ('Death to the Daleks'); 'Contemplating their belly buttons' ('Planet of the Spiders'). And near the end of her first season she reflects on her encounters with the fantastic: 'This is barmy. Here am I calmly discussing fabulous planets, giant spiders, magic crystals, as if I was talking about pussy cats, fish and chips, and the Liverpool docks.' Lis Sladen was herself making much the same move as the character: a Northern girl (in media terms, 'Northern', like 'plebeian', connotes human authenticity), she had been recommended to *Doctor Who* by Ron Craddock for her work on *Z Cars* – gritty Scouse realism again. In her personal and acting background, she fitted the role. But how generally does this apply?

One must remember for a start that Barry Letts saw Elisabeth

Sladen under exceptional conditions, late on at the end of a string of unsuitable applicants, and this must have given the decision some urgency (not that anyone has ever regretted it since!). And the previous careers of other actresses don't match their characters quite so smoothly: Mary Tamm, for instance, had appeared in *Coronation Street* for a while and had had an early film career mostly playing young innocents – strange ancestry for an ice goddess!

There *is* a link in several cases between the character devised and the actress chosen to play her, but it's subtler than we've so far surmised. You cut your jacket according to your cloth, and the casting process is no exception. A good casting decision takes account not only of the broad and necessarily rather crude dictates of the character format, but also of qualities or associations in the actress which can fruitfully expand the part; the original conception may even be modified as a result. This is probably the best view of the casting of Elisabeth Sladen, but that is atypical. More frequently the actress has presented a physical image suggestive of an already established media figure. For instance, there is a very striking resemblance between Lalla Ward and Jane Asher; the latter's media image combines sophistication with a degree of frivolity (the characteristics of the new Romana) and her association with pop culture, such as her links with the Beatles, perhaps points to the sort of orientation Graham Williams may have been seeking (or assuming) for the series. In effect, the actress seems to have been selected, probably unconsciously, as a cut-price version of a star whom a show like *Doctor Who* could neither attract nor afford.

An earlier example has more complex ramifications. Goldie Hawn's career was just taking off in 1970, the year Katy Manning joined *Doctor Who*, and the similarity between the two was remarked upon as early as 1973: the 'dizzy blonde' associations this called up were incorporated into Jo Grant. Given what can be construed of the original brief, this seems at first surprising: Jo was to be a trained secret agent, and remained handy with a skeleton key; an early *Radio Times* article called her 'a junior Diana Rigg'.

What we know of the short-list for the part shows that Barry Letts was beginning to think of softening the *Avengers* image even before he made his last-minute selection of Katy Manning. Certainly the black actress Shakira Baksh and the Swedish Yutte Stensgaard might have played the glamorous, competent woman to the hilt. However, the list also included the sometime model Anouska Hempel and (Katy

Manning recalls) Susan Penhaligon, both of them visually suggestive of Susan George, who was already successful in 'love-interest' parts like that planned for Jo with Mike Yates; the likely sensitivity of such a character was another element which Katy Manning tried to stress. Perhaps what clinched the part for Manning was the Goldie Hawn image, which supplied a last essential element that resolved the potential conflict between the characteristic of trained efficiency and the intended return to companion stereotypes after Liz Shaw, demanded by Jon Pertwee: it brought a dottiness to the character that overrode her training, substituting for the incompetence that gets *Doctor Who* companions into more scrapes than often seems humanly possible.

There's a very clear-cut recent case of this sort of casting, too. If Katy Manning is Goldie Hawn and Lalla Ward is Jane Asher, then surely Bonnie Langford is Bonnie Langford, with some of her prior 'showbiz' associations written into the part – singing in the TARDIS comes to mind.

This principle helps explain how such a mess came to be made of Peri. John Nathan-Turner has admitted the great influence of the Hollywood of his youth, and Nicola Bryant does look remarkably like a brunette June Allyson. The early character of Peri tallies exactly with the screen image of this star of the 1950s. Initial publicity characterised her as 'nice', typical of an Allyson part, and she is the same middle-class, East-coast student type. Moreover, 'Planet of Fire' also emphasises the slightly spoilt underside to such a character, evident in a number of Allyson's movies. And once Peri's stolen the 'platinum' artefact, the action follows the old Hollywood paradigm of the silly girl who gets into trouble and has to be rescued. (Would even a *Doctor Who* companion be stupid enough to try swimming whilst carrying a heavy metal object?) This raises problems: Nathan-Turner's dated treatment of the young American woman didn't last long, and Peri's image for much of Season 22 was anything but wholesome. For once, the casting decision didn't finalise the parameters of the character: somewhere along the line, Andress ousted Allyson.

This wasn't an image imposed by the press; it was purveyed to them. It takes planning to put Peter Davison into a tuxedo and swap a pink bikini for a white one; the photo call that suggested *Doctor No* most explicitly was obviously set up. Very likely the decision was taken in London during pre-production, early enough for Costume to put Nicola Bryant into a blouse knotted at the front in the style Ursula

Andress wore hers in the film. The effect here was to scupper the June Allyson character, supplying only sex by way of a replacement: the role retrogressed to the crudest level of 'the *Doctor Who* girl', and in the hands of an inexperienced actress, Peri was reduced from a person to an object, the closest a companion has ever got to another of Tom Baker's suggestions for the role, a talking cabbage.

Nonetheless Baker's is only the wittiest formulation of a common complaint, and with such a cloud of witnesses one can hardly deny that the girl's character has a tendency to devolve into a function: compared with creation, maintenance is a much neglected art. Even Mark Strickson has made the point about Turlough, and that tells us something about the experiments under Nathan-Turner. These were conceived in terms of effect and audience response rather than any deliberate attempt to change the format: girls were to identify with Tegan, boys with Adric (and later Turlough); Nyssa, brought in as another facial anchor during the changeover period, disrupted even this pattern. What the new arrangement provided, more by accident than design, was a looser structure of relationships in which character could come before function: the tyranny of the line-feed could be dispersed and the emphasis placed on naturalistic interaction.

In practice, it didn't work. For one thing the writers weren't up to it, especially (as males) in portraying female friendship in Tegan and Nyssa – Christopher Bidmead being an honourable exception. More important, there was no guidance from above: the changes hadn't been perceived with the characters in mind anyway, and Eric Saward has said that all they achieved was to split among three roles the dramatic function of one. In a diffused, gestalt form, then, 'the *Doctor Who* girl' survived – hence Jackie Marshall's point that the male companions are stereotypically 'female'. Changing a character is comparatively straightforward; but to change the type, you have to rethink the shape of the hole you're filling.

QED.

The Eternal Archetypes
Val Douglas
(*Queen Bat* #5)

The Eternals must rank as *Doctor Who*'s strangest and most mysterious aliens but are these beings who exist in the 'endless wastes of eternity' true aliens as such or something far closer to home? The name of Striker's ship provides a clue to their possible nature, for The Shadow is one of Jung's archetypes. Could it be, then, that Striker, Marriner and Wrack are manifestations of the archetypes and therefore aspects of the three star *Doctor Who* characters – the Doctor, Tegan and Turlough?

Archetypes, according to Jung, are the primordial organising factors of our psyches which manifest themselves in dreams, myths and folklore. They are common to the entire human race and have been since the species came into being and because of this they belong to the 'collective unconscious', the deepest level of the mind which is the same in everyone. Nobody, even Jung, has ever seen an archetype in its 'own' form or discovered what they do when they're at home as we only know they exist at all by the various guises they adopt in dreams and visions etc. They are 'eternal' in the sense that they are, always have been and always will be and Jung even came to believe that they 'exist not just in individuals, not just in mankind as a whole but somehow *in some continuum outside space and time*'. And like the Eternals, the archetypes cannot manifest themselves without us – it is we 'ephemerals' who lend them flesh and blood identities in our dreams while the dream scenarios and props are drawn from our own experiences and memories. We, on the other hand, have such 'brief lives' that we aren't of the slightest importance to them as individuals – here today and gone tomorrow, there are always succeeding generations of us for them to manifest through.

The human personality has three main components which can be represented by archetypal figures. The Shadow is an individual's undeveloped potential and character traits and, most important of all, his/her unrecognised worst aspects. Everyone has a dark side to their nature and it is said that the best way to discover your own shadow is to think of the reasons why you hate the person you loathe more than any other and add what you regard as the worst characteristics of everyone else.

The Self represents what could be a person's fully developed potential: for a man it is personified by The Wise Old Man (Logos: intellect, logic) and for a woman by The Great Mother (nature, life and the erotic). However, the Self is divided into four main aspects which are attributes of personality – sensation, intuition, emotion and intellect – all of which can be personified by archetypal figures with each having a positive and a negative side.

Finally we come to the Anima/Animus. No man is pure intellect because the male sex has emotions while conversely, no woman is all instinct/emotion because the female sex is equipped with the ability to reason. The Anima is therefore the archetype of everything which is 'feminine' in a man while the Animus is the archetype of everything which is 'masculine' in a woman. The Anima/Animus is also divided into four aspects with those of the Anima being the same as a woman's Self and those of the Animus being the same as a man's Self.

The Shadow, being the *sum* total of what individuals think they aren't, invariably appears in dreams as the same sex as the dreamer. However, where the other archetypes are concerned the dream character can represent an aspect of Self or Anima/Animus. Thus Wrack, although female, could personify some of Turlough's traits while Marriner, although male, could personify some of Tegan's.

But why are archetypes/Eternals so dangerous that if they are let loose with ultimate power, 'chaos will come again and the universe dissolve'?

According to Jung it is consciousness which makes us aware of the external universe – which suggests that if an individual loses his/her conscious awareness the universe will indeed dissolve from a very personal viewpoint. And this can happen because consciousness is a very new acquisition of the human race and one which we aren't even born with but have to develop as we mature from infant to adult. So, if the Ego or sense of 'I' is weak, it can be overwhelmed by images from the unconscious which leads to total insanity. This danger lies in the fact that neglected or unrecognised traits, far from going away, can erupt in a harmful form which, at the very least, leads to personality disorders. If a man neglects his 'feminine' side any one of a number of things could happen to him – he can end up totally lacking all warmth and emotion or he can be dominated by negative emotions such as cruelty and hatred, or subject to irrational moods. Conversely, a woman who neglects her 'masculine' side can become hysterically emotional or turn into a walking collection of opinions which she had picked up from her family or conventional society without examination, or end up bossy, quarrelsome and aggressive. The dark side, too, makes its presence felt, resulting in people (and groups of people) projecting their own worst traits onto others and actively persecuting them or, in extreme examples, going to war to 'exterminate' them. The Universe might not dissolve in the above cases (unless nuclear war results through the Shadow, of course) but for those who have been 'possessed' by an archetype, life is certainly chaotic when they are literally pushed around by parts of themselves which they aren't aware of: 'I couldn't stop myself'; 'I don't know what made me do it.'

'Enlightenment' can therefore be seen as the Doctor, Tegan and Turlough facing potentially dangerous aspects of themselves which are personified by Eternals/archetypal figures. The prize, 'Enlightenment', is self-knowledge, the first step to integrating the personality into a harmonious whole and, in its 'physical' form of the diamond, it is an archetypal representation of the Self.

Striker, as his name implies, is the Doctor's Shadow – the fifth incarnation is a cricketer, a batsman in particular, and in cricketing terms a striker is a batsman about to play a ball. This particular Eternal personifies both the Doctor's negative side and worst traits. The Doctor is positively bursting with energy, insatiable curiosity and intellectual inventiveness, while Striker is flat, 'dead', and mentally sterile. The only thing which livens up eternity for him is the period of excitement provided by the dangers of such activities as the race which reflects the Doctor's own drive to continually seek the excitement of adventure. The Shadow's Captain, like all Eternals, has a crew of ephemerals from which he picks up his ideas but in this instance they can perhaps be seen as analogous to the companions. The crew's lives and safety are of no importance to Striker while the Doctor tends to barge into situations without considering whether he's putting his friends in danger and the first incarnation even went so far as to sabotage the TARDIS so that he could poke around, thus risking the lives of Susan, Ian and Barbara in the process. Finally, Enlightenment for Striker is 'the wisdom which knows all things and which will allow me to achieve what I desire most', but he isn't trying to achieve it in a legitimate way because he's competing in a race for it as a trophy. The Doctor, on the other hand, wants to be a 'Doctor of everything' but is totally undisciplined in the way he goes about it. Rather than applying himself to systematic study and development he gads around the space-time continuum, picking up a bit here and a bit there and setting off again without bothering to check the consequences of his actions. Furthermore, Striker answers the Doctor's unspoken question of what it is that the former desires with 'Do not ask, Doctor, I will not tell you' which suggests that he doesn't know himself. The Doctor too doesn't seem to know what he wants either,

150

because he just drifts around with no overall purpose: even his ultimate ambition is little more than a pleasant daydream because if people *really* want something they apply themselves wholeheartedly to whatever is necessary to attain it.

Wrack is Turlough's Anima, personifying his worst emotional drives. His cruel streak which prompted him to goad his unfortunate school companion into joyriding in the Brigadier's car is reflected by her taste in play acting where she re-creates the pirates' (supposedly) traditional method of execution and by her own admission thinks nothing of hurting ephemerals by digging deeply into their minds for information which she wants. The greed which she sees in Turlough's mind is mirrored by her own in wanting Enlightenment which brings 'whatever one desires' and for her it is the power to 'create and destroy as I wish' for amusement. Turlough too has an inclination towards the mortal equivalent as Barbara Clegg states in her novelisation: 'Turlough began to imagine what he would do with a gem that size. He could buy anything he wanted. People would listen to him . . . They would crawl to him . . . He would have power'. And, as Turlough has been tempted with a piratical course of action where he is to kill the Doctor and take over the TARDIS, Wrack is appropriately a buccaneer.

Finally, Wrack is in league with the Black Guardian who aids her in her acts of destruction and while Turlough is unhappy with the bargain he, himself, struck, it was the Wrack-like flaws in his own nature which make him susceptible to the Black Guardian's influence. In the context of 'Enlightenment' the Black Guardian is also an archetype – the Devil who personifies the evil within our own natures, so Turlough's predicament is, in effect, a conflict between his worst side and his sense of morals. Significantly, the Doctor points out that Wrack doesn't control the Black Guardian for it is he who will control her in the end and the payment demanded by the Devil has always been an individual's soul.

Marriner is Tegan's Animus but what he represents is a little more subtle. He differs from the other Eternals in that he is like a child who is eager to learn – he is curious about things, forever asking questions, and he throws himself into the Doctor's activities with enthusiasm. He worries about and cares for Tegan albeit in a selfish way but as he is very immature it is the selfishness of an infant's love for whoever provides for its needs. He is therefore everything that is immature about Tegan, especially her poorly developed 'masculine' side.

Tegan's immaturity lies in her tendency to turn away from inner conflicts as illustrated beautifully in 'Snakedance' where she is possessed by the Mara. When the Doctor regresses her so that she can confront the darkness within she refuses to do so and hides in her 'garden', an archetypal symbol of the womb. And later, when the Mara takes control, she becomes a vicious, spiteful 'child' who finds the fortune-teller's terror a source of hilarity. She also has the negative 'masculine' traits in that she is bossy, aggressive and opinionated but the positive ones which she should have developed are weak because she isn't very hot on logic and reason. She is, as she once described herself, 'the mouth on legs'.

Enlightenment is therefore something different to each of the three main characters. For the Doctor it is the recognition of his own Shadow; he refuses the prize on the grounds that nobody is ready for it and, significantly, he crosses to the Black Guardian's side as he says this as if acknowledging that he is now aware of the worst aspects of his own nature. Not that he's done much about it yet because he's still gadding about the universe putting companions in danger, but admitting that the Shadow exists is at least a step in the right direction.

8: Interactive Bits

So why is fandom so queer? Why is *Doctor Who* on the same list of interests as the Eurovision Song Contest, *Prisoner: Cell Block H* and Dusty Springfield? One theory is that the Doctor is the only hero who saves the universe but (until the TV movie) shows no interest in 'getting the girl'. The Doctor's pacifist, anti-authoritarian approach also lends itself to adoption by any number of countercultural and 'minority' groups. The Williams era especially is actively camp, acknowledging as it does the priority of having fun over 'gritty realism', and its populism and high ratings allow its followers to avoid being seen as 'sad'. (Although, of course, gay fans are often just as sad as their straight friends.) Also, many of those behind the scenes at *Doctor Who* over the years have been gay.

Mind you, the reverse is also true, because, as I've said, *Who* is such a big show that it contains everything. There are fans who prefer the militarism of the UNIT stories, the right-wing individualism of Terry Nation's scripts, or indeed, think that it's just a TV series with no political content whatsoever.

The following pieces have nothing to do with all that, though, in the manner of camp, many of them are pastiches. The GCE paper is one that many fans would get high grades in, the poll results are, of course, from a poll that was never taken. Many fanzines have featured spoof TV listings, and that below is a compilation (including Bob Stanley's inspired referencing of *The Fast Show* – fandom's greatest enjoyment is often in surfing the zeitgeist to provide the most up-to-date parodies possible, for example the number of 'Reservoir Daleks' pieces in recent years). Also included is a guide to how to play the Trilogic Game, which the Doctor mastered in 'The Celestial Toymaker'.

You're going to need that information one of these days.

THE UNIVERSITY OF GALLIFREY
GCE ADVANCED LEVEL (GALLIFREYAN
CERTIFICATE OF EDUCATION)
PAPER ONE

DOCTOR WHO

Time allowed – 3 hours.

Number of questions on the paper – 25.

The paper is divided into five sections.

FIVE questions ONLY to be answered, choosing ONE from each Section.

All questions carry equal marks. (Credit will be given for diagrams where appropriate.)

DO NOT OPEN THIS PAPER UNTIL INSTRUCTED BY THE SUPERVISOR.
Copyright anytime The University of Gallifrey Th.P. 83/30 4/107

Part A – Hartnell

1. Stevenson: THE DEAD PLANET

'If the Daleks had not been introduced in this story, *Doctor Who* might have become a top ranking television programme.' Discuss.

2. Zola: THE REIGN OF TERROR

'One of the charms of this story is the inept acting by James Cairncross as Lemaitre/Stirling.' Consider to what levels acting in the programme has sunk, with particular reference to Season 20.

3. Golding: THE WEB PLANET

'There are at least fifty good reasons why this story was not successful.' Discuss.

4. Chaucer: THE CRUSADES

How far would you consider that the Lion-heart was a right dick?

5. Moses: THE ARK

Consider the implications of this story with regard to the episodes following each other two by two.

Part B – Troughton

6. Scott: THE HIGHLANDERS

'Och, Doctor, look at the size of that thing!' What does this tell us about Jamie?

7. Hardy: THE MOONBASE

'One could almost say that the Gravitron itself is a character.' Discuss, illustrating how far the Gravitron is presented as indifferent and impersonal, caring nothing for man's puny efforts to secure happiness.

8. Galsworthy: THE EVIL OF THE DALEKS

When the Doctor succeeds in defeating the Daleks, he mutters to himself softly: 'The final end!' What does this tell us about the Doctor's foresight?

9. Hitler: ENEMY OF THE WORLD

'Salamander is an evil and ruthless dictator.' Compare and contrast Salamander with Mary Whitehouse.

10. Owen: THE WAR GAMES

What do you think Jamie and Zoë have to remember of their association with the Doctor?

Part C – Pertwee

11. Dante: INFERNO

Compare and contrast with wide illustration Dante's INFERNO with the classic Houghton's INFERNO. How far do you see a clear distinction between those characters who become at odds with the Inferno and those who merge with it?

12. Wheatley: THE DAEMONS

Consider with close reference to a particular 15 seconds of episode 5, the significance of Bessie.

13. Jonson: THE CURSE OF PELADON

'I'm all dressed up for a night on the town with Mike Yates.' What does this tell us, or fail to tell us, about Captain Yates?

'Together we made a boy into a King.' How far do you agree that the word 'Queen' would have been more descriptive of Peladon?

14. Donne: THE THREE DOCTORS

'There is much metaphysical imagery in the first episode.' Consider this assertion with detailed reference to Mr Ollis and Doctor Tyler.
'The three Doctors can be compared to a three personed God: Doctor the Father (Pertwee), Doctor the Son (Troughton) and Doctor the Holy Ghost (Hartnell).' Discuss with reference to the religious beliefs of the Brigadier, Benton and Jo.

15. Forster: CARNIVAL OF MONSTERS
'The main defect in the characterisation of CARNIVAL OF MONSTERS is that there is not enough scope.' Discuss.
Consider the role of UNIT in this story.

Part D – Baker

16. Austin: GENESIS OF THE DALEKS

'Some things could be better with the Daleks.' Discuss the Doctor's assertion with close reference to the viewing figures of DOCTOR WHO.
'There are no women in the Kaled bunker and none of the men are allowed out.' Discuss.
'Underneath, Davros is very much like a Dalek.' Discuss.

17. Burns: TERROR OF THE ZYGONS

'The two main defects in TERROR OF THE ZYGONS are that it is
a) not entertaining, and
b) impossible to derive anything constructive from the story.'
Explain why you agree with these assertions.

18. Keats: THE ANDROID INVASION

'Hypochondria plays a considerable part in this story.' Discuss with reference to Crayford's eye patch.

19. Shelley: THE BRAIN OF MORBIUS

'Morbius is not a believable character as he lacks body.' Discuss.
Does Elixir come across as a sympathetic character or a medical potion?

20. Asimov: THE ROBOTS OF DEATH

'Vitality and swiftness come through in the fact that the Robots of Death are so full of life.' Discuss, with close reference to your favourite Robot.

<u>Part E – Davison</u>

21. Escher: CASTROVALVA

'The concept of "if" is banded around by the Doctor's two lady companions.' Consider whether 'if' in this story represents 'idiotic females'.

22. Elliott: FOUR TO DOOMSDAY

Contrast and compare this story with the film SATURDAY NIGHT FEVER.
'If the Doctor, Nyssa, Tegan, Adric, the TARDIS, Bigon, the Urbankans and the space ship had all been omitted from the plot, the story might have been a classic.' Discuss.

23. Byron: EARTHSHOCK

'Adric's death comes as light relief after the intensity of what has gone before.' Discuss.

24. Ibsen: ARC OF INFINITY

Consider the contribution made to the plot by Tegan's cousin's yellow socks.
'The Ergon is in reality SESAME STREET's Big Bird.' Discuss.
How does the Doctor know that the Ergon is called an Ergon if it is a figment of Omega's imagination?

25. Lawrence: TERMINUS

Discuss whether Lawrence's original premise of setting the story on a VD colony, leaving Nyssa behind to find a cure for herpes would have been more topical.

Compiled by Simon and Dominic May (*Shada – A Special*)

The Trilogic Game
Peter Anghelides
(*Frontier Worlds* #5)

The Trilogic Game is not a game invented for the story 'The Celestial

Toymaker', but an ancient exercise which is rumoured to have magical qualities. It was Peter Purves (Steven) who took home the actual game used in the programme, and on eventually disposing of it in superstitious desperation, ended a year-long wait for work with a job on *Z Cars* and then *Blue Peter*. A sect of monks are supposed to play the game using one hundred counters (the Doctor used ten), moving once a day. On completion of the last move, they believe, the world will end. (Hmm, I wonder where they're up to?) Below is a description of the game, plus instructions on how to play – and win.

Imagine a triangle with corners A, B and C. Three or more counters are used in the game, set up originally with a pile on corner A of a triangle in descending size going upwards. The aim is to transfer the pile from corner A to either corner B or C, but only making one move at a time. What is more, a larger counter may not be placed on top of a smaller one, only small ones on larger ones. To make the game even more difficult, it must be completed in a set number of moves, the number depending on the respective number of counters used in the game.

3 counters: 7 moves.
4 counters: 15 moves.
5 counters: 31 moves.
6 counters: 63 moves.
7 counters: 127 moves.
8 counters: 255 moves.
9 counters: 511 moves.
10 counters: 1023 moves.

Generally, for 'n' counters, where 'n' is a whole number, the game should take (2 to the power of 'n') – 1 moves.

The secret of winning the Trilogic Game is in knowing which order to make the moves in, and not having to waste a move by making a double move with one piece. Consider direction A to B to C as 'clockwise', and A to C to B as 'anticlockwise'. Now, by either colouring the counters alternately black and white (or, as the Doctor, odd and even numbers), start by moving the smallest counter (odd) in a clockwise direction, then the second smallest (even) anticlockwise. Always move odd clockwise and even anticlockwise, and always move the smallest counter available *unless* you have just moved it.

In playing the Trilogic Game in this manner, the game becomes one of patience rather than skill. And of course it is easier to play the Trilogic Game if you don't have to worry about what will happen when you make the final move!

Write Your Own Jon Pertwee Story
John Connors
(*Top* #3)

Yeth. It's the 1970s and the debonair, dashing Jon Pertwee has assumed the mantle of the Doctor. But what can Baz 'n' Tel do with the well-known cheetah-chaser and man of a thousand voices? Well, here's the guide they swore by.

Just choose one phrase from each section and – Hai! – it's all yours . . .

Sentence One

The Doctor is

a: Stranded on Earth.

b: On Earth because he feels like it.

c: On his way to Metebelis 3.

d: At a wine and cheese party.

His companion is

a: Stupid, but independent.

b: Very stupid, but quite independent.

c: Really stupid, and a bit independent.

d: A spaced-out Cambridge graduate.

Sentence Two

The problem is

a: A strange object which glows.

b: A strange poacher who glows.

159

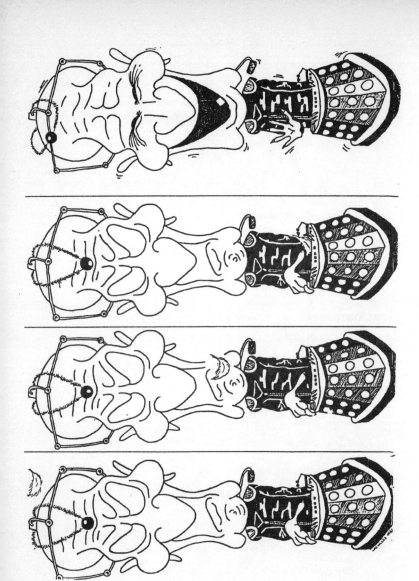

Fan artist Achilles Heel (or Nigel Thomas in real life) shares a joke with Davros, from *Cameca's Lust Issue* (one of Brian Robb and Brigid Cherry's many fanzines).

c: A poacher who dies but isn't strange.

d: A poacher who finds a glowing sandwich.

The Doctor, however

a: Is too busy fixing the dematerialisation circuit.

b: Is too busy stirring tea with a test tube.

c: Is in the shower.

d: Is on Metebelis 3 with a test tube.

Sentence Three

Just then

a: A government official turns up and orders toast.

b: Lots of people go missing.

c: Liz hallucinates about giant reptiles.

d: Liz hallucinates about giant toast.

And the Doctor

a: Tells him to 'see some sense, man'.

b: Tells him to 'talk to them, man'.

c: Tells him not to use the butter.

d: Tells him to 'pith off'.

Sentence Four

Meanwhile the Brigadier

a: Has blown them all up anyway.

b: Has talked on the phone.

c: Has set up a mobile HQ in the sheep dip.

d: Has asked Liz for some party smarties.

Then the villain is revealed to be

a: The Master.

b: The Master.

c: The Master.

d: Barry Letts.

Sentence Five

To save the universe, the Doctor

a: Reverses the polarity of the neutron flow.

b: Blows up the research centre.

c: Bores them to death with a moralistic speech.

d: Plays them 'Three Little Fishes'.

Then everyone

a: Has a dance.

b: Has a laugh.

c: Has a pint.

d: Orders a fresh round of toast.

Late, Last Minute and Just Counted Poll Results!!
Neil Corry & Gareth Roberts
(*United Colours of Cottage Under Siege*)

Yet more poll results have just been received at the *Cottage* offices.
Many of our wittier readers responded to the categories with answers
inspired by one of Brigadier Alistair Courtney's famousest lines.

Best Chart or Diagram

1. The one Norna Range finds in 'Frontios'.

2. The one Servalan finds in 'Orac'.

3. Splendid maps – all of them!!

Best Assistant's Breasts

1. Peri's breasts.

2. Victoria's breasts.

3. Splendid baps – all of them!!

Best Oriental Character

1. Ping-Cho.

2. Chin Lee.

3. Splendid Japs – all of them!!

Best Ray Gun Special Effect

1. The Eradicator.

2. The War Lords' big long guns.

3. Splendid zaps – all of them!!

Best Missing Episode

1. 'The Myth Makers' Part Three.

2. 'The Web of Fear' Part Four.

3. Splendid gaps – all of them!!

Best Water-Channelling Device

1. The pump in 'Arc of Infinity'.

2. The pipe in the Lake of Mutations.

3. Splendid taps – all of them!!

Best Knocked Unconscious Scenes

1. Sarah in 'Robot'.

2. Zoë in 'The Mind Robber'.

3. Splendid naps – all of them!!

Tonight's Television
Bob Stanley (*Something Very Wonderful and Strange* #2),
Andrew Martin (*Stock Footage* #2), Jackie Marshall &
Val Douglas (*Queen Bat* #5)

7.00 – *El Medico Mysterio*: Sci-fi drama Inglés con Juan Perthuiz.
'Scorchio' Parta 4: El Capitano habe un 'eyepatch'!

7.30 – *Terrynation Street*: Trouble at the factory tonight, as Mike
Baldwin has a premonition of the ultimate future of mankind. Later
on, the staff of the Rover's Return are split up to hurry along the
storyline, while Ken Barlow tries to find out why everybody is called
Tarrant. Drama comes to the Street when Mary Ashe accuses Malpha
of selling biscuits cheaply to Brian's new pepperpot-shaped friends
from the squash club.

8.00 – *Masters of the Universe*: Earwig Kennedy in conversation with
megalomaniacs. This week: the Master, a Time Lord from Gallifrey,
recounts more amusing anecdotes about the antics of himself, his lady
friend the Rani, and a large tyrannosaurus rex.

9: Raves

This is a chapter with two absolute paeans of praise to particular facets of the programme, in an attempt to dilute the otherwise cynical nature of much of this book. One reason for that cynicism is that fans are very aware of changing conditions at the BBC. Many fans have secretly gained positions within that organisation – secretly, because of the BBC prejudice against fans, arising from their various determined campaigns on behalf of their programmes over the years. (In public-service broadcasting, it seems, protest must be carefully contained within such shows as *Points of View*.) The BBC has also become aware that such professionally employed fans are often more loyal to their fandom than to the corporation, and so it's in the interest of those employed there not to talk about their hobby. Fans protest too much, according to the BBC, hence their nickname there: 'barkers'. The sometime-makers of *Doctor Who* are content to financially exploit fans, but not to listen to them, and thus must marginalise and characterise what they can't deal with. Some New-Labour-style moderation would be welcome here. Let's hope somebody at the BBC will one day recognise that fan organisations have a lot to offer programme makers, that we're actually the interested, active audience they've claimed to be pursuing all these years. Our bark, they may discover, is worse than our bite.

The two authors represented here are, incidentally, very much Barkers With Attitude, but here they're in loving mode. Which the BBC ought to learn to appreciate.

Love Needs No Disguise
David J. Darlington
(*Paisley Pattern #57*)

Scottish Certificate of Education
Higher Grade
1998
DODGY OLD TV SERIES

ANSWER five questions in all, at least one and no more than two from any section. Then throw a pencil at your mate and leave early with a smug expression on your face, whistling. Exams? Piece of piss. You won't find ME loading up for an all-nighter with a Robin-tub of Pro-Plus . . . any more . . .

Section A: *DOCTOR WHO*

1. Compare and contrast the equally silly and virtually identical costume-change scenes from 'Robot' and 'Time and the Rani' and outline why some narrow-minded assholes will excuse one but not the other.

2. Highlight the reasons for the superiority in depth of characterisation of the Fifth Incarnation of the Doctor, with particular reference to his relationship with his companions in the work of Robert Holmes and EITHER Eric Saward OR Christopher H. Bidmead. Illustrate your answer with quotes from The Smiths and an old Then Jericho song no-one else can remember.

> *'there's no getting over the riches that you bring*
> *and within the light that shines from you*
> *I bathe myself, I bathe myself, I . . .'*

I suppose I don't really have much cause for complaint. Peter Davison is, probably, the third least criticised of the Doctors after Pat and Tom. He always scores reasonably well in polls, and one of his stories is generally in the running for 'best story of all time'. He was used to launch the Virgin *Missing Adventures* series and was also the first Doctor to feature in two such novels. Even some of his companions are fairly popular, and his first and last seasons are generally regarded as 80s *Doctor Who* at its best.

And yet . . .

So often he is damned with faint praise. Only occasionally do we hear shouts of joy and trumpet blasts in veneration at the brilliance of Davison's character and performance. I would like – if I may – to do so now.

Consistency is a much overused word. It implies blandness, a lack

166

of excitement, the Motherwell (if English, insert Arsenal) side of a few years ago using their wild and carefree 8–1–1 formation in a succession of 0–0 draws. In the case of the fifth Doctor, however, it can be applied as a compliment. Of all the Doctors, probably only Troughton could be considered a better character actor than Davison, with a wider range of ability. The others were all excellent at certain things, certain aspects of a performance, but not at portraying all sides of a complex character. Davison is the only one of the Doctors who I think was convincing 100% of the time. In every line of dialogue and in every expression. Look at how convincing he managed to be in 'Dimensions in Time' for a start – outshining all his co-stars just as he did in 'The Five Doctors'. *Fandom Pearl of Wisdom No. 1: When Davison isn't interested in a script, he looks as if he's not trying.* When and where, exactly? To a greater extent than anyone, even Tom Baker, Davison was capable of rendering a poor script or production watchable through his performance. If he is indeed not trying, it says something for his ability that it doesn't show through in the finished show. Apparently, then, Davison on autopilot is still more interesting than any of the others.

However, we're talking here about the fifth Doctor, not Peter Davison. This is certainly not an original thought, but where this Doctor really shines is in his relationship with his companions. Mostly, he liked them. Always, he cared about them, and worried about them. *FPOW No. 2: The fifth Doctor was 'too human'.* No. Not necessarily. I'd actually suggest that he's less obviously human than the third, and anyway this implies that humans are the only species permitted to show compassion for others. You don't have to be arrogant or eccentric to be an alien, after all, and if the viewer can see and share a character's flaws and emotions, surely they should be able to sympathise and empathise more with that character. And as for eccentricity – have you ever met an eccentric? Eccentrics, particularly self-styled eccentrics, are a pain in the coccyx. I'm all for admitting to your own weaknesses and vulnerability.

But back to the companions. *FPOW No. 3: Adric worked better with the fourth Doctor.* Yes, true; perfectly true. The fourth Doctor and Adric is a team which works well in its limited run of two stories. To the fourth Doctor, Adric was a mere child and was treated as such. Adric's own personality was of no consequence. As in the case of Leela and (simplistically) Ace, the relationship was that of a teacher and pupil. Subsequent to the regeneration, the Doctor was perceived as younger by his companions, and so such a relationship would have been difficult from their point of view. The fifth Doctor tried to pay more attention to Adric, as he was now a more caring, less self-obsessed person. However it became rapidly obvious that he didn't really like Adric very much, since Adric still had, like many teenagers, the tendency to be very childish, naive and ingenuous at times. Despite this, the Doctor tried to make time for him, but often couldn't as he had two new friends to occupy his time. So, Adric became even more childish and jealous, to which the Doctor didn't really know how to respond. And then Adric was killed, trying to prove his own worth. The Doctor never properly grieved over Adric's death, which had been at least partly his fault, and so never really got over it – in 'Terminus' he decides Turlough should be given Adric's room, the pain of this being part of the healing process. He can't, however, perform this task himself, and gets Tegan to do it instead while he escapes into the heart of the TARDIS, deep in thought. The relationship between the fifth Doctor and Adric was complex and spiky, like any genuine friendship. The fourth Doctor had no trouble getting along with Adric because he made no real effort to do so. It wasn't in his character.

Friendship is something which is a major feature of the seasons 19 to 21. As has been pointed out before, seldom outside this era does the Doctor admit to having friends – the companions are so often just 'assistants'. Only the seventh Doctor's references to '. . . my friend Ace' are really comparable, since I don't really accept that the fourth Doctor's description of K9 as his 'second best friend' counts. The fifth Doctor and his early companions frequently argue; but these are real arguments, about his inability to get back to Heathrow or E-space, or the best method of destroying an android. They argue because they are having differences of opinion or attitude, but the arguments are intense and meaningful because they are actually concerned about the outcome.

> *'You could be the one alone, I know,*
> *you believe in pride and you would leave her side*
> *who could be the one to know?'*

The departure scenes of (for example) Jo and Sarah would go a long way towards suggesting that the Doctor genuinely enjoyed their company and cared about their welfare. If so, why was this concern seldom expressed at any other time? And why did the Doctor get over their departures so easily? The fifth Doctor, as I've said, never really got over Adric's death, and only accepted the departures of Nyssa and Turlough because he knew it was the right moment for them to leave, to embark on a more meaningful life where they felt they could be of use. Tegan's exit from the show is almost certainly the best in the show's history. It's less dramatic and sensationalist than those of Adric and Peri, less overtly emotional than those of Jo and Sarah Jane, but it works. It could have been a turning point for the Doctor, since for the first time ever, his attitude to his life and his travels is questioned strongly by a long-term friend, so disgusted by what the Doctor has become that she would rather walk out into the world with nothing than continue to travel with him. Unaware that she came back, doubting her own decision almost immediately, he is still brooding over this at the start of the next story, and, judging by Turlough's comments, has been for some time. Despite everything Tegan said, he is finding it difficult to accept his own responsibility for what he has done, and is blaming the Daleks for it all.

I stressed that this could have been a turning point for the Doctor. To an extent the chance was wasted by Davison's early departure. *FPOW No. 4: If Davison had done another year he'd have got even better and would be more fondly remembered.* Well, possibly. This supposes that the show would have proceeded in the same direction and, looking at Season 22, this seems unlikely. It also suggests that there is something lacking in the three seasons he did complete, and I don't see that at all. However, the difference in the Doctor is definitely tangible in (it had to come) 'The Caves of Androzani'.

1984. The Year My Voice Broke. How wonderful *Doctor Who* was in 1984; 'Caves' preceded by 'Planet of Fire' and immediately followed by 'The Twin Dilemma'. *Doctor Who* showed genuine, long-term character development for what still seems to me to be the first time. Not sudden, sweeping changes as with seasons 12 and 18, or slow deterioration as with seasons 8 to 11, but development. To really examine this it is necessary to study the show right up until the end of 1986 . . .

Immediately following Tegan's departure, the Doctor has become a little disillusioned with his own approach to life. In 'Planet of Fire', for the first time, he admits to a 'friendship' with Turlough, despite his anger at the situation he is placed in, perhaps because he has lost Tegan for reasons he doesn't really understand and is uncertain how Turlough is reacting in the same situation. Turlough leaves and the

Doctor allows him to go, surprisingly admitting that Turlough will be missed. Turlough returns the compliment by confessing that he doesn't really want to go. Peri is a spoilt American student looking for a bit of excitement in life – the Doctor is companionless for the first time since 'The Invasion of Time'. This Doctor, far more than his predecessor, needed – and relied on – company. He is ambivalent about taking on any more companions, since he has just lost two in quick succession. However, he goes along with the idea . . .

It is immediately obvious in 'Caves' that the Doctor is far more concerned for Peri's safety than that of her predecessors. The two obviously like each other, or else they wouldn't have wanted to travel together. Peri is hoping for a new exciting life, the Doctor is as enthusiastic and inquisitive as before but doesn't want to screw up his relationship with this companion – and then, of course, it all goes quite horribly wrong. In 'Mawdryn Undead', the Doctor was willing to give up his remaining regenerations to save Tegan and Nyssa. In 'Caves', he goes further, and does indeed sacrifice his life for Peri. As he himself admits, he doesn't know if he's going to regenerate or not. He doesn't know.

FPOW No. 5: It's fitting that the fourth Doctor died saving the universe, while the fifth Doctor sacrificed himself for one friend. True, but I would go further. After all, with the Watcher present, the fourth Doctor knew he still had a future. The fifth didn't, but was still willing to do what he did, for the sake of a person he'd barely met but who he knew trusted him. Throughout the story, Peri's safety is paramount in his mind – 'I'm sorry I got you into this, Peri', 'Sorry, Peri, too late', 'She's dying, Doctor', 'I owe it to my friend to try because I got her into this, so you see, I'm not gonna let you stop me now!' This last, of course, is part of one of the most popular cliffhangers the show has known.

> *'When was there any point in living without your love?*
> *or any point in living without your love?*
> *I hold on and hold on and hold on 'til the end . . .'*

I have heard it suggested that this was because the Doctor and Peri were in love. I don't agree with this, although I don't think it's intrinsically any less likely than the now apparently common agreement that the fourth Doctor and Romana were lovers. Sure, the Doctor loved Peri, the same way he loved Adric, Nyssa, Tegan and Turlough – because that's the kind of guy he was. Caring and fallible.

FPOW No. 6: Peri worked better with the fifth Doctor. Yes, of course she did. That's the point of her character. Indeed, forget the Gastropods and the super-intelligent children, since she is, in fact, the whole point of 'The Twin Dilemma'. It's superficially entertaining because of its camp value, but really the story concerns Peri adjusting to the new Doctor. This was the first regeneration ever which didn't see at least one long-running character present before and/or after – Peri and the Doctor had barely met and had been separated for much of their two previous stories. Peri really liked the fifth Doctor ('You were almost young . . . and you were sweet . . .'), and having asked to be his companion, suddenly found herself alone in the universe with someone she didn't know, and who didn't seem to care for her too much. The spats we witnessed between them for the next season or so were indicative of this – the guy's not exactly what she wanted but she's putting up with it rather than having to go back home. The Doctor is now less patient than he was previously, and is less concerned with her feelings. The initial arguments were inevitable, but had to be followed by either mellowing or divorce. By the time of 'Trial' the mellowing had begun, and then it all went wrong again. Just as the Doctor sacrificed his life for her, so she lost hers because of her trust in him – despite what he had become. This is partly spoilt by the cop-out ending of 'The Ultimate Foe', of course, but since the Inquisitor seemed to know a lot about the events of 'Mindwarp' I'm not convinced Peri isn't dead after all. If she is dead, she lost her life because of her trust in the previous Doctor, who appeared in – then disappeared from – her life so suddenly and unexpectedly. She stayed with the sixth Doctor because she wanted that relationship back, and lost either her life or the Doctor just as it was happening. None of this is in any way attempting to denigrate Colin Baker either – the contrast with Davison was necessary, and it allowed for this development of Peri as a background to the series. His brash, arrogant and seemingly shallow portrayal held great promise. He could have been just as great.

FPOW No. 7: Davison was bland and boring. This was the Doctor who cared enough to sacrifice his life for a friend. The Doctor who had such faith in human nature that he allowed on board someone who he knew was trying to kill him, secure in his belief that the boy wouldn't do it. The Doctor who got things wrong, frequently, because he didn't have any idea how events would transpire. The Doctor who was often unsure of himself in company, and didn't dominate the

Phil Bevan's Davison from *In•Vision: Castrovalva*. *In•Vision* is a fanzine which chronicles the behind-the-scenes story of *Who*, story by story. Fandom's own part work. It's intensely researched, but its meticulous production details weren't really suited to this book.

entire show, leaving dazed minor characters in his wake. And the Doctor who was utterly convincing. *All* the time.

Bland and boring are such predictable, unimaginative, bland and boring words. If you don't like the fifth Doctor, come up with some words of criticism that might counter the ones which really describe him. Subtle. Understated. Convincing. Beautiful.

> *'It's so easy to laugh, it's so easy to hate,*
> *it takes strength to be gentle and kind.'*

(With thanks to Derek and Robert for their contributions re. 'The Caves of Androzani' and 'The Twin Dilemma' respectively, even if – as I suspect – neither of them agree with me.)

That's What I Like
Kate Orman
(*DWB* #122)

I'm standing at the photocopier, pressing against the plastic warmth of the cover with the palms of my hands. Hot pages flick out of the machine to my left: government reports on domestic violence, the psychological details of the battered woman syndrome. I'm writing a *Doctor Who* book.

Since when did *Who* get so serious, so real-world, so adult? Since the series got its second wind in 1987. The Doctor regenerates, the series *regenerates*, given a new lease of life. JN-T, already on his way to fresh fields, is called back to the BBC. He has no Doctor, no Script Editor, no scripts, and perhaps nine months before transmission. But the disappointments of the 'Trial' are behind the series, as are the disruptive conflicts between Producer and Script Editor. The slate has been wiped clean. And it is the late nineteen eighties.

When Andrew Cartmel arrived in the middle of January 1987, most of the preparatory work on 'Strange Matter' had been done. It was not the type of *Doctor Who* he wanted to make. Cartmel was 'a young, 'right-on' type of bloke',[1] influenced by British SF, British comics, British headlines. He and JN-T immediately struck creative sparks, agreeing on some things, disagreeing on others.

Between the two of them, a new kind of *Doctor Who* began to form. The series was brought back to Earth after its excursions into space opera. Its mythology was junked or rewritten. And it was aimed at a more adult audience – and at the more sophisticated children of the 1980s. These innovations are what makes the era of the Seventh Doctor my favourite.

> I think that by the time I was doing the re-writes on 'Dragonfire' we knew what we were after. To begin with we only knew generally, and early attempts didn't quite hit it. In Season 25 Andrew knew exactly what he wanted from the start and could ask writers for that. (Ian Briggs, *DWM* #147)

JN-T has described Season 24 as 'running on the spot'.[2] Everything was moving at breakneck pace. The new Doctor was announced to the world on 27 February. Rehearsals for 'Time and the Rani' began on 30 March, the OB taping on 4 April. There was no time to discuss what direction the series should move in. But it was already moving.

Before you take a tin-opener to your copy of 'The Trial of a Time Lord', take a moment to consider the ingredients: Gallifrey and the Time Lords, the Matrix, the Master, Sil, two appearances by Glitz . . . the series had become tired, contemplating its own navel.

Andrew Cartmel, who had 'hardly watched it at all'[3] before he came, brought a badly needed fresh eye to the show. There are reprises in Season 24: JN-T's first act in creating the season was to contact Kate O'Mara, and Glitz replaced a similar character in the original draft of 'Dragonfire'. But 'Paradise Towers' is the first story since 'Vengeance on Varos' to contain no references to previous *Who*. It was a 'conscious junking of the old mythology',[4] a trend which would continue with 'Delta', 'Patrol', 'Greatest Show'. When the old mythology *did* reappear, it was not the old mythology. The Daleks were sharply redefined, Skaro destroyed, UNIT brought up to date. And most importantly, the Doctor himself came full circle, back to the character he was when the series began: 'Not sinister, but slightly more dangerous'[5] than he had been for years. In some ways, 'Remembrance' is a rewrite of 'An Unearthly Child', presenting us with the same mystery: who is this alien, and what is he up to? We thought we had all the answers. But not only did we not know the Doctor's past, we did not know the Doctor.

> I wanted to bring back that mystery, and Andrew Cartmel agreed. It was funny, both of us having the same idea at the same time. But such things take a long time. With the first season over, the second was well into the pipeline, so in a sense, what we were discussing

Character development is not normally a feature of *Doctor Who*. No matter how great the crisis in one story, there will always be one more . . . Companions come and go, more or less poured from the same mould, and the Doctor's actions are usually pretty much what you would expect.

This is the most daring and the most exciting thing about the Seventh Doctor: the sharp swerve away from the humorous, the predictable, the *comfortable*. This Doctor was compassionate, but also manipulative; concerned but distant, humane but not human. If the right thing to do was a terrible thing to do, he would do it. For me, the Seventh Doctor is the most real. One of the first pictures I saw of him was the *DWM* cover on which he straddles a motorbike; I remember being quite stunned by the down-to-Earth image. This Doctor was not a science fiction cipher wandering pristine white corridors. His stories were set in the real world, or in fantasy worlds with the flavour of reality, 'that had garbage on the floor and graffiti, and felt like a real, lived-in environment.'[6] The Seventh Doctor does things which a real person might do: sing, dance, make puns, read banged-up Penguin books, panic, mourn, listen to jazz. The heroes in his stories are feminists, and Communists, and the boy next door who distracts a Cheetah long enough to save Ace's life. And he fights the kind of monsters you might *really* find on the loo in Tooting Bec.

Down the end of my street someone has painted a swastika over the Keep Left sign: a cheerful sight to greet the local immigrants. But we have it easy in Sydney. The last time I was in London a seventeen-year-old Pakistani was beaten nearly to death, and there were riots in the streets.

The Daleks are, of course, Terry Nation's vision of the Nazis. But the neo-Nazis are the threat now, and that's what 'Remembrance' is all about: the cosmic fascists are mirrored by their Earthly counterpart, the Association. The same analogy was drawn between real Nazis and the Cybermen in 'Silver Nemesis', and 'Survival' contrasted the Darwinism that produced the Cheetahs with the tatty Social Darwinism of Patterson and Midge. While the alien Doctor confronts alien Nazis, his companion fights human Nazis. Manisha's story in 'Ghost Light' is one of the series' most sensitive scenes, beautifully underplayed despite Ace's seething emotions. There is no lecture here, no *Ninja Turtles* moral. All Ace says is, 'White kids firebombed it,' and we're told everything we need to know, the single line painting a broad stroke of human pain.

This is a *Who* which is very aware of the world in which it is broadcast. Thatcherism was parodied in 'The Happiness Patrol' – and the television industry (and, cheekily, fandom) in 'Greatest Show'. The Doctor's description of nuclear warfare in 'Battlefield' still chills me – the cold war may be over, but the missiles are still there. That's why I'm standing here photocopying stuff about battered women: it's that kind of *Doctor Who*.

At Panopticon this year, Janet Fielding was brave enough to tell an audience of fans that it might not be such a bad thing that *Who* was no longer on our screens: perhaps a series which perpetuated such cardboard female stereotypes as the companions didn't deserve to go on. Sitting in the audience, I felt a pleasant smugness. Janet had not seen Ace.

There have been strong female companions before, but there has never been a companion as three-dimensional as Ace, a companion who visibly changed in character over the course of two years. If the Doctor was to become more mysterious and alien, his companion had to become more ordinary, more human. With her working-class background, her boombox, Ace is firmly 'placed' in the real world. Her personality is drawn from three teenage girls of Ian Briggs' acquaintance, her costume from the pages of *The Face*, her situation from the newspapers. Ace is almost a political statement. Her feminism is not the fake loud-mouthed variety of a Sarah Jane Smith or a Tegan Jovanka, the male image of the strident suffragette. Ace is an eighties woman who's learned to take care of herself, and if you give her any aggro, she'll rivet your kneecaps together.

Sophie Aldred's on-screen rapport with Sylvester McCoy is one of the delights of the era; it reminds me most of the relationship between the Second Doctor and Jamie. They were made for one another, and if Ace is a political figure, so is her mentor: 'The Doctor is quite political – he's a pacifist, a man of principle and he abhors corruption and wants to help the world, which he loves. I should imagine he might be a member of Greenpeace!'[7]

It doesn't surprise me that for years before he landed the role, people were telling Sylvester that he'd make a perfect Doctor. I was fuming when Colin was so rudely and pointlessly shown the door. It took Sylv to make everything alright again. The instant he jumped off that table and started babbling about the flicker in sector 13, I knew the Doctor was back.

Even in those earlier, lighter stories, Sylv's relentless energy shines through. His Doctor is magnetic, drawing your eye: Alan Wareing describes him as 'a great instinctive performer. He's also very inventive and creative, and rehearsals with him are both exhausting and rewarding ... He's very keen to create his own Doctor and he's always looking for new angles to develop.'[8] Sylv can play the Doctor both comically and seriously. In Season 24, despite the laughs, he's not all sweetness and light: there's a hint of what's to come in 'Delta' and in 'Dragonfire' when he confronts the villains, especially when he talks Kane to death. On the other hand, in Seasons 25 and 26, he's not entirely serious. In the midst of a battle with the universal force of evil, he drops a brick on his foot. His versatility makes it possible for his Doctor to have many sides.

And he's *cute*, too.

'Ghost Light' is, of course, the greatest *Doctor Who* story ever made. It's also the most adult three episodes of *Who* ever conceived. Not adult as in sex-violence-'n'-swearing, but adult as in *complicated*.

This is a characteristic of the era: the audience is assumed to have a flicker of intelligence, enough perspicacity to follow the narrative without having everything spelt out in black and white. Watch, say, 'The Monster of Peladon', and you'll get politics: you'll also get someone explaining the plot to you every couple of minutes. 'Peladon' is classic children's television. 'Ghost Light' is classic television.

There were, of course, behind the scenes problems which contributed to the staccato pacing of some of the Seventh Doctor's stories, 'Ghost Light' included. Watch the first episode of 'Patrol', and you'll see some of the tightest editing ever done on the series – and no surprise, given that Sylvester was having to turn up to rehearsals in costume and make-up between taping 'Greatest Show' in the Elstree car park. Strikes, accidents, and the asbestos scare all chewed up rehearsal time vital to getting the timing right.

But the script of 'The Happiness Patrol' was overlong at every stage of production: the crew must have known that some of it was going to end up on the cutting room floor. In fact, that's par for the course; whole scenes were harmlessly lopped from 'Frontios', for example, and most of the extra footage in the extended 'Fenric' is non-essential.

> 'I like episodes sharply cut, with a strong narrative drive . . . you really want to get on with a whole lot of story development – not just to hold the attention of the audience, but to make what you are handing them more substantial.' (JN-T, *DWM* #153)

For me, the tight editing on some of the Seventh Doctor's stories actually makes them *better*. 'Ghost Light' in particular is like having a wave break over your head: there are so many references, jokes, bits of business, so much *stuff* going on at any given time . . . it is more substantial than a story that's padded, or has a great deal of exposition. It's a literary multivitamin. And, as Marc Platt has pointed out,[9] the necessary exposition *isn't* missing: it's all there, if you're watching. The only story for which editing causes genuine narrative problems is 'Silver Nemesis'. This is television for adults, and adults can follow complex stories without having explanations spoon-fed to them. Stories like 'Ghost Light' are fractal. No matter how many times you watch them, you will notice something new: how many viewings did it take me to spot the line, 'Uncle Josiah knows about as much about its secrets as a hamburger knows about the Amazon Desert'?

When I entered fandom, Season 24 had just been screened in the UK. *Doctor Who* was about to become an important part of my life, along with university and writing.

I was lucky enough to become a fan when *Doctor Who* was entering one of its most creative periods. The era of the Seventh Doctor is innovative, daring, complex; there's a lot to chew on, to think about. 'Delta' made me rethink *Doctor Who*. 'Fenric' made me rethink *religion*.

Because the Seventh Doctor's stories are adult, because they talk about the real world, because they re-created *Doctor Who*: that's why I'm photocopying these pages. Because that's the kind of *Who* I want to write – and the kind I want to watch. *That's* what I like.

1 Sophie Aldred, *DWM* #139
2 JN-T, *DWM* #153
3 Kevin Clarke, *DWM* #146
4 Stephen Wyatt, *DWM* #146
5 Sylvester McCoy, *DWM* #142
6 Stephen Wyatt again
7 Sylvester McCoy, *DWM* #130
8 *DWM* #161
9 *DWM* #158

10: Days Out

Before there was the Dwas, there was the *Doctor Who* Fan Club. From their charming photocopied *Monthly*, which must be one of the earliest possible fanzines, comes the wonderfully innocent and gushing set visit below. Imagine, if you will, what Nick Cooper, the scaldingly pomo author of the latter piece in this section, would have made of the opportunity afforded the author of the former. He'd have stayed in the bar. And good luck to him, because this convention report gets to the heart of what those sweaty, hormone-driven, overemotional experiences are like. PanoptiCon is the Dwas's annual convention, the official get-together for fans from all over the world (but for several years now less impressive than the independent, and rather more exciting, Manopticon, held in Manchester). At conventions, fans watch 'celebrity' panels, buy merchandise from dealers, buy fanzines, queue for autographs (if not too cool to do so), but mainly hang out in the bar. These days the ultimate cool, and rather sensible, position is just to hang out in the bar, without bothering to attend the actual event.

Carnival of Monsters
Keith Miller
(*DWFC Monthly* #14)

In issue 12, you will remember I told you about my second visit to the BBC to see the filming of 'The Three Doctors'. Well now the DWFC proudly presents another report, on 'Carnival of Monsters', my first visit!

I met Sarah Newman at the *Doctor Who* Office where she had been working, answering letters and so on. The office overlooks Shepherds Bush Green and is just along from the BBC TV Theatre where Basil Brush comes from. I entered the room only to come face to face with a Sea Devil! I took a step back then saw a Mutant! I was just about to run for the hills when Miss Newman picked up one of the head-pieces and handed one to me. It was the head of the Sea Devil. It was thick and rubbery and I pitied the actor who had to work in one of those. But time was pressing on as we collected our things together and stepped out into the midday traffic. A short walk later, we rounded a corner and the giant circular building of the Beeb loomed up in front of us. We entered through a side door and started our journey through the vast network of corridors which spread out like a spider's web over the complex. Walking through the brightly lit corridors, it suddenly sprung to mind where I had seen the inside of this place before! It bore a remarkable resemblance to the interior of the Star Ship Enterprise!

At the end of the trek, Sarah pushed open the double doors of the studio and we entered. The studio was quiet, apart from some scenery workers hammering over the other side of the hall. In front of us stood the inside of the Scope, with its glowing corridors and shiny floors. Sarah guided around the studio showing first the Scope and then the hold of the ship of Major Daly and his crew. Then again I came up against another monster – a Drashig! It was standing four or five feet away, its teeth showing a fearsome white grin. But not to worry. The Drashigs are really only four or five feet long! They're superimposed onto the main picture by a special camera process (see *The Making of Doctor Who*). At this time, camera men began to come in and take up their positions at the back of the colour TV cameras. Miss Newman decided it was time to leave them to their preparations so she showed me up to the BBC canteen where we had lunch. I looked around and saw Ronnie Barker and Ronnie Corbett sitting at the next table. Marching through the doors was the weather man Bert Ford. Behind him was Donald Eccles (Krasis from 'The Time Monster') and Neil McCarthy (Barnham from 'Mind of Evil'). It was all very exciting but it was time to go back to the studio. We re-entered the corridors and made our way back.

We sat in the Producer's box and watched the rehearsals taking place. Shooting was out of phase at that time – that is scenes were being shot which don't follow each other on the TV screens – out of sequence, so this made the following of the storylines very difficult.

But then Jon Pertwee, Katy Manning, Jenny McCraken, Tenniel Evans and the rest of the actors came onto the sets, dressed in their everyday clothes. Katy, of course had her question mark with her and it is her lucky charm. The rehearsals went pretty smoothly then we returned to the canteen for dinner where I was introduced to Barry Letts and Terrance Dicks. Ask your Mum or Dad if they remember a TV serial called *The Silver Sword*. If they do, they'll probably remember Barry playing one of the lead roles in it. In fact he's done quite a lot of acting in films like *Boy, Girl and a Bike* and numerous other TV programmes. We discussed the history of the programme like when the very first episode was repeated the second week following. How many of you remember that?

Everything is hurried in the BBC so before we knew it was time to get back and see that the final preparations were made before filming.

We sat down again at the TV set and watched Katy and Jon, now in TV gear, hurry through the Scope trying to find the way out and escape from the Drashigs. You may remember that the Doctor and Jo rushed down a corridor with a very shiny metal floor which I mentioned earlier, with the tubes of coloured plastic positioned along the sides. Well, the acting was going very well with Katy running along with Jon behind. They came to the end of the ramp and Katy quickly turned the corner and headed in a new direction, but the surface was slippery and Jon's boot skidded from beneath him sending him toppling into the tall, coloured plastic tubes. There was a terrible clatter and the screen went dead. Seconds passed and nothing was seen. Then there was a curious puffing sound and Jon's head suddenly appeared on the screen. He seemed to be okay, then Katy rushed forward and helped him up. She asked if he was all right and he replied yes but his leg hurt for some time after that. But things restored, the play went ahead.

The next scene was when the Drashig reared up through the ship and into the forward hold. This called for the crew to have firearms – in this case rifles. But although they are equipped with blank bullets, the guns can still be dangerous with the empty cartridge shells flying through the air. So extra precautions have to be made to ensure complete safety for the rest of the crew. The practice shots rang through the air, with Jon and the sailors firing at the monster, but there was one little chap who was going berserk! He was firing at everyone except the monster, waving the gun about like a madman and jumping up and down like a thing possessed. Barry, who was directing this particular adventure as well as producing it, wondered what on Earth this little man was up to, so they had to take him off and replace him! He was still jumping up and down when they took him away . . .

And so the rehearsals continued until the last scene was played – through where Major Daly and Claire were saying goodnight to each other in the final episode – then there was a coffee break for 15 minutes.

Suddenly, Sarah rose to her feet. 'Come on,' she said. 'This is our chance,' and she whisked me out of the room, down a small corridor, into a lift, down a couple of floors, then out into another corridor. I then discovered that this was the dressing room area. We walked down the long corridor and a small figure stepped out in front of me, and I nearly bumped into her. I said I was sorry and the little lady turned round. She wore a smile I have seen countless times before. It belonged to Jo Grant! 'That's okay!' she said, then Miss Newman introduced us. She asked me if I was enjoying myself and I said yes, tremendously. She then said she had to see Jon about something then led me down into another dressing room where another friendly face greeted me. The face of the Doctor! He stepped forward and shook my hand. 'I thought you would have been down here at the lunch break!' he said bursting into that broad grin which makes his face so distinctive. I explained we were talking to Barry Letts then and we couldn't make it. We then went on discussing how things were going and what he had to do. But a few minutes later a message came telling him he only had a few minutes to get back on the set, so I said goodbye and he replied that he hoped one day we might get together for longer. We returned to the box, my head still in the clouds.

And so there it was. My day was almost complete and the hands on the clock said it was ten o'clock. Sarah showed me down to the entrance where I stepped out into the cool night and into the taxi, ending a very exciting day with *Doctor Who*.

A Solitary Vice
A Sordid Tale of Sex, Drugs and All Night Stapling at Panopticon 1990
Nick Cooper
(*Purple Haze* #2)
THE (*ridiculously overlong*) PROLOGUE

It was the best of times, it was the worst of times. It is also a long story . . .

It was ten months since the great January 7 Editorial Committee Massacre, which left *Star Begotten* limping away, not exactly gutted, but missing a lung, a kidney, and half its heart . . . It also seemed to have suffered a partial testectomy and I felt much the same. I felt like lying low for a bit to lick my wounds (that's a cat metaphor and *not* an 'oo-er!'). I had planned to go to Carousel in June, but since Tim, Simon and Mark were attending, I decided not to risk it (while recent events have proven that one quarter of the former EC still bears a grudge to an extreme and dangerous degree), while the fact that I just bought a new VCR and was also propping up *Star Begotten*'s finances meant that even if I'd wanted to go, I couldn't have afforded to. But I DID want to go to at least one convention in 1990 and I figured that by Panopticon, I would have both enough cash and also a new *SB* and the debut issue of *Weird* ready for sale. I considered this shrewd financial planning since David Gibbs had given the impression in past *FHE*s that Panopticons were better for sales than other conventions (some weeks before the event he admitted that this was a complete lie – the bastard!). Previous assurances had also led me to believe that Messers Gibbs and Berriman might be attending (this also turned out to be a complete lie), along with occasional *SB* hacks Philip Packer and Sandra Pascoe, and some other fans I knew. As the convention drew nearer the list was whittled down to just Packer and Pascoe.

Panopticon for me really began the week before the event as I attempted to finish both *SB* 14 and *Weird* 1 before the Thursday – the last day I could print anything before leaving for Coventry on Friday. At 03.00 on Sunday, I had staggered from my attic study (*très chic!*) to the bathroom, stuck my head under the cold tap and told myself I was losing it – there was no way I could finish both zines in time. Looking at the unshaven face that stared back at me in the mirror, I argued back that that wasn't the sort of attitude that HG Wells had had, and so staggered back and chained myself to the PCW. Fate smiled on this particular struggling hack and I managed to get the zines printed bit by bit as each new set of pages was completed. The last part of *Weird* I finished at 09.00 on Thursday, before taking two Pro-Plus and departing for work. 19.00 that night saw me half-dead on my feet nursing an overheated photocopier at Park Lane College Students Union. To relieve the monotony I rang Sandra Pascoe to check that she hadn't changed her mind and to explain that I'd probably be up all Friday night stapling fanzines together. Laughing, she said she'd give me a hand since there'd be nothing else to do (this was *also* a complete lie). *(Ay, up, I hope he's going to elaborate on THAT later!)*

Friday dawned, and I was still guillotining and stapling various issues, so I was also resigned to the fact that I *would* have to finish the job in Coventry. I grabbed a mere hour's sleep, took two more Pro-Plus and (shaking slightly) waited for the taxi. Annoyingly, it arrived on time, so when I got to the coach station I had an hour's wait ahead of me, but at least I could catch up on reading the latest *DWB* in between falling asleep and being accosted by a stereotyped Irish tramp (still, he was amusing, so I gave him a quid). Otherwise the time was employed in that traditional fruitless activity: Trying-To-Spot-Another-Fan-Going-To-The-Same-Convention (preferably female, but that's just me *(not JUST you, Nick)*. No-one reacted to the Colin Devis lookalike reading *DWB* (not even to rip it up), so I reasoned that the journey would be a lonely one. Still, it meant I could catch up on some sleep . . .

15.00. I was jolted awake as the coach trundled through what seemed to be the suburbs of another drab Midlands town. I pulled off my headphones (damn, I'd left it running!), but if the steward had announced the stop, I'd missed it. The desolate coach station hinted at the place as being the second favourite stopping-off point of the Luftwaffe after they'd had a few down the *bier keller*, while the name on a sports centre opposite confirmed it. Once off the coach, I retrieved the SBS (I expect steward's hernia has healed by now) and then spent ten minutes waiting in the drizzle before a taxi turned up. I use the word 'taxi' in its vaguest sense – in Leeds we're used to Ford Escorts and Sierras; this looked more like something out of *Quatermass IV*, except that the wire mesh was on the *inside*! I hurled my bags into the back, registered the presence of the driver's apparent bodyguard, and asked to be taken to the Leofric Hotel. Eventually the taxi pulled up next to what appeared to be an ordinary 1950s shopping precinct and the driver turned around and demanded payment, while the bodyguard looked mildly more intimidating. If there was a hotel in sight, I couldn't see it, and asked as much as I parted with my cash. 'It's over there,' he replied. I looked round and finally spotted the tiny lettering above a doorway identifying it as the Leofric.

I staggered into reception (with no excuse of drink) and checked in. This caused some panic among the staff as they didn't have any single rooms ready. As I waited for them to find one, I spotted the still-cherubic Philip Newman and Friends coming in. He grinned and waved in my direction, but not being sure it was intended for me, I merely smiled in return. The receptionist strung out the paperwork as much as possible.

'How will you be settling your account, Mr Cooper?' she asked.

'Credit card,' I said coolly.

'Would you like a newspaper in the morning?'

'No . . . er, yes . . . a *Guardian*.' Damn! Fluffed that one.

'Has anyone seen Andrew Beech?' one receptionist asked the other and my blood chilled. Was there a chance they'd find me a room before . . . arrgh! Too late! The Legal One turned up, flustering like a headless chicken. The receptionist came to my rescue by suggesting I waited in the bar. No sooner had I ordered a coffee (I needed caffeine and I don't suffer from Gibbsicosis) than the receptionist came over with my room key. I drank up and waddled to the lifts, which turned out to have none of the quaintness nor eccentricity of the Wiltshire's (ie, they worked!). The room turned out to be a *real* single, which meant that Packer would be sleeping on the floor. Still the bathroom and TV were up to the required standard, although the hotel lacked the Bath Hilton's XXX-rated movie channel (Falcon '88). The Leofric had BSB instead, although Galaxy was later replaced by *another* service . . .

It was now 16.30 so I decided to recce the immediate vicinity of the hotel, ostensibly to find some extra-high-speed film and a camera battery. I enquired at reception if there was a photographic shop nearby and was subsequently given directions that were almost, but not quite, entirely useless, and I then spent 45 minutes going round in circles (it seems Coventry town planning is based on the Castrovalvan model). Still, I managed to find one cheap processing shop with the film and another with the battery. I also noted the location of the local MacDonalds and (joy!) Kentucky Fried Chicken for future reference . . .

Returning to my room, I decided to pass the time until Pascoe turned up by starting with the stapling. I switched on the TV with the intention of giving Galaxy a whirl, only to find the channel replaced by a revolving Prydonian Seal and a caption fading in and out telling viewers that 'panoptiCon TV' would be on 'the air' later in the evening. Oh dear.

By 18.30, I was sick of rolling a marker pen over the folds of *SB* 14s and decided to see what was happening in the bar. As I clipped on my Walkman™ there was a knock at the door. Cue *Twilight Zone*

music. Who could it be? Who knew I was there? Had the manager come to investigate the strange noises coming from Room 321? I opened the door to find a grinning bespectacled fannish female outside – Miss Pascoe, I presumed. I was shocked to discover she had got my room number from reception. The lack of discretion horrified me – what if other less welcome attendees found out where I was? Would the unknown maniac who had rung me up nine months before to call me 'a bastard' appear at night with more material assaults?! We then spent an hour *not* stapling fanzines *(ay up!)*, but rather discussing the breakup of the Staraker Editorial Committee *(oh.)* and how I now had conclusive proof that Mark is – in fact – the Anti-Christ.*
Around 20.00 we went to MacDonalds and played Spot-The-Fan. Returning to the Leofric, Sandra excused herself on the grounds that a) it was very late and b) she was very tired, and so vanished in the direction of the over-flow hotel. Left without the promised helping hand, I decided to stop off in the bar for a fortifying drink before tackling the remaining several gross fanzines (and boy, do I mean *gross*!).

Halfway through my first pint, I was getting pissed off with Coventry's loud token yuppies ('Oh yah, well the first firm I worked for, the money was shit, the boss was a shit, the company was shit . . .') and because they didn't serve Grolsch. There were other fans in evidence, but being mostly the DWAS élites I didn't want to intrude on their egos. On the way to the bar and my next pint, I made the mistake of recognising the name on the badge of a regular *SB* reader. He seemed to have downed more than George Best in a BBC hospitality lounge, so I had to contend with his swaying figure for fifteen minutes while he told me how good *SB* was and asked me three times whether I was still living in Halifax. When he staggered off for another drink I decided to risk a quick escape before he returned. At this point a not-as-smug-as-it-used-to-be voice called out. 'The conversation's not too bad over here, Nick!' To my surprise it was Philip 'Auton' Newman, and so, figuring one should never look even a *cherubic* gift horse in the mouth, I dropped into the empty armchair at the table around which were sitting Philip, IDWN supremos Stefan Gough and Neil Every, a strange militaria collector and a couple of others. Two years on from our last encounter, Philip seemed to have mellowed somewhat – maybe it was his not being as involved in the

* *Ed note; he isn't.*

DWAS anymore? Anyway, at least it was someone to talk to until Packer turned up and Pascoe got a bit more conversational. Much was discussed, including Philip's bewilderment at a report in *SB* of the '89 Honeycomb, which he'd heard about but not seen – I told him to buy a copy tomorrow. The discussion group broke up around midnight and I wobbled back to my room. After a little experimentation, I found that stapling on the floor would cause the least noise for other guests and it was 04.00 before the majority of the task was completed.

SATURDAY

I was having a dream. In the distance I could hear a telephone ringing and I was running towards it. I then realised that there really *was* a telephone ringing and I clawed my way up through the waves of sleep until I broke surface, scrabbled for the handpiece and tried to remember whether I'd asked for an alarm call or not.

'Hello?' I said, heart pounding in the manner of rapid awakenings.

It was Sandra; 'When are we supposed to be setting up this table then?'

'What time is it?' I asked.

'A quarter to nine.'

My inner being screamed. I had intended to be having breakfast at 08.30, but obviously the sleepless week was catching up on me. Fighting the fuzz from my brain, I asked where she was. When she said she was in the first floor lobby outside the Dealers' Room, I told her I'd be down in fifteen minutes and went and threw myself in the shower.

At 09.02 I was down in the lobby, where I found Sandra and a friend of hers named Kate. After a quick recce of the Dealers' Room, where everyone else was almost ready, I found the 'Staraker' table between *Fan-Mail* and ex-Exec member Julian Knott, but at least *Private Who* wasn't there! By 09.15 the table was set up – damn, too late to grab some breakfast! While waiting for the doors to open, I wandered round the Dealers' Room checking out the opposition: Trevor Ennis and *The Key*; Gary Leigh and his unfeasibly large stock of Target books; *SKARO*; John McElroy selling the last of his photos (oh, for shame, BBC Enterprises!); *Fan-Mail* (who had booked 2 tables, one either side of the room, but weren't occupying the one next to me); John Fitton; JJB, CMS, and lots of merchandise. That wasn't too bad; a 50/50 mix of fanzines and dealers, but just five fanzines – two A5, two A4, one 'abstract A5' (right Paul?) – was a depressing reflection of how the field has retracted in recent years. I was somewhat surprised that *The Frame* and *Private Who/Proteus* were not represented, but I was to find out the reasons later on . . .

The thing about attending a convention as a fanzine editor is that you actually get to see very little of the convention, especially if there's no one with you to take your place occasionally. This was my position until Philip turned up, and Sandra seemed a bit distant this morning, so I decided it best not to ask her. The gulf between the events and the dealers was further exacerbated because the Dealers' Room was separated from the main hall by some one hundred yards, with the lobby and a large ante-room (where the hotel were serving refreshments) in between. This could have been alleviated somewhat by a better use of the video monitors, but it seems DSL didn't think the Dealers' Room mattered.

The Dealers' Room opened earlier than billed because everyone was ready and a queue was building up outside – the fact that the first event was nothing more exciting than episode one of *Ghost Light* may have helped. I know the morning was supposed to be devoted to the story, but actually screening it seemed a bit dumb because I daresay virtually everyone had it on video at home anyway. The bewildered attendees then wandered into the Dealers' Room and I had to contend with the usual vaguely patronising down-the-nose looks as they filed past on their way to buying the sort of merchandise they can get at the same prices anytime.

Philip Newman appeared and demanded to see the Honeycomb report. I indicated the last printed copy of *SB* 11 – I've found bulging eyes such an amusing sight, which is more than can be said for Philip's reaction. Still, he did go and fetch me one of the enamel Prydonian Seal badges that were on sale in the foyer, but declined to actually *buy* the copy of 11 and continued to do so for the rest of the weekend. Packe turned up at around 10.30, looking relievingly normal – older than he sounded on the phone (sorry Phil!), and thankfully quite willing to atone for his reviews in *SB* by helping to sell a few. Another contributor to show his face – albeit momentarily – was Mark Freshney (who designed *Purple Haze*'s glorious logo), who proved that the final frame of the 'Doctor Fuckwitt' strip in *Weird is* a self-portrait! Mark collected his complimentary copies and I was able to tell him that a number of people had observed of his contributions to *Weird* that he ought to be working professionally. Heavy irony.

Julian Knott turned up around lunchtime to claim his empty table and proceeded to cover it with copies of the reissued *Blacklight* cassette (which has annoyed the DWAS so much!) and his new Paddy Kingsland tape – *The Corridor of Eternity*, which I eventually bought once the Staraker Publishing takings had passed break-even point, along with a couple of advertising posters for the abortive *Aliens Special Edition* tape, a copy of which he was auctioning off. For an ex-Exec member, Julian turned out to be quite an okay sort of bloke. As did *Proteus* editor Richard Bignell, who browsed past at one point and ended up staying for a long chat on the mechanics of fanzine production and the idea that even A5 photocopied fanzines can and should try to attain the design and presentation standards of 'real' magazines as the A4 'glossies' do. He told me that *Private Who* was now officially dead, so I guess that leaves a little more room for the *real* fanzines. Trevor Ennis' 'professional interest' in fanzine production extended as far as wanting to know how I could print *SB* so cheaply that I could charge only £1.65 for it! I just smiled enigmatically and said that would be telling . . . John Freeman browsed past at one point, asking what was all this about his cheques not bouncing (see *SB* 11), but I managed to persuade him it was nothing to do with me.

Some less welcome passersby were two *CT* merchandise reviewers – both of whom seemed totally shocked when I refused point-blank to give them a free copy of *Star Begotten* 14 so they could review it! I offered them a discounted copy (I don't produce *SB* for the benefit of pompous DWAS types), but in the end they went off in a huff, shortly before Martin Kennaugh appeared and bought one without being prompted. He subsequently semi-panned it in *CT* – ah well, I guess that's the free press for you!

The Dealers' Room closed at 18.00 and the convention was suspended while 80 lucky attendees enjoyed the Celebrity Dinner. Phil and I hadn't booked for this, so we dumped the stock in my room and wandered over to Kentucky Fried Chicken for a *Non*-Celebrity Dinner. Back at the Leofric, we switched on Panopticon TV in time for *Auf Weidersehen, Doc* – part of a clips tape that was the 'rare, nay unique' material promised in all the advertising. Next was the untransmitted *French and Saunders* sketch. After the first few minutes it became obvious that the reason it hadn't been shown was because it just wasn't funny! We returned to the main hall just as the screening started of the *Rock and Roll Years*esque sequence of telefantasy title sequences and clips set to pop music that was shown at the 1990 TellyCon. Knowing how insular *Who* fans are, it was interesting to see which series did or did not elicit a response. Utter silence greeted *Terrahawks*, for example, while *The Box of Delights* got the opposite . . . but they were cheering Patrick Troughton, not Cole Hawlings. *Star Cops* gained a smattering of applause. I muttered, 'Small-minded sods!' under my breath, turned to Philip and said: 'If they don't include *Knights of God*, I'll scream.' The *KoG* titles produced even less response than *Star Cops*. 'The bastards would've wet themselves if they'd shown a clip of Pat,' I confided in Philip as the tape moved on to the next series. Not a bad little piece, but it was too *Time-Screen*-approved to break any new ground.

The bar was quite full, but most of the people waiting to be served turned out to be non-residents and so were refused service, including one despite his protests about being on the sound crew and one of the convention organisers. Heh, heh, there is some justice in the world, after all! When the young lady behind the bar turned to me, I held up my room card and asked with slow deliberation: 'A pint of lager, *please*.' After a couple of pints I staggered back to the Main Hall to find it plunged in darkness and perhaps only fifty people scattered around, close to the side monitors. Finding Philip sprawled on a couple of chairs, I collapsed on to a few and fell asleep. I woke up to find episode one of 'The Best of Both Worlds' ending and managed to stay awake for the first few minutes of part two before Morpheus got his fingers around my throat again. I re-woke as part two finished (a bit of a cop-out I thought, but a nice final scene) and 'Horror of Fang Rock' began. By episode three I'd had enough and dragged Philip away from the screen. Reaching my room, I threw the bedspread on to the floor for Philip and retired for what was left of the night.

SUNDAY

In contrast to the previous morning, I woke up in time for breakfast, which was okay as far as hotel breakfasts go (no black pudding though!). Philip kept wandering backwards and forwards between the Dealers' Room and the Main Hall and told me as I restocked the table that JNT was going on stage again. I figured this would be a laugh and so asked Julian Knott to watch my stall and went to see. Still in a Hawaiian shirt and with a Dunhill at hand, the ex-producer seemed almost human again, especially since he conceded that he *had* made a few mistakes. He also said the real reason for the 85 suspension was that the BBC had needed £7 m to finance Daytime TV and so axed it along with a lot of other programmes/slashing episode counts (e.g. *Crackerjack* (' C R A C K E R J A C K ! ') *Pop Quiz, Juliet Bravo*, etc). They then had to find a public reason for doing so – like needing £7 m wasn't valid enough. He said he'd hate to go down in history as the person who'd killed off *Doctor Who*, while his disgruntlement about the series' lack of future endeared him to the fans somewhat. Oh, what short memories we have!

Next up with *The* Doctor himself, Jon Pertwee, who delighted us all from the start by means of a bright shiny object and a few lines of that ol' Venusian lullaby. Despite his various convention appearances Jon didn't appear worn-out panelwise at all, and included some hilarious (but very probably untrue) anecdotes about scuba diving Irishmen. One fan asked him if there was any news of *Starwatch*. 'Yes,' he declared, 'it's dead!' Before Jon finished, I went back to the Dealers' Room, in anticipation of one final rush of custom before its impending closure at 14.00. Despite an extension to 14.30, however, this rush didn't come because they announced it *while* Pertwee was still on stage! After the interview finished, Philip later told me Jon had decided to leave through the hall rather than be whisked away from the fans via the TARDIS 'entrance' at the side of the stage. This caused Andrew Beech a minor fit as he grabbed a microphone and urged the fans to 'let Mr Pertwee exit'!! One steward rushed after him and tried to lead him back to 'safety'. 'Why?' he asked. 'I wanted to meet all these lovely people . . .'

I took what was left of the Staraker stock back to my room and returned to the Main Hall to await the arrival of Sylvester McCoy. The Short One did his stand-up comedy routine for an hour or so, inciting the audience on the subject of the non-return of the series in the process. This wound up around 17.00, when McCoy started signing autographs and the convention sort of petered out at this point. After saying goodbye to Sandra and Kate in the foyer, Freeman walked past and I called after him that I hoped he was going to 'Give us a good plug'. Now I meant a plug for *SB* in the Monthly, but he must have misunderstood me because he called back: 'Yeah, what room are you in?' Philip and I exchanged worried glances and quickly went to

Kentucky Fried Chicken for a bite or seven before he caught his train, and I returned to a relatively empty hotel. As I started cashing and packing up, someone in the next room started playing an electric guitar and didn't stop until after midnight . . .

MONDAY

Ho hum, I felt *really* pissed. Post-Convention Blues with a vengeance. On my way to breakfast I spotted Sandra lurking around the lobby and my cheery 'Still here then?' turned out to be the last time I saw her! While waiting for my breakfast who should descend for theirs but Andrew Beech and Friend. 'Successful weekend, Mister Beech?' the waitress asked as she took their order. 'Everyone seems to have enjoyed themselves,' Beech smiled. Well, he would say that, wouldn't he? Speak for yourself, Andrew . . .

After packing, I went for a wander round the immediate vicinity of the hotel to find a poster tube in which to get the two *Aliens* posters home safely. I was also tempted into coughing up for a *ST-TNG* video and also a couple of cassettes to get me through the journey home. Wandering back to the Leofric, I found it in the first throes of a Safeway Sales Conference, so I checked out and had an obscenely large lunch courtesy of Colonel Sanders, before squeezing into a taxi. I then spent 2½ hrs waiting in a Portacabin™ at Coventry coach station. When the coach did turn up, I had the good fortune to sit next to a rather charming young lady, but unfortunately she got off at Nottingham, so I was forced to don headphones and start scribbling bits of this review.

Old Wolfgang Amadeus did this bit (well, if Wagner works for Ian Levy . . .). By Chesterfield, *Mass in C Minor* had raised my spirits somewhat; I was up to *Eine Kleine Nachtmusik* as the coach pulled into Sheffield and starting to feel human again, and as the lights of Leeds appeared through the night, *Divertimento in F Major* was finishing the job. In the words of Harry Perkins MP, 'A man who's weary of Mozart is weary of life.' And not even the DWAS could disprove that . . .

11: Leftover Bits

L eftover fanzines worth a mention: *Private Who* (started off as satire, then followed *The Frame* into pro printing and serious set visits); *Metamorph* (part of the vast subculture of Midlands fandom, the place where the wars seem to get most intense); *Eye of Horus* (an A5 'zine with two editors which begat *Zygon* when they split); *Androzani* (with awesome production values); *Auton* (spiteful, in-jokey to the extreme, and thinks it's too cool to be part of its own culture, all of which makes it rather wonderful); *Fan Mail* (an A4 'zine with great cartoonists and comic strips, including Doctor Duck and his arch-foe the Hamster); *The Doctor's Recorder* (now ten issues old: a few years ago that would have been a record); *Eye of Harmony* (which had some of the jaunty invention of *Skaro*); *Star Begotten* (solid, dependable, hard as nails and always concerned with the politics of fandom); *Experiential Grid*; *Varos*; *Synaptic Adhesion*; *Traken*; the *New Whovical Express* (good fiction and cartoons); *Chronic Hysteresis* (which claimed to travel in time and thus printed issues out of order. The team also once produced an issue without the editor Peter Ware's knowledge and announced he was dead); *Opera of Doom* (named after a fan *rumour*), the current fave *Mayfield* (poetry, fan lifestyles and silly photo story recreations of episodes, set in Bristol) and we haven't even started on the 'zines produced just for the Fitzroy Tavern, like *The Hippo and Bowling Ball* . . .

Leftover articles worth printing: one of the best-loved sections of *Cottage Under Siege* is the fake newspaper columns, such as 'A Room of My Own' with Omega, and 'My Kind of Day' with the K-1 Robot. Scott Grey, now a Marvel mainstay, did one of my favourites, featuring the villains from 'Tomb of the Cybermen'. Val Douglas is underrepresented in this collection, and I couldn't resist her poem. Jim Smith's mob are one of the newest gangs to create an A5 fanzine, the (obviously) radical, noisy and third-Doctor-hating *Rassilon's Rod*. Finally, something from one of the many one-off 'zines of the media pirates Brian Robb and Brigid Cherry (they were once given the editorship of the Dwas newsletter *Celestial Toyroom* you know – lasted about a week!) – the self-mocking *Doctor Eye*. The best people in the universe, it seems, are a culture who do nothing but laugh at themselves.

How We Met: Kaftan & Klieg
Interviews by Scott Grey
(*Cottage Under Siege* #2)

BETTY KAFTAN: I cannot remember the exact day Eric and I first met. We were approximately 5.72 years old and were both attending Guildford Neo-State Physics Grammar School. The students were always seated in alphabetical order, so Eric and I found ourselves together a great deal. We were approximately 10.67 times more intelligent than any of our teachers and frequently amused ourselves by reprogramming their financial records, wiping their bank balances, doubling mortgages etc.

Eric was really something of an outcast in those days, quite unlike the suave debonair man he is today. All of his hair fell out by the time he turned three and, as if that was not enough, he had contracted Linguiscolleximia, a rare disease that affects the vocal cords. It caused Eric's voice to take on a strange Eastern European accent, despite his being born in Scunthorpe. My heart went out to him as I watched him walk home from school. The other children would laugh and jeer and throw live lobsters at him, but I could see Eric was meant for greatness.

By the time we were approximately 9.29 years old we were firm friends. We spent long summer afternoons going bike-riding, playing volleyball and imagining what the world might be like if it was ruled by us and an army of ruthless silver alien cyborgs.

Such happy, innocent days could not last forever. Eric and I eventually parted: he to pursue a career as a freelance mathematician; I to become a quasi-lateral physicist and part-time television presenter.

I spent most of the next 20 years exploring the possibilities of dual-

Betty Kaftan and Eric Klieg by Scott Grey.

state warp mechanics and putting letters on a board on *Countdown*. My thoughts often returned to Eric – he had dropped out of sight. One day I found him on a street corner, offering quick calculations for spare change. Eric had fallen on hard times – there was a recession on and little need for a man who could calculate axiom systems based on integrated logical proofs. I took him home, gave him a bath and suggested we form an organisation of like-minded souls – brilliant scientists with razor-sharp intellects and no social skills whatsoever. He agreed, and the Brotherhood of Logicians was born. I feel my bond of friendship with Eric shall never break, unless, of course, he ever dares to betray me.

ERIC KLIEG: I am blessed with total recall and can remember my first meeting with Betty in minute detail.

We were students at the Grimsby Advanced Quantum Mechanics Academy. We were both 8.17 years old. Betty was seated next to me and was a shy young thing. I asked her if she had a pocket calculator and she replied that only craven fools with chemical imbalances in their thyroid glands needed such primitive devices. I liked her immediately.

I was enormously popular at school – the other children were fascinated by my bald head and exotic accent – but I reserved most of my time for Betty. She found making friends difficult. I believe the main obstacle was her sense of humour – one of her favourite jokes was to offer £50 to any boy who could keep his head inside a microwave oven for 15 minutes.

I remember going to Betty's house for the first time to listen to her Johnny Mathis collection. I walked in and there it was: a huge poster of the Cyberleader on her bedroom wall. It was a striking moment – I realised I had found a kindred spirit; someone with the same drive, the same goals, the same gross disregard for human life as myself.

We were both big fans of the Cybermen – I remember we once drugged one of the servants at Betty's house, lobotomised him and put him in a silver jumpsuit. He just wandered around, going 'Excellent' all the time. I suppose all children play such pranks, but we felt pretty special all the same.

After graduation Betty and I lost touch. I went from success to success as a freelance mathematician – everyone wanted to hire me: nightclubs, concert halls, bar mitzvahs … I had a great season at Caesar's Palace in Las Vegas. I would calculate the spatial configuration of an inverse ratio of alpha particles and wind up the evening with my rendition of *I Will Survive*. It was a real show-stopper. Eventually, the lure of more serious work led me to found the Brotherhood of Logicians. When Betty heard of my group she begged me to allow her to join. I'm glad I did – she is a popular figure at our annual conventions, which can get pretty wild at times. Put 1,500 mathematicians in a hall, bring on the tonic water and look out!

By the time you read this, Betty and I will have returned from a secret trip to Telos and the Earth will finally be a very logical place to live. But I'd better not give away any surprises!

Betty Kaftan, 38, is a major figure in the field of trans-dimensional warp mechanics. She is also a respected, well-known children's television presenter, agony aunt and Liberal Democrat candidate for Surrey South East.

Eric Klieg, 38, was educated in the finest universities of Sleasford Barnstable and Cheddar. Founded the Brotherhood of Logicians and is the author of the best-selling book 750 Reasons Why Bald Men Are Sexy.

A Poem for your Edification and Delight
With apologies to Mrs Hemans
Val Douglas
(Frontier Worlds #17)

The boy stood on the freighter deck
Whence all but he had gone;
Upon a lone, dead Cyberman
Control bank lighting shone.

Yet muttering to himself he stood,
A proud and noble sight,
'Though clad in working garments rude
Of sunshine yellow bright.

The planet loomed – he would not flee
Until the codes he'd cracked;
He'd done two – now for number three.
(He was a stubborn brat.)

The ship blew in Earth's atmosphere –
Young Adric – where was he?
Ask of the man who sweeps the sets
Down at the BBC.

Manning's Milk
(Rassilon's Rod #1)

Renowned scientists Sam Barlow and Jim E. Smith have spent many months investigating what they have termed the 'Manning Factor'. We now proudly present an edited transcript of their notes.

Following a tentative hypothesis developed by Professor Barlow, we began to see the effect *Doctor Who* episodes featuring Katy Manning had on various quantities of milk.

For example, a half pint of milk was placed 6 inches in front of the television screen, and then the video player was engaged. The chosen tape was 'Terror of the Autons'. During the first few minutes, starring Roger Delgado, the milk showed no signs of anything (except being milk) but upon the scene switching to UNIT headquarters, some startling results were observed. At the exact moment Ms Manning entered the Doctor's laboratory, the milk slowly began to curdle, ultimately turning sour on the line: 'you mean like Frankenstein . . . Ugggh!' and requiring evacuation of the test site.

The milk had curdled completely in just under four minutes.

Further tests were begun a week later, when, using the same video player, different milk, the same glass, and keeping it exactly six inches from the screen, we played the milk 'The Daemons'. The milk curdled instantly upon the line 'but it is the age of Aquarius!'; under two minutes from the start of the episode.

Further tests with 'The Green Death' and 'Planet of the Daleks' showed the milk curdling in between 3 and 7 minutes.

To test the hypothesis we showed various bottles of milk 'The Gunfighters', 'The Caves of Androzani', 'The Creature from the Pit', 'The Greatest Show in the Galaxy' and read *Timewyrm: Exodus* to one. No curdling was evident. We therefore conclude that, without question, Katy Manning curdles milk.

Colemanballs
5p paid for contributions
(*Doctor Eye* #646)

'The Doctor's nightmare opening "The Time Monster" serves a similar function in much the same way.'

Justin Richards. 'Now We Can Begin', *Stock Footage* #2

'Bonnie Langford – ready to do to USA conventions what the A-bomb did to Hiroshima.'

J. Jeremy Bentham. 'News from Great Britain', *Whovian Times* #14

'I wouldn't want a girlfriend who was in the DWAS. She might know more than I do.'

Dominic May. Private conversation, made public.

Epilogue: The Moment Has Been Prepared For

So what happens to fandom next? Without a show, the island has become, suddenly, a free country. In Australia and New Zealand there's a growing enthusiasm for the New Adventures as a new subject for study and love, in fanzines such as *Broadsword*. As the books have also now passed away, and are thus safe to adopt as beloved objects, fandom in Britain may go that way too. The contraction of fandom as a result of there being no new series may already have stopped, and even reversed a little as small kids get into the videos and grow up. There were *families* at the last Manopticon. The dialectic of *Matrix* and *Skaro*, the radicalism of 'zines like *Mayfield* and the rigour of *Spectrox* all continue undimmed. New 'zines (like *Sutekh's Bum* and the latest, vaguely newsstand-friendly version of *Sonic Lance*) keep springing up as well. The only difference is, most of them don't specialise in *Doctor Who*. Instead, they bring the particular language and culture of this fandom to all manner of new subjects and series – loving, for example, *Babylon 5*. (One of the first, most radical gestures of the New Fandom, all those years ago, was to embrace and write about *Star Trek: The Next Generation*. These days, fandom assumes that dealing with other series was something it always did.) In the end, the latest fanzines are concerned with the business of getting on with, and having, lives.

I'm part of fandom, and I think I'll remain so. It's a good culture to find yourself in, in all senses of the word, and more and more artists and thinkers will come from it. Rather than try to make any hypocritical attempt to step out into the wider culture around us, I think fans can achieve much satisfaction from watching our cultural parameters expanding: we apply a fandom turn of mind to everything, and the wider culture itself (as is happening more and more) adopts a fandom perspective.

The bits I'm signing off with include a few that are mentioned whenever fans get together and talk about A5-era fanzines: one of the regular telefantasy agony columns of *Queen Bat* and the infamous 'missing line' from the Christmas episode of 'Dalek Masterplan'. Add to that an index of an average fanzine's content, and a pinch of *Spectrox* . . . and we have ourselves a culture and a book.

You edit the next one.

Dear Auntie Nicer
Jackie Marshall
(*Queen Bat* #3)

Dear Auntie Nicer,

I am a dedicated scientist whose important work is being put in constant jeopardy by the antics of a dark, bearded, heh-heh-heh-ing megalomaniac and his silly feud against a man with no dress-sense whatsoever and a lamentable taste in companions. Much against my better judgement, I was coerced into assisting the megalomaniac but not only did he refuse to listen to my advice, he then added insult to injury by stationing himself on *my* TARDIS. How can I get rid of this unwanted pest so that I can continue causing mayhem in the interests of science?

Infuriated of Gallifrey.

P.S. Talking of unwanted pests, do you happen to have any handy household hints for disposing of a large tyrannosaurus rex?

Auntie Nicer illustration by Amanda Kear.

200

Dear Infuriated of Gallifrey,

As a fellow scientist, I sympathise deeply with your problem. The large Tyrannosaurus Rex is no problem as I have found Harmonious Hairspray very effective in ridding oneself of this nuisance. It may also work on the dark, bearded, heh-heh-heh-ing megalomaniac, but if not, I suggest you leave him to his own devices and seek refuge for a time elsewhere – I've heard that Denver, Colorado, is very nice. Then, the next time he gets himself into a terrible pickle you can use your handy remote control to summon your TARDIS to you, thus abandoning him and teaching him a much needed lesson about 'borrowing' other people's property.

Extract from an 'Ark in Space' review
Tat Wood
(*Spectrox* #8.5)

American movies have all Amurrican generals to blast the flying saucers out of the sky: over here we've got Nick Courtney, always looking as if he's just about to realise that it's a silly way to make a living. It's an approach which bears comparison with someone like Paul McCartney or Ray Davies plonking an un-rock'n'roll word like 'pataphysical' or 'caterpillar' in a lyric instead of 'mama' or 'baby', or Eric Idle inserting 'Rutland' for 'Hawaii': something solid, familiar and defiantly unglamorous (sod Lowri Turner, Pertwee wasn't remotely sexy) but in the place where glamour should be and treated as if it were. The extreme of this, possibly the ultimate imaginable, was 'Earthshock' supplanting Sigourney Weaver with Beryl Reid. What's funny is the assumption that they are equivalent and interchangable.

Drama Extract Plus
Researched by Justin Richards
(*Frontier Worlds* #17)

The first in a series which transcribes moments from Doctor Who *stories which for varying reasons were altered – albeit very slightly – on final transmission. At last we can reveal such secrets as why the Shadow was a pain in the neck for the Marshal; just what those Cybermen were doing in St. Paul's; and the question on everybody's lips: why did the brontosaurus take offence, and what exactly was it that Adric said to him? What precisely was the bicycle pump for? This issue we take a look back to the classic story 'The Daleks' Masterplan'.*

The Doctor closed the door carefully behind him and carried the tray towards Sara and Steven, taking care not to spill any of the wine in the magnificent seventeenth-century French crystal glasses which he had picked up cheap in a small shop in Amboise. 'We so rarely get the chance to celebrate,' he explained to his companions as they looked up, puzzled. After all, what with the Daleks and all that excitement, it was all go.

'Celebrate?' asked the bemused Steven – God, this boy was dim.

'Don't you remember?' asked the Doctor, trying not to let his contempt get the better of him. 'In the police station?' Still no response from the moron. Oh well, might as well spell it out for him. 'It was Christmas.'

'So it was,' realised Steven at long last, taking the fullest of the glasses and allowing a few drops to trickle down the side. The Doctor handed the least full one to Sara, who inspected it rather dubiously.

'Here's a toast,' said the Doctor, the bottle and a half he had drunk to check that the wine was still okay beginning to cloud his mind. 'A happy Christmas to all of us.' Suddenly, an idea took hold of him. Now was his chance to annoy everyone tremendously, but not too seriously, at the same time. 'And incidentally,' he added, a twinkle in his glazed eyes, 'a happy Christmas to all of you at home ... You can edit that out, can't you, Douglas?'

Index
David Gibbs (*Five Hundred Eyes* #5: an accurate index of that issue!)

'The most merciful thing in the world, I think, is the inability of the human mind to fully correlate all its contents.'

– H.P. Lovecraft

ace electric....................................11–14
ancient conventioneer.......................14
appendectomy...................................53
back cover...84
back issues...3
baker, tom...18
berriman..................14, 34, 36, 53, 77
bestiality...24

bidmead, christopher.........................18
blackeyes..61
blank pages....................................2, 83
boy's own paper....................67, 68, 69
bureaucracy..................................29–33
burt, jonathan.................20–23, 55–59
café munchen....................................26
cannabis..68

cartmel, andrew............20
chegwin, keith............53
chemistry............11
clapp, nicole............36–48
cliffhangers............15–18
conventions............14, 49
copyright............3
credits............81
creeping terror............77
daleks............60
deadly grapefruit............24, 53
dr who............4–34, 36–67, 77–80
draught cider............29
drugs............34–35, 67–76
editorial............3
eyes............36, 61
eyes are the window............36
fandom............18, 26, 54, 63, 77, 79
fanzines............19, 81
fiction............24, 34, 36, 61
five hundred eyes............76
flowchart............60
forbidden planet............26
fragment, a............14
frame, the............19
front cover............1
green condoms............80
hinchcliffe era, the............19
hippies............34, 69
historical stories............20
holmes, robert............19
hunter-watts, tom............15–18
illegible print............3–82
index............82
joy of dr who, the............79
knees, ian reddington's............51
kinda............19
kinky sex............24, 79–80
lalla love you............36
lesbian lavatory lust............53
letters............4–10
levy, ian............67–76
ley, shaun............29–34
libel............55
longleat revisited............26
lsd............34, 68, 75, 76
marijuana............67–76
marvel............26
mcgrade, paul............18–20
men from the ministry............29
missing stories............20
mr benn............34
narnia............1, 14, 19, 52
narrow minds............54
nerds............14, 26, 54, 79

nietzsche............68
o'brien, stephen............4, 5, 79, 81
obsession............77
oddballs............21
officialdom............29–33
o'mara, kate............20
orgasm............15
out-of-date............11–14
1001 things............53
paranoia............77–78
pearson, alaister............27, 51
pertwee............20, 29–33, 55–59
perversion............24
poetry............14, 36
police boxes............77
pornography............24
rancid spit............53
recursion............82
redon............74
reprinted article............24, 53
riding whip............36
roe, jackie............5, 26, 49, 63
seducing sue pollard............53
sex............24, 79–80
sexist comments............17
sinclair, paddy............54, 60, 79
small brains............54
space buns............20
spaghetti............79
sploing, sploing............53
stiffs............19
story review............55–59
talons of weng-chiang............19
technophilia............24
teenage girls............12
time and the rani............53
time monster, the............55–59
time storms............11, 20
titan books............26
tharils............36
toast............33
tristan und isolde............68
underpants............53, 80
unit............30, 56
untouchables............18–20
van gogh............70, 71, 72
vermeer............74
wagner............68
when was dw good?............63–67
winnie the pooh............107
wizard of oz............12
woolley, jamie............3, 84
woolworths............79
zygon............49–52

How to get Fanzines

Many of the fanzines and fanzine writers featured in this book are still going. Experiencing the culture first-hand is, of course, much more satisfying than any book could ever be. Here's how to find some of our subjects. Given addresses are correct at time of going to press, but are, of course, subject to change.

The following back issues of *Spectrox* are available from Tat Wood, 28A Arcadian Gardens, Wood Green, London, N22 5AD: #6 (48 pp.) for £1.50; #7 (32 pp.) for £1.50; and #8.5 (60 pp.) for £3.00 all inc. p&p. There may, one day, be a #8.

The new issue of *Skaro*, #13, is out now for £2.60 inc. p&p. Back issues of #7–12 are available for £2.90 inc. p&p. Cheques payable to V. Bishop at 4 Vernslade, Upper Weston, Bath, NE Somerset, BA1 4DN.

The latest issue, and many back issues of *Matrix* (now ten years old!) and its fan-fiction sister publication *Silver Carrier* are available from Jeremy Daw (secretary) at 103 Canning Road, Southport, PR9 7SW, price £2.50 each plus p&p. A catalogue is also available which lists everything currently in print. (They do a range of fan novellas, and published the first version of Lance Parkin's *History of the Universe*.)

Happiness Patrol is the Fanzine for Lesbian and Gay *Doctor Who* Fans and Friends. Editors: Mel Fitzsimmons and Sarah J. Groenewegen. Address: PO Box Q952, Queen Victoria Building, Sydney 2001, Australia. Send an IRC for details. Or e-mail: melsarah@mpx.com.au.

The latest issue of the gorgeous *Mayfield*, current spiritual descendant of *Purple Haze*, mixing articles about pop and comedy with a photo-story recreation of the TV movie, is available for £2.50 inc. p&p from Clayton Hickman, 35 Raynes Road, Ashton, Bristol, BS3 2DJ.

Liam Brison still has some copies of *Pickled in Time* #3 available, for £1.80 inc. p&p from 16 King Street, Spennymoor, Co. Durham, DL16 6QQ.

#2–5 of Allan Toombs's fanzine of comic-strip *Who* stories, *The Tomb*, are still available. The whole bundle costs £5 inc. p&p (cheques to A. Toombs) from 8 Morkinshire Lane, Cotgrave, Nottingham, NG12 3HJ (allan@escritoire.demon.co.uk or http://www.escritoire. demon.co.uk/splink.html).

#3 of *Rassilon's Rod* features a 'Best Of' the first two issues as well. It's £2 inc. p&p for over a hundred pages. Jim Smith and co. also produce a fan fiction 'zine, *Squide*, for £1.50 inc. p&p. from Jim Smith, 20 Stapleton Road, Studley, Warwickshire, B80 7RH. (jim.smith1@virgin.net).

The editors of *Cottage Under Siege* and *Sarah Jane* would like to announce that they're completely sold out. So there.

Bob Stanley, of 15 Harradon Road, Walton, Liverpool, L9 0HE is offering #2 of *Something Very Wonderful and Strange* for only 50p plus an A5 SAE. And what wonderful value that is, too!

The following back issues of *Circus* (an excellent current fanzine, rather underrepresented here, and a cracking start to any exploration of New Fandom) are available from Colin Brockhurst, 73 Vann Road, Fernhurst, Haslemere, Surrey, GU27 3NP: #1 (£2.50), #2 (£1.50), #3 (£2.20), #4–5 (£2.50 each), all inc. p&p. There's also a fan-fiction 'zine, *The Story Zone*, for £3.

Nick Cooper's current fanzine is *625*, devoted to all television. Again, there should have been more from Nick in this collection, and I can heartily recommend this 'zine. It costs £2 inc. p&p, and is available from 31 Gipton Wood Ave, Oakwood, Leeds, LS8 2TA.

All ten issues of *Queen Bat* are available (£1.60 each, £10 for the lot, inc. p&p) from Jackie Marshall, Flat 3, Queen's Cottage, St Nicholas Place, Sheringham, Norfolk, NR26. There's also a multimedia fiction 'zine, *Rat's Tales* (£1.40 each, £5 for all three).

Five Hundred Eyes #5 is still available from David Gibbs, 38 The

Meadows, Cherry Burton, Beverley, E Yorks, HU17 7SD for £1.50 inc. p&p. There will also (yes!) be a new issue out soon for the same price.

The scandalously brilliant new issue of *Anti-Matter Chicken* costs £2 inc. p&p and is available from Lee Binding, 3 Larkspur Way, Clayhanger, W Midlands, WS8 7RA.

November Spawned a Monster sums up everything in this book brilliantly, and is available from Alistair McGown, 20 Southpark Avenue (Top Floor), Hillhead, Glasgow, G12 8HZ, for £1.25 inc. p&p.

Kate Orman would like to say that you can access *Bog Off!* on the web at: http: //www.ocs.mq.edu.au/~korman/Bog_Off/

Broadsword, the fanzine of the New Adventures, costs $6 (Aussie) for a six-issue subscription, from: 153 Wardell Road, Dulwich Hill, NSW, 2203, Australia.

Fans of the gorgeous art of Phil Bevan will enjoy the extraordinary fan novel that features many of his pieces: *The Electric Catholic Bible* is available for £4.00 from Nikolaos Kanales, 64 Capstone Road, Malmesbury Park, Bournemouth, BH8 8RP.

You can contact the New Zealand *Doctor Who* Fan Club at PO Box 7061, Wellesley St, Auckland, NZ (enclose an IRC). A year's subscription to *TSV* costs $16 (NZ), $20 (Aus.), $22 (US/Japan), $26 (UK). All funds by bank draft in NZ dollars. I know more people in the NZDWFC than I do in the Dwas . . . probably because of their brilliant fanzine.

In•Vision is available for £3.25 an issue (specify story title) from 13 Northfield Road, Borehamwood, Herts, WD6 5AE.

If you think I've been talking rubbish all through this book, don't let that put you off fanzines. Try this hardy mainstream variety: the latest issue of *The Doctor's Recorder* is available from Andrew Hardstaffe, 42 Rosebank House, 217 Belle Vue Road, Leeds, LS3 1HG, for £2 inc. p&p.

And if you want to join the Dwas (everybody should experience it once), write to: Dwas, PO Box 519, London, SW17 8BU, enclosing a SAE.

Also available:

I CAN'T BELIEVE IT'S AN
UNOFFICIAL SIMPSONS GUIDE

Warren Martyn and Adrian Wood

The Simpsons must be considered one of the most bizarre success stories to emerge from American TV. From its roots as a series of inserts on *The Tracey Ullman Show*, it has gone on to become the longest running animated show in the world.

But just who are the Simpsons? How did they manage to top the charts with 'Do the Bartman' – a song written by Michael Jackson himself? And why do celebrities fight to join a list of guest stars that includes Elizabeth Taylor, Michelle Pfeiffer, Meryl Streep, Winona Ryder, Leonard Nimoy, the three surviving Beatles, and the entire cast of *Cheers*?

This unique book examines the *Simpsons* phenomenon as never before, looking at the high points of all the episodes and the people who made them. Everything anyone would want to know about America's most dysfunctional family is covered – including many things you didn't want to know but will be pleased to find out.

ISBN 0 7535 0166 X

THE BABYLON FILE

Andy Lane

Babylon 5 is unique: a science fiction TV show with a predetermined story arc. The closest thing to an SF novel conceived for the small screen, the programme has been hailed by fans and critics alike as one of the best and most complex genre series ever.

Incisive, helpful, comprehensive and occasionally irreverent, this is the book that will unlock the show's secrets as never before. It features an extended essay on the programme's roots by its creator J Michael Straczynski himself as well as a detailed episode guide and an exploration of all aspects of the world of *Babylon 5*. This volume is essential reading for all dedicated fans of the show – and an invaluable guide for recent converts who must be wondering what they have missed.

ISBN 0 7535 0049 3

'This is a remarkable feat and is equally entertaining whether read from cover to cover or just dipped into at random.'

–TV Zone

X-TREME POSSIBILITIES

Paul Cornell, Martin Day and Keith Topping

This book presents a unique analysis of the *X-Files*, the programme that has transformed our perceptions of the paranormal. Though sometimes humorous in tone, it is also a serious study of all the elements that have made the show what it is today. As well as a detailed and complete episode guide, the book pieces together, step by step, the nature of the series' conspiracy – the first attempt to discover just what the 'truth' behind the series is.

From Mulder's astonishing leaps of logic to the tendency of characters not to make it through the pre-titles sequence, this book covers all the hitherto unexamined aspects of one of the world's most popular science fiction shows.

ISBN 0 7535 0019 1

'This is a refreshing change from the usual po-faced attitude of *X-Files* literature. There's an extremely high possibility that you'll enjoy it.'

–Dreamwatch

ALSO AVAILABLE
IN
THE NEW ADVENTURES

OH NO IT ISN'T!
by Paul Cornell
ISBN: 0 426 20507 3

Bernice Surprise Summerfield is just settling in to her new job as Professor of Archaeology at St Oscar's University on the cosmopolitan planet of Dellah. She's using this prestigious centre of learning to put her past, especially her failed marriage, behind her. But when a routine exploration of the planet Perfecton goes awry, she needs all her old ingenuity and cunning as she faces a menace that can only be described as – panto.

DRAGONS' WRATH
by Justin Richards
ISBN: 0 426 20508 1

The Knights of Jeneve, a legendary chivalric order famed for their jewel-encrusted dragon emblem, were destroyed at the battle of Bocaro. But when a gifted forger is murdered on his way to meet her old friend Irving Braxiatel, and she comes into possession of a rather ornate dragon statue, Benny can't help thinking they're involved. So, suddenly embroiled in art fraud, murder and derring-do, she must discover the secret behind the dragon, and thwart the machinations of those seeking to control the sector.

BEYOND THE SUN
by Matthew Jones
ISBN: 0 426 20511 1

Benny has drawn the short straw – she's forced to take two overlooked freshers on their very first dig. Just when she thinks things can't get any worse, her no-good ex-husband Jason turns up and promptly gets himself kidnapped. As no one else is going to rescue him, Benny resigns herself to the task. But her only clue is a dusty artefact Jason implausibly claimed was part of an ancient and powerful weapon – a weapon rumoured to have powers beyond the sun.

SHIP OF FOOLS
by Dave Stone
ISBN: 0 426 20510 3

No hard-up archaeologist could resist the perks of working for the fabulously wealthy Krytell. Benny is given an unlimited expense account, an entire new wardrobe and all the jewels and pearls she could ever need. Also, her job, unofficial and shady though it is, requires her presence on the famed space cruise-liner, the Titanian Queen. But, as usual, there is a catch: those on board are being systematically bumped off, and the great detective, Emil Dupont, hasn't got a clue what's going on.

DOWN
by Lawrence Miles
ISBN: 0 426 20512 X

If the authorities on Tyler's Folly didn't expect to drag an off-world professor out of the ocean in a forbidden 'quake zone, they certainly weren't ready for her story. According to Benny the planet is hollow, its interior inhabited by warring tribes, rubber-clad Nazis and unconvincing prehistoric monsters. Has something stolen Benny's reason? Or is the planet the sole exception to the more mundane laws of physics? And what is the involvement of the utterly amoral alien known only as !X.

DEADFALL
by Gary Russell
ISBN: 0 426 20513 8

Jason Kane has stolen the location of the legendary planet of Ardethe from his ex-wife Bernice, and, as usual, it's all gone terribly wrong. In no time at all, he finds himself trapped on an isolated rock, pursued by brain-consuming aliens, and at the mercy of a shipload of female convicts. Unsurprisingly, he calls for help. However, when his old friend Christopher Cwej turns up, he can't even remember his own name.

COMING SOON
IN
THE NEW ADVENTURES

GHOST DEVICES
by Simon Bucher-Jones
ISBN: 0 426 20514 6
Publication date: 20 November 1997

Benny travels to Canopus IV, a world where the primitive locals worship the Spire – a massive structure that bends time – and talk of gods who saw the future. Unfortunately, she soon discovers the planet is on the brink of collapse, and that the whole sector is threatened by holy war. So, to prevent a jihad, Benny must journey to the dead world of Vol'ach Prime, and face a culture dedicated to the destruction of all life.

MEAN STREETS
by Terrance Dicks
ISBN: 0 426 20519 7
Publication date: 4 December 1997

The Project: a criminal scheme so grand in its scale that it casts a shadow across a hundred worlds. Roz Forrester heard of this elaborate undertaking and asked her squire to return with her to sprawling and violent Megacity – the scene of her discovery. Roz may be dead, but Chris Cwej is not a man to forget a promise, and Bernice is soon the other half of a noble crime-fighting duo.

TEMPEST
by Christopher Bulis
ISBN: 0 426 20523 5
Publication date: 15 January 1998

On the wild and inhospitable planet of Tempest, a train is in trouble. And Bernice, returning home on the luxurious Polar Express, is right in the thick of it. Murder and an inexplicable theft mean that there's a criminal on board; the police are unable to reach them; and so the frightened staff and passengers turn to a hung-over, and rather bad-tempered, archaeologist for much-needed assistance.